HOW TO CATCH
SALMON

HOW TO CATCH
SALMON

DENNIS REID

ORCA BOOK PUBLISHERS

Canadian Cataloguing in Publication Data
Reid, D.C. (Dennis C.), 1952-
How to catch salmon

Includes index.
ISBN 1-55143-030-4

1. Pacific salmon fishing. I. Title.
SH686.R44 1995   799.1'755   C95-910212-4

Reproduction of information from Canadian Hydrographic Service *Sailing Directions* in this publication are for illustrative purposes only, they do not meet the requirements of the Charts and Publication Regulations and are not to be used for navigation. The appropriate *Sailing Directions*, corrected up-to-date, and the relevant Canadian Hydrographic Service charts required under the Charts and Publications Regulations of the Canada Shipping Act must be used for navigation.

Contact the Canadian Hydrographic Service to obtain information on local dealers and available charts and publications or to order charts and publications directly:
Chart Sales and Distribution Office
Canadian Hydrographic Service
Department of Fisheries and Oceans
Institute of Ocean Sciences, Patricia Bay
9860 West Saanich Road
Sidney, BC V8L 4B2
telephone: 604-363-6358   fax: 604-363-6841

Cover design: Christine Toller
Cover photograph: Al Harvey/The Slide Farm
Back cover photographs: Dick Williams (left), D.C. Reid (centre), Dave Lockyer (right)
Interior illustrations: Jim Ketilson

Printed and bound in Canada

Orca Book Publishers
PO Box 5626, Station B
Victoria, BC Canada
V8R 6S4

Orca Book Publishers
PO Box 468
Custer, WA USA
98240-0468

10 9 8 7 6 5 4 3 2 1

For my father, Mr. N.L. Reid,
who generously allowed me the use of his boat
to catch the fish about which this book is written

♦ CONTENTS ♦

◆ 1 ◆
INTRODUCTION:
FISHING FOR THE WILY AND ELUSIVE SALMON

As most fishers know, when you go out fishing, you get up in the darkness well before dawn, nurse down a cup of coffee as the car bumps around the endless turns on the way to the marina, spend a zillion dollars on the final bits and pieces of gear you somehow forgot and then dodge the logs en route to what you hope is endless zings of adrenaline all day long. You can almost feel the fish in your blood; just under the boat they're practically fighting one another for the chance to be the first on the lure you are sending their way.

And then an hour goes by and expectation disappears like a flock of birds. Doubts begin to surface. Then more hours go by and you finally have to admit that the only things you are going to come back with are a sheepish grin and a greater than usual need for a shower and a shave. After your ego has taken this dashing, it doesn't do any good for someone, quite often your bright-eyed partner, to remind you that fishing is really very simple. All you have to do, that person will tell you, is use the right thing in the right place at the right time. Unfortunately, this person is pretty much right, and if you do not become good at figuring these three things out you are destined to go home skunked for a long time to come.

Fortunately, there is something that you can do to change your luck. The more you learn about fishing, the more likely it is that success will come your way. Becoming consistent can take a lifetime, but it's sure a good feeling to know that you can go out virtually anywhere knowing your chances of bringing home a fish are fairly good.

Once you have some of the basics figured out, luck seems to come your way more and more regularly. Not long ago I was asked to take out a visiting writer and scholar—and dead keen fisherman—from Zimbabwe. He spoke in dignified, stentorious tones not unlike a subtle blend of Abraham Lincoln and Nelson Mandela. Of course, I thought I was in deep trouble. We got onto a discussion of religion and politics, then digressed into witchcraft, Satanism and voodoo—you know, the usual subjects one discusses when fishing.

Intermittently, I made bleating excuses like, "Well, the fishing hasn't been that good this summer," and, "Gosh, too bad we got out rather late in the day," so as to prepare him gently for what I thought was the inevitability of getting skunked. Then, of course, we caught a fish—a pink salmon. This was in an even-numbered year—a year when pink salmon simply do not swim through the Strait of Juan de Fuca where we were fishing.

This hapless salmon had swum three hundred miles out of its way to be in just the right spot at just the right time to take just the right thing that had been thrown overboard for it. It was eerie.

That day we were lucky. The skill part of luck comes with hours and hours of fishing (which isn't half bad), thinking really hard about fishing and learning whatever you can. This book can help you along the way. It has a lot of basic information that you should find useful in the pursuit of your quarry. The luck part of luck you will have to solve on your own, whether it be with incantations, rabbit's feet or whatever.

This book contains a lot of background information: about the five types of salmon and their habits, about the ocean and its biology, about deciphering fishable water, about fishing and boating gear, and about mastering the various fishing techniques. Some of the summarized information you will find as "rules" here and there about the book. Here are a few that I follow faithfully.

- *Let the captain have the first fish!*
- *Buy two of everything that you fish with.*
- *Phone ahead for local information and patronize the business.*
- *Use lures that have caught fish in the previous few days.*
- *Binoculars are your most important piece of gear.*
- *Take more clothes than you can shake a stick at.*
- *Fix your gear or throw it away.*
- *Trim knots close to the tackle.*
- *Do not go out in a boat unless it has a compass.*

- *Buy the biggest net in the world.*
- *Stay out on the water as long as you can.*
- *Make a plan before you go out and have a backup plan.*
- *Be adaptable if you are not having any luck.*
- *Listen to your CB radio for current information.*
- *Even though they are insufferable, take lucky people out with you.*

As for me, I am neither the luckiest nor the best fisher in the world; there are plenty of fishers who catch more fish than I do. I have, however, been fishing for thirty-five years—close to twenty of those for salmon. I catch (or I should say that the total number of fish caught on my boat is) about one hundred salmon in an average year, and I have gotten to the point where my catch statistics are related more to the number of times that I go fishing than to any other factor. People have been telling me for years to write a book on salmon fishing, and so I finally have.

Boiled down to one phrase, as I said earlier, it seems to me that salmon fishing is really about using the right thing in the right place at the right time.

In my experience, the most important of these three considerations is using the right thing, and this includes making sure that the lure is functioning properly in the water. A great deal will be said about this in Chapters 6 through 9, which cover the various fishing techniques, but I think it is important to say it right up front: taking the time to perfect your lure's action beside the boat can be the most productive few minutes you can spend in all your fishing hours. Each fisher develops different skills and will often outfish other people by perfecting just one or two things. Good luck originates from making subtle adjustments to your gear, and this can take years to learn.

Possessing brains the size of peas, salmon are not very bright. However, they know exactly what they want. The difference between a bite-tantalizing lure and one that might as well be a Twinkie can be so insignificant that a human being can hardly perceive it at the side of the boat. Yet over the years, you will see again and again that small differences can have dramatic consequences in the number of fish caught. To give you one example, I once told someone how to fish a certain technique, what depth to fish at and so on. I tied his lures for him, sharpened his hooks and fished right beside him. By the end of the day, I had my limit of the most mammoth slabs you've ever seen. He, on the other hand, was skunked—something that did not make any sense at all. It made a bit more sense when I examined his gear and found that the flasher he had used to attract the fish had been put on the line backwards and was not working right. This was all it took for the results to differ for the two of us even though we were fishing in the same way in other respects, and in the same place.

As I have said, being in the right place is also very important. Two aspects of "rightness" of place should be noted: you need to know whether there are actually fish in the area you intend to fish, and exactly where the fish are likely to be.

Finding the fish is very hard, even for the expert. Let me illustrate this point with an example that is commonly encountered in fishing. There are successive runs of salmon on the west coast of British Columbia, twelve months of the year. The fish in each run are usually of different species, have different habits and may be headed for different destinations. In the winter, for example, it is not uncommon to be fishing for small coho salmon—called blue-backs—on the surface, while 150 feet down there lurk schools of resident chinook. The coho are one-pound one-year-old fish freshly emerged from fresh water and bound for the open Pacific. The chinook can be ten to twenty pounds, two to four years old and may never venture far into the open sea. They may simply be fattening up in preparation for a spawning run up the nearest river in this coming or a succeeding fall. Hard as it may be to believe, the fish in one school may not even know that those in the other school are there, though they are geographically in the same place, only a hundred or so vertical feet apart. To complicate matters, other than these two schools, there may be ten miles of fish-empty water all around you, and if you don't find the two schools you will get skunked.

The third consideration in catching more fish is fishing at the right time. Usual times include tide and current changes in the area in which you are fishing. Solunar tables can give valuable fishing information as well—almost as valuable, some believe, as tide tables. In addition, most fishing spots have bite periods associated with the crack of dawn and also the last couple of hours of light. Going out after work in the summer can be the most enjoyable, calm time you will have for fishing in the whole year. This is the time of day that the very air seems to soften and the light goes amber. Moistness rises into the sky and the coastal mountains look like they're cut from layers of blue tin. It can be lovely.

It's probably a good idea to read this book a couple of times every year for the next few years. While I have tried to make it user-friendly, it is easy, with this much information coming at the mind, to miss something on the first reading. Some information here may not sound all that important the first time through until it falls into place with other information from the book.

I am also hoping that you will take the book out in the boat when you go fishing. When you encounter a problem, open the book and find the most common solutions. If you feel, for instance, that lack of success stems from your boat moving too quickly through the water, the book can tell you how to effectively counter boat speed, even if the engine won't idle any slower.

Some of the information may also surprise you or not seem believable. When I was told that salmon do not bite as well on a full moon, I found it hard to accept that this could be true. Over the years, however, I have come to realize—because I record every fish I catch in a logbook—that this is true. You may catch fish on a full moon, but you won't catch as many. I do not have a good explanation for this phenomenon. I have heard it suggested that the fish eat all night under the light of the moon and are fat and happy by the time you get out there. I think this is fairly unlikely; I can't remember the fish being any more full of food in a full moon. Perhaps they just go a little crazy.

Which gets us back to fishers. They must also be a little bit crazy to get up in the middle of the night, spend all that money, suffer the perpetual boredom, punctuated by brief highs of adrenaline rushes (or, even worse, Sartrian nothingness all day), and still come back for more. I hope this book will help you catch a few more fish so that you keep coming back hooked and happy. Tight lines and best of luck.

◆ 2 ◆
GENERAL INFORMATION

Going out on the ocean can be terrifying at times, and it can be intensely fascinating and enjoyable at others. Paying attention to expected conditions usually leads to a better than average time, particularly for those who haven't that much experience with boating. This chapter makes some general observations about the ocean and the weather that you may wish to bear in mind. Tidal and current action also contribute to one's sense of ease, as well as to fishing action. Among other things, prepreparing for a fishing trip, going out with people who catch fish and keeping fishing logbooks will result in greater success on the water. It is worthwhile to repair your gear regularly, to try and keep your kids happy campers and to keep on-the-water beer intake to a minimum. These and other general comments are made in this chapter.

A PORTRAIT OF THE FISHER
AS A SLIGHTLY CRAZED HUMAN BEING

Fishing can be described as the closest thing to gambling since gambling. You put down a lot of money, you agonize as the wheel spins, then you suffer as the croupier rakes off your dough. But wait, there comes a tug on the line; the reel screams freely; you are completely hooked.

That's what fishing is all about. It's in the viscera. It has nothing to do with the brain. The fight-or-flight reflex takes over, and while I'm not into beating drums, the Klingon in me howls for fish.

Spouses and friends know this well, but fishers do not seem to be able to embrace this image of themselves, even when it's staring them in the face. I remember a time when this almost happened to me. It was pink salmon season. The pink season can be heartstopping, from absolutely no action to a breakneck triple-header in an instant.

One afternoon, I and five hundred other guys were fishing cheek by jowl. I was playing idly with my gutting knife, balancing it between my fingertips, when my rod got a bite. I dropped the knife and grabbed the rod. After awhile I noticed blood gooshing around the bottom of the boat, but the fish was screaming here and screaming there so I did not pay any attention to it. When I started sliding around the boat, I started paying attention—and discovered that the blood was pouring from my own foot. Though I hadn't felt a thing, when the knife dropped it had turned so that the tip of the blade was pointing directly down. It had driven through my running shoe and deep into the bone above my big toe.

My friend took off my shoe and I put my foot up on the transom. Blood was pouring everywhere, so he took off my sock and tied a tourniquet around the arch of my foot with it, including a great big bow. I, of course, continued battling the huge pink salmon, foot balanced high in the air, while he got the net ready. About this time, I noticed people in nearby boats looking my way from the corners of their eyes, at the blood on my leg, the bow on my foot and the rod in my hands, their faces wearing a this-guy's-got-it-real-bad expression.

In due course, we landed that fish, and another eight. I hobbled around with the sock tied to my foot all afternoon. Due to the enormous slugs of adrenaline in my system, I didn't feel anything until three o'clock the next morning, when I was in such agony I had to drag myself to Emergency. They did their Mengele needle and suture stuff, gave me a ghoulishly Vincent Price-like tetanus shot and sent me home to bed.

The important thing to remember, I believe, is the moral of this story: I did not give up the fishing rod even though I was bleeding to death. To other human beings, this may illustrate the crazed nature of the fisher quite well. Personally, I don't think this is quite an accurate portrait of me at all. Not really.

COLD SEA AND SALMON FISHING AS A YEAR-ROUND SPORT

The image most people have of salmon fishing is of a 30°C afternoon, the sun beaming down from a perfectly blue sky, a frosty cold beer, fish practically jumping into the boat and someone leaning back, saying, "It don't get much better than this."

This is a very nice image, all right, but it doesn't happen very often. The usual day of fishing includes going out in a parka, even in summer, and cups of coffee sliding all over the place: the ocean just isn't very warm in this area. Winter temperatures in the inland waters average 6°C to 8°C. Summer temperatures rise only a couple of degrees, producing water that is still very, very cold; falling in on a 30°C day is as much an exercise in survival as on the coldest day of the winter. It is unlikely that you will survive even a few hours unless you are wearing some sort of survival jacket. Even then, survival past twenty-four hours is slim.

Common wisdom has it that the cold currents coming across the ocean to the coast of Vancouver Island make our waters cold. In fact, this isn't true. It is the mixing—by the very strong currents in the Juan de Fuca and Georgia straits—of colder, deeper water with surface waters that gives our area its extremely cold water year round. In addition, the northwest wind blowing down the west coast of Vancouver Island in the summer also contributes to up-welling of colder, deeper water on the Pacific side of our shores.

The sea is so cold in and around Vancouver Island that temperature-sensitive fish do not come into these waters in any numbers. These fish include mackerel, sunfish and dangerous sharks. Normally, these fish are fifteen or so miles out in the Pacific Ocean on the other side of what commercial trollers sometimes refer to as "the blue line." This is where the warmer surface waters from the tropics run into the colder water that local conditions have up-welled to the surface. The cleaner tropical water is indeed bluer than coastal water, which is green or greeny brown. Coastal waters bear a lot of river runoff and organic material that plankton feed on, and it is the presence of these organics that gives our waters their characteristic colour.

These prevailing water temperatures are affected about every four years by the El Niño current, a warm plume of water rising from South America. During these periods, temperature-sensitive fish come onshore and gobble up local herring stocks, as well as juvenile salmon that are migrating to the open sea. Anyone who has been out on a day when the mackerel are about can attest to their persistence. They snap up virtually anything thrown in the water.

Even during El Niño conditions, water temperatures are very cold and one has to dress warmly for the cool winds that blow down the straits. However, since the ocean does not freeze in the winter, and because there are successive salmon runs twelve months of the year, salmon fishing is a year-round sport in B.C.—something many visitors to the coast and many British Columbians are not aware of. Even many fishers do not know that winter fishing, usually for feeder chinook, is often more reliable than summer fishing—even with its huge spawning runs. Bluebacks—immature coho heading out to the open Pacific—can also abound in the winter months.

Turn to page 52 for a description of the usual twelve-month pattern of runs of the five types of Pacific salmon on this coast. It's really quite fascinating how these patterns repeat themselves year after year. The successive nature of salmon runs is so regular that in any given area a good local fisher will be able to identify at least a dozen different runs of salmon that move through, one after the other, the whole year round. He or she will know the various methods by which they may be caught as the year progresses. Many of these people are perfectly willing to take you out. So get your woolies out of mothballs and have a good time whether it is summer or winter.

WEATHER AND FISHING

Everyone knows the commonly held belief that fishing is at its best in the rain at the crack of dawn—conditions in which you are likely to be feeling rather glum, wondering why the heck you aren't in a warm, cozy bed. I recall a fishing derby in Saanich Inlet one dreary March morning when it poured. Even with a hardtop on my boat, the heater going full blast and a canvas roof over the rear end where the fishing gear was set out, I was soaked and catching nothing. Like a long train of children's pull toys, a hundred boats followed one another around Brentwood Bay. Rain fell on the water like steel pellets. And beside me there was a pale, wet guy in a twelve-foot aluminum cartop boat looking as lugubrious as a catfish. Light began filtering through the arbutus into a sodden world, and it dawned on me that there was a million dollars' worth of boats going round in circles in a bathtub-sized bay, catching absolutely nothing. I just shook my head at all of us foolish people. I didn't, however, stop fishing. A fisher is the ultimate optimist; "Things," I thought, "might get better." At least I wasn't in the cartopper.

Usually it isn't that bad. If you put on your long woollies, a little rain will not normally dampen your day on the water. Over the years, I have fished in a great variety of conditions. Although uncomfortable, I have caught my limit many times in five-foot waves. I have caught fish in the pitch dark, in snowstorms, in driving rain, in fog so thick I couldn't tell where I was. I have been hailed on, attacked by eagles and nearly run over by commercial fishing boats. I have watched my tackle box fly off the table at least 356 times, pitching every last swivel and hook all over my boat.

And I have experienced some paradisaical days. In only shorts and sunglasses, I have caught countless big, beautiful, silvery chinook at two in the afternoon. On a sea so smooth I could walk on it, I have pulled in fish after fish that were swimming like little torpedoes, dorsal fins poking from the surface like herds of sticks.

You can go out fishing any day of the year in virtually any condition and still catch fish. Having said this, there is one condition to which constant attention should be paid: the wind. Wind can ruin fishing and is the most prevalent danger on the sea. It should never be ignored.

Lightning, of course, is more dangerous than wind. When you are out there alone—the highest gas-filled lightning-attracting thing for miles around—static builds inside your skull until it is simply too scary to stay out. Fortunately, lightning on water is rare.

Wind, on the other hand, should be expected every time you go out and can have a terrible effect on fishing. Wind builds waves and also blows a boat across the water. In a relatively small wind, mooching and drift-fishing become impractical because it becomes difficult to get the gear down to the fish. Trolling can be accomplished in much higher winds, particularly if you troll with the wind. But even trolling is affected by wind. As the boat rises and falls over waves, the action of fishing lures is greatly affected. The gear goes through a cycle of speeding up and being whizzed around in circles much too quickly and then being stopped dead in the water, only to whiz forward again away from the salmon. Consequently, you will often catch fewer fish in windier weather.

It always astonishes me how a boating situation can become dangerous in the snap of the fingers. If a wave turned your boat over, would you be able to get out of it? Would your radio work? Would you be able to go into a water-filled boat and rescue your children? What would be the possibility of retrieving your flares if they were under water? How would you light one if you were in the water? Who would see it? And are you confident that your boat will float? These are just some of the questions that worry me when thinking about fishing in the wind. It's not a bad idea to wear your life jacket when fishing alone on a windy day. I have almost fallen out many times.

So before going fishing, it is wise to make it a rule to:

+ *Phone the weather line.*
+ *Check the weather channel on the TV.*

My habit is to start checking the weather a couple of days in advance of going out, so that I get a feel for the pattern of fronts that is developing. When the morning for fishing arrives, I want to be sure of the current and forecasted wind speeds and their direction, as well as the readings at the various weather stations up and down the coast—most importantly, the stations in the direction from which the wind is coming.

Over the years, you will notice that weather reports are sometimes wrong. I have been out on days when it was supposed to be calm and seen the wind pick up from zero to fifty miles per hour in less than an hour and been battling seven-foot seas before reaching safer water. Many fishers, myself included, check the weather channel on their VHF radios while fishing. It is best to keep on guard. Most experienced fishers have the unconscious habit of keeping an eye on the horizon at all times. A black line indicates rising wind, regardless of what the weather report may say. A line of white indicates calm water.

You should also know the daily and seasonal wind patterns in the area you will be fishing. Generally speaking, wind is lighter at dawn. It speeds up as the day progresses and usually blows onto the shore. Just before dark, the wind begins to slow and night is often the calmest time. Seasonal variations can also influence fishing decisions. On the Juan de Fuca Strait, for instance, the winter wind is generally from the southeast. It changes to southwest in April, and back to southeast in November. Depending on land configuration, the change can be as much as 180 degrees. So one may decide to seek out a lee shore (a shore that the wind is blowing from rather than onto) for more comfortable fishing.

Sometimes, no matter how good the planning, one will get caught out in rough, windy water. If this happens, try one of the following.

+ *Turn and go with the waves until you find a sheltered place to anchor and wait it out.*
+ *When going with the waves, cross them at a slight angle.*
+ *When going with large waves—say, above six feet—it is quite dangerous to do anything other than go directly with them.*
+ *When going against the waves, keep your bow up by backing off the throttle or the trim, and go directly into them.*

+ *Avoid travelling at right angles to the wave direction. Your boat is in extreme danger of having a wave wash over the gunwhales, or a standing wave pitch the boat right over.*
+ *Have confidence in your boat; it is often far more seaworthy than the captain.*

Let us hope you don't get caught out in any dangerous situations. Long before being in real danger, however, many people can experience difficulty with seasickness. If anyone on board becomes sick, it may help them to stare balefully at the horizon. This helps the inner ear maintain equilibrium and thus prevents that greasy sick feeling. It's not a bad idea to have a set or two of seasickness wristbands. These bands have a small bead that is pressed into the wrist, and will keep many people feeling okay until land is reached. I know this sounds a bit like hocus-pocus, but I have a set, and it definitely works. Perhaps my next purchase will be a set of acupuncture needles or snake oil.

TIDES AND CURRENTS

I am originally from the prairies, and when I moved to the coast I was immediately fascinated by the tides. On the prairies, the wide line of earth and the limitless blue sky are constants of nature. It is the limitlessness of the landscape that impresses the mind. On the coast, the hills, the rain and the ocean dominate. Having lived in a changeless landscape, I can't describe how I felt coming to one in which one of the largest elements changed constantly. I used to sit on the shore and marvel at how the water advanced or receded, even in the space of five minutes. It was as though the very elements of the world were alive; the sea was breathing in and out. Almost two decades later, I still retain the same sense of wonder and find myself watching the endless variety of the swirling sea each time I am out.

I feel this way even though I know that the tides are simply the ebb and flow of the ocean caused by the sun and the moon. Each of these bodies exerts a gravitational pull through the blackness of space. Water, being made of matter and fluid, is attracted and actually moves toward them. This produces a high tide on the side of the earth closest to the heavenly bodies. On the opposite side of the earth, there will be a low tide. See the diagram on page 13, as this concept is easy to understand in a drawing.

The moon is much closer to the earth than the sun, so its pull on the oceans of the earth is stronger. During the period of its cycle

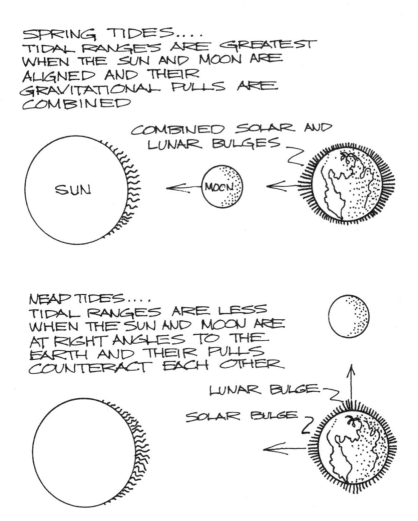

SPRING TIDES....
TIDAL RANGES ARE GREATEST
WHEN THE SUN AND MOON ARE
ALIGNED AND THEIR
GRAVITATIONAL PULLS ARE
COMBINED

COMBINED SOLAR AND
LUNAR BULGES

SUN   ← MOON ←

NEAP TIDES....
TIDAL RANGES ARE LESS
WHEN THE SUN AND MOON ARE
AT RIGHT ANGLES TO THE
EARTH AND THEIR PULLS
COUNTERACT EACH OTHER

LUNAR BULGE

SOLAR BULGE

when the moon lines up between the earth and the sun, the highest tides occur (ie., the highest variation in water height along our shores). As the moon continues to circle the earth, these high tides slowly give way. Because the moon moves around the earth in a set cycle of twenty-eight days and then begins a new lunar cycle, the tidal pattern—both the timing of the tide changes and the difference in their height—can be predicted. The tide and current guides published by the Department of Fisheries and Oceans contain very accurate predictions of tidal heights and timing of changes in given locations along the coast.

At this point, the explanation that I am giving gets a bit more complicated. It may have occurred to you that because the earth turns around once in a day, the sun and moon will cause two tide changes in a day—a high tide and a low tide. This is generally true for much of the world and on the high seas, but not in the west coast waters. The tide charts indicate that on most days there are four tide changes, although on some days there will be three or two and, on very rare days, only one.

The extra tides are caused by the flow of water around and over land structures under the water (locally referred to as reefs, although there is no coral in these waters) or sticking up from it as islands. These impediments slow the water while the earth continues to spin, thus resulting in an altered tide pattern. Normal tidal rhythm for this area is a little over six hours between tide changes, and so the normal pattern generally advances slowly through the day as the lunar cycle progresses. In a typical day there will be a very high tide—usually referred to as the high high—followed by a very low tide (the low low tide), followed by two intermediate water marks— that is, a lower high tide (the low high tide) and a higher low tide (the high low tide). As the tide cycle progresses, some of the tide changes "catch up" with one another and blend together, producing unusual patterns or fewer than four tide changes per day.

I hate to make matters seem more complicated, but superimposed upon the tide-change picture I have described, there are also current changes. In many areas there are both tide charts and current charts. When you are on the water, you will encounter situations where the tide is flowing one way, but the current is flowing in the opposite direction. Tide currents result most often from the constrictions on water as it flows around the land masses of the west coast. A typical example occurs when the tide has been ebbing to the point where it has stopped and, under the influence of the sun and moon, begins to flow back in. While this may be happening, there is a still a body of water that has not been able to completely ebb because the islands in its way have impeded its flow. As this water is higher than the water in its path, the gravitational pull of the earth is pulling it to the lowest point. Consequently, this produces a situation where the tide is rising, even though the current is falling. Boats on one side of the resultant tiderip move like freight trains in one direction, while boats on the other side steam off in the opposite direction. In some situations you can actually see that the water is flowing downhill—fascinating.

And, oh yes, there is yet another complicating factor. The flow of some of the greater rivers on this coast, such as the Fraser River, create natural currents. Much of the water of the Fraser moves south and out the Strait of Juan de Fuca. Thus there is a constant natural flow in this very large area moving out to the open sea, superimposed upon the current pattern, which is superimposed upon the tide pattern. Very complicated. For these reasons, the slack water associated with a tide change may not be a time of completely still water; slack water will actually be moving.

I am sorry for this rather dry explanation of phenomena that are actually much more complex and interesting than indicated. But there are reasons for understanding some of the basics about tides and currents:

• *Salmon-bite periods are related to tide and current changes (see Chapter 3).*
• *Tidal flow and wind can produce dangerous conditions.*

TIDAL FLOW AND WIND

The tide moves the sea like a river. Water swirls around islands and over reefs, creating back eddies, boils, tiderips and whirlpools. The latter can be quite dangerous, and Ripple Rock north of Campbell River, which was blasted to smithereens decades ago by the largest-ever peace-time explosion, is still a deadly spot in certain conditions. And there are the sixteen-knot currents of the Sechelt Rapids, where the land shakes with the thunder of the running sea. I have seen a huge telephone pole-sized log, three feet thick at the butt, stood on end like a giant spoon and simply sucked out of sight. The power of the sea is very frightening, and in the case of that log, I quickly moved, because sooner or later it was going to come flying back up, right through whatever was in its path.

The power and roughness of the sea are greatly affected by the prevailing wind. I have often seen dead-calm water just a few miles from rough water, the only difference being the speed and direction of the water in relation to the wind direction. Wind as high as twenty knots can be fishable, provided it is blowing off a shore or is moving in the same direction as the tide.

Winter fishing off Victoria is best in a high-pressure system when the wind is blowing off the shore. I once wrapped two hundred feet of wire downrigger line around my prop, and with no one else around, had to lean out over the back end and cut it off. The offshore breeze moved me further and further away from land and into choppier and choppier water, while I hacked with a pair of sidecutters and finally had to remove the prop in three-foot waves. One second I was high above the water, the next I was up to my armpits, trying to prevent myself from falling overboard and also to retain my pipe wrench, the prop bushing and cotter pin. All the while I was shouting encouraging comments to my five-year-old daughter that we were in no danger. After a hair-raising hour, though, the repair was complete, and we motored back into the lee shore and continued fishing in the same breeze in very flat water as though nothing had happened. In fact, had the repair been unsuccessful, our likely fate would have been to be carried out until a wave swamped the boat.

Water conditions become their wildest when the wind moves directly against the tidal flow, producing standing waves. This type of wave has a deep, narrow trough that rises as steep as a mountain to Katmandu, then drops precipitously down the other side. Such waves are often encountered near ripples, where tidal flow is directed straight up from an underwater obstruction or reef. Virtually all standing waves are associated with bottom structures, and in not-too-extreme conditions, you will usually find safer water by moving into deeper water—usually off shore—rather than by giving in to the natural reaction to crowd closer to land, risking even greater danger from reflected waves.

When caught in standing waves, it is extremely dangerous to motor directly into one that is six or more feet high. At the crest of the wave, complete control can be lost as your propeller comes out of the water. I have seen a thirty-five-foot boat turned 180 degrees on the top of a standing wave. Your chances of coming through standing waves safely are better if you turn and motor with them. The rule of thumb with standing waves is:

* *Once through the first wave, never go back; ride it out.*

I discovered the truth in this rule the day I made my most foolish boating mistake. Coming out of Victoria harbour, I was travelling east into a falling tide that was being pushed toward me by a southeast gale. Waves were about three feet, and I reasoned that as soon as I turned north into Haro Strait, the gale would be funnelled into a northeast direction as it passed around the various bodies of land in its path. This would put the wind at my back and make my ride much smoother. What I failed to consider was that the tide was running full force in a southeast direction, directly into the gale.

That day I learned the hard way that once through the first twelve-foot wave, there was no going back. Twelve- to fourteen-foot standing waves followed me all the way up the strait. One second I was falling over the steering wheel and staring at the bottom of the sea as the bow pointed virtually straight down and the stern of the boat rose up the front face of a huge wave. Each wave crashed green and dark into my side window, and then, without warning, I was hanging from the steering wheel to prevent myself from falling out the back of the boat as the bow pointed directly at the sky. The most terrifying moments were those when sliding down the wave's back side and watching the wall of water grow in front of me, first up to eye level, then up above the boat, then growing so high as to obliterate the distant bluffs, and then rising almost twice that height while I prepared desperately for the next wave to lift the rear end of the boat.

For well over an hour, I was sure I was going to die. I knew that if I made one mistake on any of the thousands of waves that passed under me, nothing could save me. I had never felt this way before, nor have I since. Finally, in the distance, I could see Saanichton Spit and, every now and then, a brightly coloured kite-like thing flying above the waves. When I got closer and the waves were down to about eight feet, I realized it was a windsurfer. As we roared by one another, each of us wore an expression of terror and complete shock at seeing someone else out in this water. It was still too rough for me to have helped him. We were both on our own, and he, I surmised, was safer than I.

The relationship between the wind and current changed once more during this trip. Half an hour later, as I turned north into Saanich Inlet, the sea became as calm as glass. It was bizarre, but the reason was simple: this inlet did not have any current, and the gale had been deflected away by the peninsula that separates the inlet and Haro Strait. In other words, the sea condition changed vastly three times in what is normally a two-hour trip, simply because the wind and tide changed three times.

PHONE AHEAD FOR LOCAL INFORMATION

The salmon in one school or run usually have the same habits, so you can improve your chances of catching them by finding out what gear has been successful in the days preceding your fishing trip. A day before all of my trips, I phone the marina or the local tackle shop and find out what is working. I mull over the information, look at previous years' records and then make a fishing plan. I also go out and buy the gear I do not have in order to be completely ready in the morning. There is nothing more annoying than standing in line at the marina as the bite period disappears.

Current advice is often more valuable than logbook records of previous years' catches. Once when phoning ahead, I was told that someone was on the dock with a limit of chinook taken at 170 feet off a certain point of land on a gold squirt. I assumed that the person telling me the information was mistaken, because in all my years of fishing I had never ever heard of a fish caught on a gold squirt in that location. Furthermore, my records from past years indicated different gear and a different location for the fish. Nevertheless, I bought a gold squirt and the next day put it on the line. Much to my surprise, I picked up a limit of salmon just after noon on a beautiful 30°C summer day at 170 feet, exactly where I was told they would be. I caught every fish on the gold squirt and did not get a bite on any other lure. This pattern continued for the next three weeks until that run of salmon moved on. In the many years since, I have never caught another fish on this lure, even though I use it faithfully each year at this spot and am still confident that sooner or later the descendents of these fish will pass by again and also be genetically disposed to gold squirts.

Now, the important thing to remember is that had I not found out and used current information, I would have been skunked. This is the value of phoning ahead. When you call, be polite and try to determine the following:

- *specific lures that have been hot*
- *flasher or dodger*
- *lure size and colour*
- *whether the fishing was spotty or good*
- *method of fishing (e.g., mooching)*
- *whether to fish close to shore or offshore a ways*
- *location of the fish*
- *fish depth*
- *leader length*
- *best bite period in the day*
- *species of salmon*
- *use of weights or downrigger*

Exactness is the key. I have often thought I got it all, only to get skunked. For example, fishing an unfamiliar area recently, I was unaware that it was common practice to use a five-foot leader between bait and flasher. Nary a bite came my way until, using my binoculars to check what other, more successful fishers were doing, I spotted the correct leader length and adjusted my gear.

While you should always get information before going out, it is better to get it the day before rather than as you are rushing to get away from the dock. This allows you to make a plan and to pick up gear you may be low on. I can't count the number of times I have gone to the trouble of getting red-hot information, then gone out at the crack of dawn only to discover, much to my horror, that I didn't have any treble hooks or a hootchie bib or some other up-until-that-instant insignificant piece of equipment.

You will catch hundreds of fish over the years if you phone ahead. In my opinion, finding out current information is almost as important as perfecting lure action beside the boat. And remember, once you have called, it's only fair to patronize the marina.

MAKE A FISHING PLAN AND A BACKUP PLAN

The chances of catching fish are improved if you have thought out a plan of action for the day, something you should do every time you go out. This is a more scientific way to go about things, and even if you are not successful, your plan will have told you what does not work. Salmon are creatures of habit, and current information, combined with catch statistics from your own logbooks, will normally result in more fish in the boat.

Salmon runs occur on an annual basis; therefore, you should be able to haul out your records for a particular month for a particular area and catch fish on the same lures. Much of my own fishing success comes from keeping meticulous logs, because the patterns that emerge are remarkably consistent for specific runs of fish, year after year. For example, I know in June to try a bright blue-and-green squirt on a 36-inch leader and flasher when fishing in Saanich Inlet. If this lure is successful in June, it will be successful for the rest of the summer. If it is not successful in June, I don't waste valuable bite-period time on it for that summer. I would, however, keep it in mind for my backup plan. It should be pointed out that I do not use this lure in other areas during the summer unless my logs support that use.

After consulting your logbook and phoning for local information, your plan should include the following considerations:

- *The specific lures you are going to try out. Have a minimum of three.*
- *Based on tide and current changes, the time the fish are most likely to bite. (See Chapter 3 for a discussion.)*
- *Based on charts, the location the fish are most likely to be.*
- *The habits of the salmon species in the area.*
- *How deep you should fish. Be prepared to raise your lines if it is cloudy, and to go deeper on clear days or on full moons. Fish are often deeper after stiflingly hot calm days, as well as in the winter.*

In the event that the fish do not cooperate with your well-laid plans, be flexible enough to try a new plan. During your thinking the night before, you should also have prepared a backup plan that includes the considerations above, plus some new angles. Many times in the fall, when I feel sure there are fish there but they won't take a lure on a downrigger, I will automatically change to slip weights to get the lines further away from the boat and its engine noise. This often results in fish in the boat when I would otherwise get skunked.

There is no point fishing doggedly for six hours without changing terminal tackle. If the fish haven't taken your lure after an hour, they aren't that likely to take it for the rest of the day, and this is even more true in winter than summer. Accordingly, you should always be willing to change your plan. And this includes coming back to your original gear if nothing else works. Although it complicates things a bit, it's not a bad idea to remember that if you haven't come out at the peak bite period, you may have the best tackle on and still not get more than a bite or two.

If you have a CB radio, keep it on. Guides and successful fishers often tell one another about a lure that is working. If you catch a message, put the lure on. The one and only time I caught fish on a purple hootchie, I picked the tip up from CB information. I did not receive a bite on any other gear that day.

In formulating a backup plan:

- *Glean past records for alternative gear.*
- *Reconsider your initial interpretation of tide and current guides and charts.*
- *Keep an eye out for diving birds and seagulls.*
- *While fishing, ask other fishers how things are going. If they have caught fish, ask them the same questions that you asked to get local information. You will normally only have time to ask about the type of lure and depth. Congratulate them and immediately switch gear.*

+ *Use your binoculars to determine where fish are caught, the gear used and depth.*
+ *Sometimes the crowd does know where the fish are. Find them if you are not having much success.*
+ *Listen to your CB radio.*
+ *Steer clear of sea lions and killer whales. Harbour seals are pesky but okay.*

I normally write down my initial plan, and then my backup plan. In these plans I also consider jigging for rock cod or bottom fishing if there are younger people or others needing more consistent action to keep them happy. Throw out your crab trap on days when excitement is needed. A handy tip to remember is to keep a fish head from your last trip for bait. Before putting it in the freezer, tie a large loop of monofilament line through the gills and mouth to provide a method of tying the head to the trap while it is still frozen.

And remember, no matter how well laid the plan, there are days when the fish simply won't cooperate. If you keep thinking about your plan and backup plan, however, some of these slow days can be turned into fish-catching days. To give you an example, on a summer day when I expect coho, I plan to fish higher in the water, fish faster and with shorter leaders. If I catch a sockeye, I then slow down the boat, move to a red lure and lengthen my leaders. There have been many days when an on-the-water change in plans has resulted in as many as eight salmon.

LUCKY PEOPLE

I have this friend who ceases to be a friend when we are fishing. I taught him to fish long ago when we were teenagers, including tying the knots, putting on the swivels, selecting the lures, baiting the hooks and the whole nine yards. Since that day decades ago high in the Rocky Mountains of Alberta, fishing in the icy robin's-egg-blue waters of Bow Lake, I have never, ever caught as many fish as he when fishing together. I grind my teeth in dreams just thinking about it.

That very first day we caught only two fish, and he caught them both. The first he snagged in the back, with a hook I had sharpened, as the fish was just swimming by the spot where his first cast was being retrieved. The second fish wound itself in his line so thoroughly that all he had to do was lift it out of the water, where it hung in a little harness like a trussed up chicken, perfectly horizontal. You simply could not have done a better job of it had you tried. And this is how our fishing relationship has gone over the years. The odds on his grotesquely good luck are impossible to believe.

Needless to say, there are without a doubt lucky fishers in the world. They drive the skilled-but-non-lucky fisher crazy. I have chewed off many knuckles in jealousy. I cannot explain the paranormal, but I know that these guys can catch ten-pounders in pails of water. And while they may be insufferable as they laugh at you, the rule about such people is:

 • *Take lucky people out fishing with you.*

You will catch way more fish with them on board than without, and as the object is to catch more fish, it is worth the ribbing. You can save face by remembering that you are far, far more skilled. If that doesn't work, try and get them to pay for your gas.

FISHING LOGBOOKS

Salmon have very definite habits, and salmon of a certain species or from a certain run have a tendency in succeeding generations to do the same things that their ancestors did. Informing yourself of current fishing trends may be your best source of information, but the next best source is the records you keep.

Memory is a dimming thing. I can't recall how many times I have thought I caught such and such a fish on such and such a lure under such and such conditions, only to find, when looking over my fishing logbook, that I have not remembered it at all correctly. So, improve your catches by making it a practice to:

 • *Log every fish that you catch and look at your logs every time you go out.*

The purpose of a logbook is to record all the pertinent information about the fish you catch so that in following years you can refer to your logs of the month in which you are fishing and glean information about proper gear, fish location, etc. Patterns will begin to emerge as many years of information build up; for example, different runs of salmon will become discernible, even within the same species. The dates fish move in and and then out of your fishing area are often very exact; sometimes the fish arrive and depart on the same day every year. Your logs will also list lures that local information will not give you, and this can help when you are deciding your plan of attack and backup plan the night before each of your fishing trips. I have found, for instance, that the most under-rated lure on the market for summer fishing is the red Krippled K spoon. Other people use them from time to time; I seldom fish in the summer without throwing one out for a try.

I keep paper on the boat and write down information at the time each fish is brought on board. Then I transfer it to a permanent log at home. The type of information that is relevant includes:

- *salmon species*
- *salmon weight*
- *leader length*
- *use of flasher or dodger*
- *depth of water under boat*
- *exact location each fish was caught*
- *lures bitten on, even though fish were not landed*
- *size of weights/feet of line let out*
- *depth on downrigger counter*
- *lure type, size, colour, etc.*
- *time caught*
- *time that tides and currents changed*
- *water conditions*
- *miscellaneous*

Under miscellaneous, I write down other observations. For example, after some years fishing, it dawned on me that if resident winter salmon wouldn't take a lure in an hour, they were not likely to take it for the rest of the day. Summer fish are more capricious, and coming back to a lure that you have taken off the line sometimes spells fish in the boat. I have also noted in the winter that if you are not catching fish, it is better to move on in search of the salmon, rather than doggedly circling the same spot.

The miscellaneous entry also contains information I get after fishing—mostly about lures—from people on the dock, from the newspaper and from the marina. It's amazing how valuable these tidbits can be in future for backup plans or simply as clues to colours to try, even if you are using lures other than the locally recommended ones.

So the second rule of fishing logs is:

♦ *Ask for information on the dock and at the marina after you come in, and write it down.*

On the days when you get skunked, the information you get from successful fishers on the dock may be all that makes the day worthwhile. Be polite, congratulating them on their fish, and you will find that most people are only too glad to tell you what they did. So after a skunk, don't just skulk off home, or you may be ensuring another skunk the next time out.

STAY OUT FISHING LONGER

The observation that you will catch more fish if you stay out longer may seem straightforward, yet it is surprising how many people quit fishing and go in before the bite comes on. Despite all we know about salmon, they do have bite periods that do not correspond to the expected patterns, and individual salmon will snap at something that goes by every now and then. It is these salmon that you will pick up by staying on the water longer. If you check the catch statistics at a marina, or talk to people with fish, it is surprising how many forty-pound Columbians are caught at nine o'clock in the morning, rather than on a tide change or four hours earlier when the sun came up. How many times do you hear, for instance, that a fish was caught just as the lines were being picked up?

When you decide to stay out an hour or two longer, use the extra time to reexamine what you are doing, find out what other fish were caught on or perhaps alter your gear or approach. Quite often I will decide that as part of my backup plan, I will move from the area in which I have been fishing into a new one to end the day, and then, after a spotty morning, discover that the fish were in this other area. Had I been in a rush to get in, I would have overlooked fishing the area. These hard-worked-for fish often separate the so-so fisher from the better one.

I often discover that fishing success improves as I get to know an area over a few years—the nooks and crannies that hold fish, the tideline into which fish will drift on a slowly dropping tide, the rock that fish hide behind in a back eddy.

Stay out that extra hour or two, come back to the lure that worked earlier in the morning and do not rush to get back to the dock. Remember, you are only rushing home to do the chores that your partner wants you to do.

GO OUT WITH PEOPLE WHO CATCH FISH

It is no accident that eighty percent of all salmon are caught by twenty percent of the fishers. Most people who go out get skunked, while that small percentage just keeps coming back with fish. Most of these people are not unduly lucky. What they have done is figure out a few things—usually many things—that the average fisher does not know. Guides, for instance, will often out-produce the average fisher because most were very good, knowledgeable fishers before they became guides. It can prove a very good investment, indeed, to go out once with a guide, learn what you can about fishing an area, and then put this knowledge into use on your own.

It is surprising how small mistakes can lead to poor results. Many times I fish with people who do not custom-bend drift-fishing lures before putting them into the water, who don't sharpen hooks religiously, who choose hootchies because they like the colour, and, most important, who throw a lure into the water without making sure that its action is correct. Subtlety is the key, and most good fishers are flattered to be asked to give you a hand. The most obvious thing to do is ask a fisher with consistent luck if he will take you out fishing. Tell the person you will pay for the gas. This twenty-dollar investment is a bargain, considering all that you will learn. Another thing to remember is that most people who catch a lot of fish are only too happy to give you a fish or two at the end of the day because they don't need them themselves or because the chinook portion of their licences is filling up.

When you go out with good fishers, watch what they do and ask questions. Why are they fishing over here and not over there? Why they have chosen this depth for their lure? Why are they smoothing out the fur of a bucktail? Pick their brains; they won't mind. If they are bait-fishing fiends, memorize what they do to achieve the action they like. Have them show you exactly what to do, then do it and have them comment so that you can duplicate the action exactly. A small tip you may pick up, for example, is that you will increase your catch considerably if you anchor an anchovy in a bait holder with a toothpick, or mount a wire off the holder to keep a nice smooth curve in a herring. It will help you to recall this information if you sit down at home and write down what you were told as soon as you return. Once you have absorbed what you can you, will have picked up the point of view of some successful people. Then you can go out with others. When on your own, make a point of memorizing your tackle every time you get a strike. Soon, fish-producing patterns will start replacing the unsuccessful ones you have been perfecting for so long.

INSPECT AND REPAIR YOUR GEAR

Closely related to cleaning out your tackle box is making sure that the rest of your gear is working properly. Repair it, replace it or suffer the grief.

I have had more than one downrigger mounting bracket break on me. One breakage led to one of my expensive downriggers jumping off the side of the boat and disappearing, never to be seen again. The last evidence of its departure was my rod snapping straight up in a good-bye salute as the release clip—for once—released properly and the downrigger rocketted to the bottom, 107 feet away. If such a thing happens to you, try to think quickly: grab the rod and swing it far forward in an attempt to wrap line around the downrigger or its line, and release the tension on the reel to cushion the jolt.

Many other things have broken on me as well. Another downrigger mounting bracket came apart in my hand as I was putting the downrigger on the boat. Many times I have broken my heavy wire set-ups by snapping the rod in two at the joint and watching the rod tip disappear down the line, leaving me to play a fish on a rod butt. I can't count the times that a loosely seated reel has fallen off and skittered about the boat until line has wound around the handles and broken off the fish. Even an eight-pound fish can rip hooks out of its mouth or break a knot in 25-pound test line.

Repair rod guides frequently, as they often pop off in the heat of the action and will easily catch in the line. This includes sanding down the grooves that the line wears in them over time (line frays in passing over these grooves, and it seems to break only when there is a fish on the line). Ceramic rod guides do much to reduce friction, but are notorious for popping out when tapped by something.

Tackle boxes also have their problems. Ones with loose latches seem to break only when you have them over the dock, dumping hundreds of dollars of gear into the cold, dark water. All in all, it is best to:

• *Anticipate problems and fix your gear before it fixes you.*

This includes boating gear. Recently, and without warning, the engine mount for my small engine delaminated. I was in rough water and there was a very real danger of my small engine being jolted off the boat. Of course, this occurred after my main engine had conked out, leaving me dependent on the smaller engine. My advice is that any boating gear that could compromise your safety should be fixed; it is vital that it work when you need it. It could save your life.

I once took the boating vacation from hell. After tootling through the San Juan Islands and out into Rosario Strait, my main engine conked out due to an inaccurate fuel gauge. In connecting up my small engine—usually called a kicker—I discovered that the petcock on its fuel line to the main tanks was frozen and would not draw fuel from the twenty extra gallons of gas in one of the onboard tanks. No problem, I thought, and hauled out my carefully set-aside third tank of 2½ gallons. By the time we crossed over to Whidby Island, this fuel was used up and the kicker died. The anchor would not hold, and we were being dragged into the rocks.

I jumped overboard, up to my chest in water, to keep the leg from smashing to pieces on the rocks. There I was, holding a one ton boat up with my arms (never mind that this was pretty foolish), the engine leg crunching down between my toes. My kids were cowering in the cockpit. My wife was hitting me with a paddle. I was black and blue everywhere by the time some kind soul came along and hauled us in.

I found out later that my money was lighter than water. All of my vacation money rose from my pocket and simply floated away. The rest of my holiday was spent down on the boat fixing what should have been fixed before setting out. It seems fitting, although only in retrospect, that the pass where we had our problems is called Deception Pass.

DRINKING AND FISHING

In my opinion, it is more dangerous to drink and boat than to drink and drive. Being impaired in rough water can become life-threatening, and when in trouble, one cannot pull over and stop; the ocean, unlike a road, is not flat, straight or benign. It swirls with unpredictable currents, deadheads and rogue waves—those huge unexpected waves that loom overhead and swamp the boats in their paths. Avoiding such hazards requires split-second judgement—something that drinking drastically impairs. I cringe when I see people coming down the dock with a case of beer in either hand.

It is truly surprising that more people aren't killed from drinking in the waters off the west coast. Apparently, the body most commonly pulled from the Great Lakes is a male between twenty and forty with his pants undone and high blood-alcohol content. Presumably, the guy climbs out to relieve himself, falls overboard and drowns because he is too drunk to swim. Even in the more usual cases where drinking boaters survive the fishing trip, they endanger other lives on the road home after leaving the marina.

You should be aware that the fines for impaired boating are quite severe. Impaired boating and impaired driving are offences under Section 253 of the Criminal Code. Most people do not realize that the penalties for both offences are exactly the same. In other words, penalties on a first offence of impaired boating may include a $350 to $500 fine, losing an automobile licence for up to a year, points assessed to that licence, the boat being impounded until the boater is sober and the possibility of a jail sentence.

Impaired boating should be as socially unacceptable as impaired driving. So please, leave the beer behind and enjoy nature as it was meant to be enjoyed—unanaesthetized.

FALLING OUT OF YOUR BOAT

Local waters range in temperature from 6°C to 10°C year-round, and the chances of surviving for more than an hour are slim. Falling out of your boat, then, should be treated in the same category as walking off a mountain.

Even if survival suits are beyond your financial reach, you can improve the likelihood of coming through alive. When fishing with others, particularly children, be sure they know the safety procedure you would like them to follow in an emergency, and have them practice to make sure they are comfortable performing it:

+ *Shut off the key.*
+ *Throw a life jacket overboard.*

For younger children or inexperienced boaters, shutting off the key may be the only, or best, method of ensuring that the boat remains closeby. The person overboard retrieves the life jacket and should be only a short distance from the boat, which, after all, will stay in the vicinity as it is floating in the current at the same speed as the victim. The less experienced boater should follow this procedure as well, because it is very easy to turn and run over someone, thus cutting them into spaghetti with the engine.

There are, however, many times when you fish alone. I fish by myself most of the time, and when the water is rough, I wear my life jacket to give me a bit of a chance if I fall out. Many times I have slipped and would have fallen overboard if my foot had not caught on the engine cover or my hand had not grabbed the stay for the canvas roof. Be sure to wipe up all fish slime and blood as soon as it gets on your boat; it is extremely slippery.

In the unlucky event that you fall out, try to grab a fishing or downrigger line as it goes by. If you do subsequently get close to the boat, be sure to stay clear of the engine. This is because it creates a back eddy that will pull you into the spinning propeller blades. These blades will cut you up like butter, and many people have been killed by bleeding to death in the sea. Should you get sucked into the engine, try to get your feet up. They are better sacrificed than your chest, and may just stop the engine, giving you a chance to pull yourself up.

If you are not able to grab a line and the boat gets away from you, do not swim for shore unless you are in dead calm water; you will never ever outswim even the slowest tide. It makes more sense to pull up your knees, conserve body heat and use your very bright day-glo-coloured hat to attract the attention of a passing boat.

On occasion, though, some boaters get lucky. One local tale concerns a very lucky fisherman who fell out as he was beginning to turn his boat, and it came around in a complete circle, allowing him to get back on board. The odds against this happening are hard to compute. Another story concerns a very lucky guide I know who was fishing in the fog by himself. Someone on a boat nearby heard the splash and came to investigate as the boat moved off out of sight into the fog. The guide was retrieved, and they spent the rest of the morning tracking down the boat that had disappeared into the fog. In both cases, these men were very lucky; both could have been killed.

BOAT NOISE

Sound travels well in water, and fish react immediately to sounds around them. These are received through the fish's lateral line, the line running down the length of the body between the darker upper and lighter lower halves.

Good hearing helps a fish to avoid being eaten and, in turn, to find prey. As water depth increases, light dims rapidly; accordingly, an animal's hearing needs to be finely tuned. The Buzz Bomb drift-fishing lure and other sonic lures are based in part on attracting fish via vibrations passed through the water, even when the fish cannot see the lure.

Seals also have finely tuned underwater hearing. In pitch-darkness, they can separate the vibrations of a fish on a line from all other sounds, close in on it like a bat, separate the fish from the hook and make off with it. Ling cod can also distinguish the sound of a struggling fish. They will streak out from the rocks they lie on—even from around a corner—and grab the small rock cod on your line.

Most ling cod are caught this way, with a rock cod in their mouths.

I have often seen salmon, lingering by a herring ball, disappear instantly when someone moves in the boat or drops something heavy. So, when you are fishing, it's a good idea to:

+ *Wear soft-soled shoes.*
+ *Choose quieter, four-stroke engines.*
+ *Reduce noises on board, especially those where contact is made with the hull.*
+ *Buy a boat with a carpeted floor.*
+ *Leave your ghetto blaster at home.*

The noise of rushing water is so loud that it drowns out many boat noises and nullifies their effects on fishing. To satisfy yourself of this, kill your engine some day when in an area of high tidal flow, and you will be surprised how loud moving water sounds. In the presence of this noise, of course, the sounds of your engine and other sources are swirled away. In the absence of water noise, the effects of boat noise increase dramatically. It is my experience that fish are spookier in calmer water; this is more noticeable with resident fish that are not on the move.

Some level of boat noise is unavoidable but its effects can be minimized to some extent. Generally speaking, fish move away from boat noise, then turn and swim back to where they were before. If your lure is the correct distance behind the boat, they will swim back almost on top of it. So when fish seem spooky, try slip weights, as these get your gear further away from the boat at the same depth.

BOAT ELECTRICAL POTENTIAL

The sea is filled with minerals and ions, which essentially make it an enormous battery with electrical potential sluicing here and there. This potential is passed through the water around any metal on the boat, including engines and propellers, trim tabs and swim grids, and also from electrical sources in the boat that are not directly in contact with the water, such as blowers, navigational lights and generators. Passage of electricity through metal parts eventually eats them away, and in an effort to prevent this occurring to useful parts of the boat, zinc plates are mounted in various spots. The zinc absorbs the initial charge and passes it along. In the process, the plates are eaten away. They are usually replaced annually.

Boaters who leave their boats in the water know very well the effects of electrolysis. I once had our boat in a marina that had a lot of people living on their boats, using shore power; my zincs were eaten away in three months. At that time I was unfamiliar with the effects of electrolysis and left the boat another six months, until its usual time for bottom painting and changing of zincs. In this six months, the electrical potential in the water ate through the propeller until it looked like Swiss cheese. It was so brittle that pieces shattered with a tap from a hammer. Much more significantly, the leg had to be replated from the pitting it had acquired, a repair costing the better part of $2,000.

Electrical potential also affects fishing. Researchers have determined that salmon, and most other fish, are particularly sensitive to electrical charge and will avoid areas of negative charge, a circumstance that occurs quite often. Once zincs are more than half eaten away, a negative charge may develop around the boat and the downrigger lines. To counteract this and develop a positive charge, a new, expensive, high-tech gizmo has been developed, which senses and adjusts the charge around a downrigger line to a fish-attracting range.

Recommended voltage for chinook salmon is .60 volts, for coho it is .65 volts, and for sockeye, .75 volts. Tests have revealed that salmon are attracted to a well-modulated mooching setup from as much as 300 feet away. The larger the fish, the lower the voltage, and as little a change as .025 volts can have dramatic results in attracting big chinook.

How well does this pricey bit of magic work? Commercial fishers have been using such technology for forty years. Since the recent introduction of much "cheaper" units for sportsfishing, virtually all guides have switched to these "black boxes," as they are called. Results indicate at least a two-to-one increase in numbers of caught fish. One operator told me that the fish have a tendency to turn and follow the boat so that a school begins to show on fish finders. It's not hard to see how one's catch statistics would climb if the fish actually followed the boat in order to be bathed by this positive ion aura. Sounds positively sexy to me.

I have caught literally thousands of salmon over the years and do not have a black box to modulate electrical charge around the boat. Perhaps I would have caught thousands more. The guides I have talked with tell me that you can adjust the positive charge down slightly and single out the big fish in the school for a bite! Now this needs further investigation.

KIDS AND FISHING

During the period you are introducing young kids to fishing, you may find your patience extremely tried. Even the most fishing-crazy among them will find their attention wandering when there isn't a fish on the line every half-hour (ie., most of the times you go out).

I make a point of allowing younger fishers the thrill of pulling in the shakers and looking them over before putting them back in the water. They can find this every bit as exciting as catching a larger fish. When fishing is slow, pull over to a reef and jig up a rock cod or two. Who knows? This may result in a big ling cod as well. Alternatively, promise them a few minutes of fishing on the dock. I carry some number 8 snelled freshwater hooks for this purpose and cut up a tube worm for bait. While I wash and close down the boat, they fish. Shiners and bullheads become lifetime memories and can occupy—and ultimately hook—virtually any child for hours. On a recent vacation, my daughter put a hefty dent in the local bullhead population and would have stayed on the dock all day long if she had been allowed.

But, of course, there are many other things to do.

- *Put out a crab trap.*
- *Play "I Spy."*
- *Leave a bag of crayons and a colouring book on board.*
- *Leave a six-pack of pop and a bag of cookies (in a freezer-lock bag) on board.*
- *Take a pack of gum or twizzlers and dole them out when the action goes as grim as Scott's ill-fated trip to the South Pole.*
- *Chop up a herring and fish for a dogfish. Give them an impromptu biology lesson. Kids love the gore of chopping things to bits, particularly the strange rostral brain in the nasal part of the skull.*
- *Ask them unusual questions and see what they can come up with: for example, what would the world be like if we had no thumbs, or, what if there were no trees?*
- *Homework (not likely to be a big hit).*
- *Have a contest. Make up a game you may actually win, such as listing famous pop composers of the '60s.*
- *Take a big bag of bread crusts.*

The bag of bread crusts is the most fun thing to do. We save up our crusts for months, and then stagger down the dock like Santa

Claus with his sack. Save this one for when the boredom becomes as terminal, say, as listening to Data give a poetry recital on "Star Trek." Spot a seagull and heave a piece of bread overboard. In no time flat you will have a huge following. Hundreds and hundreds of seagulls will come squawking after the boat, diving in the water and milling about in a feeding frenzy. This one would make a very good picture from another boat; as you putt along, a long line of seagulls stretches out behind for hundreds of yards, like a living cloud.

AFTER LEARNING ALL SORTS OF GOOD STUFF ABOUT FISHING, IT'S ALWAYS GOOD TO HAVE SOME GOOD OLD DUMB LUCK TO MAKE YOU LOOK LIKE A PRETTY SHARP FISHER

Some days, it pays simply to be out there with your rabbit's foot, even if what you are doing isn't working that well. One day I was straining every brain cell, every synapse and dendrite, every ganglion and nucleus in my reticular activating system, reading fish after fish on the depth sounder—and still catching a whole lot of nothing. I watched the dark sky lighten, saw a magenta sun lift through a bloody dawn and turn the whole sky brilliant. And I thought, well that's pretty nice, but I smell a skunk here and I'm not happy.

One of the local guides went roaring by and off into the distance, looking like he knew where he was going. After awhile, taking my advice from earlier in this chapter, I reconsidered my plan and then tossed out it and my backup plan. Sheep-like, I turned toward the western horizon and meandered along with the tide in the direction that the guide had gone. As I putted along, I picked up an eight-pound coho. After some time, I espied the guide on my binoculars, many miles offshore. I turned to go out and was lucky enough to pick up a thirteen-pound northern coho. Still feeling they were hauling in the fish and I was not doing that well, I watched the guide roar off to another location. I turned again and putted after him, picking up another eight-pound coho as I went.

I arrived back on the dock to find a very disgruntled client handing across hundreds of dollars to a guide who had gotten skunked. At that point, I felt pretty good standing there beside them with my boxful of fish, the big one being so large that its snout hung out one end of the fishbox and its tail out the other end. Innocently, I agreed that it wasn't such a bad one after all, was it?

It must be admitted that there was a bit of skill operating here. I was a more experienced fisherman than the client and had landed all three bites I had received while the client had lost all four of his bites due to binding down on the reel. The luck part for me was that I had essentially conceded a skunk for that day and was fishing through water I would have thought devoid of fish. The moral of the story is that when all is said and done and all the skill in the world won't work, it's nice to know there's a bit of luck in the universe. May it shine on you.

♦ 3 ♦

KNOWING SALMON

BEING IN THE RIGHT PLACE AT THE RIGHT TIME

I have already said that the essence of salmon fishing is using the right thing in the right place at the right time. This chapter concerns itself with determining the right time and place to fish. It makes little sense, after all, to fish at a time when fish are not going to bite, or in a location where there are no fish.

If you picture the ocean for a moment as an empty sky, your lure is much like a kite being towed all alone through a distant galaxy. Here and there, far under the boat, dottings of fish drift across a whole lot of unfilled space. In other words, if you could see the fish and your lure, you would readily appreciate the vast emptiness of the ocean. In reality, though, we cannot see the fish because we cannot see far into the water. If there aren't any fish where you're fishing, the chances of catching one are about as good as the duck hunter who goes out in May, points his rifle at the sky, closes his eyes and pulls the trigger.

Catching fish more frequently than a duck hunter results from understanding the various factors affecting the locations of salmon schools and their feeding behaviours. Ocean biology, tides and their interactions with land masses all affect fishing, as does the food chain. Each of the five Pacific salmon species has different habits, and these habits influence where each will be found and its readiness to take lures. At many times, other animals can give clues to where the salmon may be found—even the semi-pesky seagull, squawking over a herring ball or contentedly pecking at euphasiid shrimp, which in turn are feeding on even smaller, hapless denizens of the food chain.

THE FOOD CHAIN

One of the most magical sights in the ocean is produced by plankton on calm summer nights. If you trail your hand through the sea, certain species of plankton release phosphorescence as a green and sparkling light called bioluminescence. The light sways here and there hypnotically. Many nights my kids have lain on their bellies on warm wooden docks, sweeping a hand through the water, conducting their own private universe of stars.

Every type of plant and animal life in the world belongs to a food chain, a group of plants and animals that depend on one another for their food. The most important level of all, strangely enough, is the first level; without photosynthetic plants, all life on earth would die in very short order. The salmon food chain begins with plankton, the soup of very young and larval stages of life, as well as algae and other light-fixing plants. The ocean teems with microscopic life. If you take a close look at a bottle of our coastal seawater, you will see transparent life beating this way and that like junks in an Oriental harbour, as well as a lot of floating particulate matter that is contributed by our rivers. Under a microscope, even smaller life is revealed. The water is simply jammed with small animals of varying grotesque but edible shapes.

This plankton—phytoplankton and zooplankton—floats with the tide and is the first step in the food chain. Mixed in with the smaller plankton are maturing animals of endless variety, some of which are feeding on the very plankton from which they recently emerged: larval shrimp moving about with as-yet-unsettled barnacles and mussels and other mollusks of every description, itty-bitty jellyfish and on and on.

The sea is a vast incubating ground for all the life on our shores and in the deeper water. In a kind of cosmic orgasm uncensored by any government department, many creatures get together in the millions and joltingly release eggs and sperm into the ocean in the billions. The eggs and larvae are then on their own among all the other planktonic forms. Because of their sheer numbers, enough plants and animals survive to carry on the next generation, despite the billions that get eaten.

The next link in the food chain is comprised of the various baitfish that feed on plankton, and these include herring, anchovy, needlefish, or sandlance, and eulachons. These omnivorous animals are important to the fisher, as they are the primary food of some species of salmon. Along with plankton, baitfish form virtually the entire diet of all five species of salmon. Some salmon will also eat squid and small octopus. Euphasiid shrimp are the easy prey of coho, and any salmon that eats plankton will at some point bite on pink or red lures depending on the time of year. Coho and chinook are the carnivorous salmon and have plenty of hand-slitting teeth to prove it. Chum feed almost entirely on plankton, as do sockeye, although the latter—along with the the omnivorous pink—are commonly caught on baitfish.

The final level of the food chain includes the largest carnivores—humans, killer whales and sea lions. Fishers compete with killer whales and sea lions for salmon, and sometimes this competition is intense—sometimes the sea lions get more of the salmon you hook than you do.

A CLOSER LOOK AT SALMON FOOD: BAITFISH, SQUID, SHRIMP

Herring and anchovy are free-swimming fish that school in vast numbers where plankton is heaviest. This seems to occur in areas of higher tidal flow, something that at first glance doesn't seem reasonable. In fact, such areas are associated with greater numbers of most species, largely because the tidal action promotes much better oxygenation and this in turn promotes growth. Kelp, for instance, will not grow in quiet areas even though its chances of staying rooted to the bottom are much greater. Quiet areas are often rearing grounds for salmon and other species including baitfish, but these then move to areas of greater turbulence in search of food. Passes between islands are often likely areas to fish. Schools of baitfish, most often herring, will be found where the much more passive plankton will be transported by the tide. Plankton is more likely to be found pushed against an underwater structure or reef, off the end of an island or in a back eddy. Feeding on these, the herring and anchovy grow from about 1½ inches to as much as 12 inches.

Needlefish are much more slender fish of 4 to 6 inches and tend to stay on the bottom, rooting around in what they find down there. Bottom bumping of drift-fishing lures can be deadly in such areas. Needlefish, also known as sandlance and candlefish, generally feed on flat bottoms of sand or, more often, mud in the first fifty feet. They are much less common over rock bottoms or on steep drop-offs. This contrasts with herring and anchovy, which are more far-ranging, sometimes being found miles offshore and also descending as much as 150 feet from the surface, depending on the amount of sunlight hitting the water.

Salmon eat a variety of other baitfish, but only in small quantities. These other baitfish may include eulachons, smelt, shiners and perch, most of which are found close to shores or estuaries and under docks—areas salmon do not frequent.

Squid mass in midwaters in huge schools, and while I catch relatively few fish with squid or octopus in their stomachs, I expect the schools of squid in the open Pacific are enormous. This would explain why most salmon have large appetites for the lures that represent squid—squirts and hootchies (something that would not make much sense if squid were not a common natural food source). Octopus, on the other hand, are few and far between and rather solitary by nature. They are associated with the rocks, reefs and crevices around our shores—any place where they can hide and wait for hapless crabs to come their way. Octopus likely form little of a salmon's diet.

Swimming among the plankton is one other large component of the salmon's diet, particularly the coho's: euphasiid, or young, shrimp, which mass at depths greater than 150 feet in winter and rise to the surface in spring. These are next to impossible to see from the boat, but tiny Vs wrinkling the water's surface and heading away from the side of the boat are evidence of these near-transparent shrimp. When you see these Vs, or seagulls sitting on the water and pecking at them, it's not a bad idea to throw out a pink or red lure right on the surface to see if there are coho in the area. You will notice, if you empty a coho stomach, that the only colour in these shrimp is the pink of their eyes and extremities.

HERRING BALLS

Herring, and sometimes anchovy, display one unusual form of mass behaviour: they swim together when attacked by predators and form a huge ball of living, sparkling tissue. Herring balls are seen all year round, but are much more common in summer when surface-running spawners, particularly voracious coho, are about. When predator fish encircle a school of herring, the baitfish instinctively draw together into a smaller and smaller space, as each desperate herring tries to get into the centre of the mass, until they are a living mass of twisting tissue. Surprisingly enough, this is a survival mechanism; baitfish on the outside are the first to get snapped up. Salmon take turns charging through and snapping the bait or crippling it by cracking their tails. The salmon then hang around underneath, leisurely picking up the dying herring which spiral, like wounded diamonds, into the depths.

The herring balls we see are formed against the surface of the water. The air makes an inescapable border for the school, and thus it is cornered by the salmon herding it from below. The most common way to find a herring ball is the "herring ball" squawk of seagulls attracted for lunch. Seagulls have various different squawks, and when they find a herring ball they make such a racket that it can be heard for miles on calm water. Quite often you will hear evidence of a herring ball before spotting the seagulls. These are such wild sights that when you enter the cloud of seagulls it stirs the blood in a primordial way: the noise, the hundreds of seagulls looping and diving like a storm of paper, the herring dripping from mouths of frenzied birds. Sometimes the terrified herring push so hard they lift the seagulls on top of them right up and out of the water.

You can see seagulls attacking herring balls from miles off. You should move directly to them, as nine times out of ten they are associated with salmon (although, on occasion, dogfish, seals or diving birds will herd the herring together). I keep a casting rig and drift-fishing lure ready to go at all times so that I can cast past or to the side of the ball and possibly pick up a salmon. I am always astonished by the speed of salmon. Many times, standing high on the bow of my boat, I have witnessed salmon streak straight down from a herring ball and out of sight in an instant. When watching this, I am struck that the ocean is a three-dimensional world, and that we human beings, as we cannot fly, live in a two-dimensional world and are just a little humdrum.

Any time you come upon an area of seagull feathers on the surface, look down. If there are scales in the water, you have found the remains of a recently dispersed herring ball. Stop and fish this spot, either trolling back and forth or drift-fishing, because salmon will often drift down to pick up the crippled and dying herring below. Afterwards, like Marlon Brando as the aging godfather, they will descend to the bottom and sit, digesting their meals. At such a time, they might be teased into picking up a lure dangled in front of their noses.

TIDES AND THEIR EFFECTS

Probably the most remarkable thing about the ocean is the tide: the natural sloshing of billions of tons of water around the islands of the west coast every few hours. Fishers are keenly interested in this sloshing because the tides have a tremendous effect on where salmon will be found and when they will bite.

I cut my fishing teeth at age five in small trout streams in Alberta. Salmon and trout come from the same phylogenetic class of higher bony fish, osteichthyes, and what I learned in streams applies directly to salmon fishing. Two of the basic but important observations that I learned about trout are that they swim pointing into the current, and that they have a tendency to seek calmer water so that they do not have to be expending energy by constantly battling to stay in one place. Salmon exhibit the same two behaviours. It often surprises me that although they seldom come in contact with the bottom, salmon seem to know they are being moved by the water. I doubt they know they are being carried or care where they are going, but their tendency to swim into a current influences their location and, hence, our tactics for catching them. As they are trying to save energy, they will be found directly in front of or behind an obstacle, or in a back eddy formed by points of land, reefs or passes between islands.

I am always amazed that salmon and trout, as well as other species, can sense an increase in water speed and will expend a great deal of energy trying to stay out of it. In streams, this means you will most often find trout exactly below where fast water enters a pool or at the tail end of that pool just before the water shallows and speeds up, before falling over the next section of rocks. When they enter calm water, trout and salmon normally rest for a bit and then slowly swim up to the point where the water coming into their faces increases speed. Accordingly, fish are more commonly found at the head of the pool rather than at its tail end, presumably to get the first chance at any food flushed their way. Fish are seldom found in fast water; they either go with it to a slow area or stay ahead of it.

The tide in the ocean is much like the flow in a stream. Water flows downhill, and you can see, if you look closely, that the tide is indeed flowing slightly downhill. This is most pronounced in and around islands or in tight straits such as Sansum Narrows, Porlier Pass or Active Pass. Unlike in a stream, though, the tide may change direction as many as four times in twenty-four hours, and the changes have two important effects on fishing: plankton, baitfish and salmon are moved around; salmon increase feeding dramatically.

Plankton drifts passively with the tide and will be concentrated by the tide in back eddies. These commonly form behind islands and points of land: as the current rushes past the point of land, part of the water spills in toward the land, turns close to the shore and returns toward the point of land. Overall, the effect is a slow circular pattern which concentrates plankton, and hence, baitfish. In addition, baitfish, like salmon, recognize that a back eddy is moving at a slower speed and tend to rest in it as they slowly drift around in a circle.

Sometimes bait and salmon can also be found in front of an obstacle. This occurs for the same reasons as already discussed. First, water that is flowing directly into a land mass has to at some point split and go around it. The space between the split and the land will be an area of reduced flow into which salmon will move. Boulders in streams, for instance, often contain a bulge of slow water in front of them, which acts as a lens. If you look closely, you will often see a trout directly in front of the boulder, swaying and magnified as though waiting to leap like a bullet almost right into your eye.

The second circumstance in which salmon will be found in front of an obstacle occurs when an underwater reef obstructs a current. The water must speed up to move over the obstruction, much like water leaving the tail end of a pool in a stream. Salmon will hold here trying to stay ahead of the current of increasing speed. Since they have turned 180 degrees, and more and more fish are swimming into this area at all times and they then also turn away from the higher-velocity water, more and more fish come to "hole up" in front of the shallow area. I have often had unusually good fishing for migrating fish on strong in-flow tides in such areas where the bottom becomes shallower.

On the open ocean, there are few land masses or reefs to influence animal behaviour. Tidal movement of baitfish can be even more pronounced. Schools of baitfish are commonly moved miles by a tide. A four-knot tide can move over twenty-five miles in a six-hour period, and thus can greatly affect baitfish location. In hot pursuit of the bait, salmon will drift with it, staying in contact with lunch.

Tide changes, whether out in the ocean or in our coastal waters, have the important effect of triggering the salmon to feed. More times than I can remember, I have sat out there engrossed with cleaning my fingernails or captivated by the varnish peeling off my boat; I would bet my last dollar there were no fish in the sea. And then the tide changes and the fish go wild. Think of tide changes as nature's way of being friendly to fishers.

Why salmon bite when the tide changes is anyone's guess. Conventional wisdom has it that as water speed drops, fish become more active: they swim around more freely, as they no longer have to battle the current in a hunkered-down-in-a-bunker mentality. At the same time, the plankton, which has been curling around the back side of a land mass, all of a sudden starts to move off in another direction around the other side of the land mass. This is supposed to stimulate the bait to begin feeding, something I am not convinced of. I think it's more likely that the baitfish also find it easier to swim around, and venture forth. At the next level of the food chain, salmon begin feeding, either on plankton or the bait. It makes sense that they would be hungry after sitting without food for some time, and finding the food must be something of a chore in itself, as at least fifty percent of the fish I catch have nothing in their stomachs.

Regardless of the reason, the effect is most noticeable. It is very eerie when you are on the water feeling that everything is pregnantly dead—like waiting for the Viet Cong in *Apocalypse Now*. The sea is limp; seagulls are nowhere to be seen; you haven't had a bite in hours; your sandwich wilts like Salvador Dali's watch; even the sun droops in the sky. And then ... all of a sudden something changes. It's as though a light switch in the sky has been flicked. Seagulls begin squawking, the sea gets greener and you sense as you've never sensed before that even the inside of the air is getting fishy. Salmon can be voracious when it hits. This happens every day, every time the tide changes. Your previously unnoticed lure looks like the tastiest morsel on the shelf.

♦ *In most waters, the bite period occurs before a high tide and after a low tide.*

I don't know why the bite pattern should be this way but it is. The high-tide bite is often short and intense, while the low-tide bite can take some time to build and then tails off. To take best advantage of the bite, plan to get to your boat at least two hours before the bite, so as to be sure your gear is in the water, working properly, an hour before the bite. Start fishing at least two hours before a high tide and at least one hour before a low tide. Most of the rest of the day, other than first or last light, will be wasted time in terms of fish production.

One final point is worth considering. As discussed in Chapter 2, some areas have current changes as well as tide changes. Currents have the same effects on fishing as do tides and can result in extra bite periods in the day. Current tables list the times that currents change and also their maximum velocity. The higher the velocity, the greater the amount of water that has to be moved through the channel. Periods of high current velocity—like periods of very high tides—are generally associated with depressed fishing action, as the fish tend to be dispersed or pushed around. I also suspect that increased speed reduces the performance of your gear, something that will be addressed in the chapters on fishing technique. Periods of high tidal and current action also markedly affect boating conditions if it is windy.

TIDELINES

Tidelines occur when one stream of moving water flows into another stream of water going in a different direction or at a different speed. Tidelines are also caused by the natural billowing action of a single stream of water breaking up to move around obstacles such as reefs or islands.

Tidelines are important to fishing, because as the streams of water come together, they naturally bring plankton and baitfish into them and hold them there. One stream of water forces the bait into one side of the tideline while the stream coming into the other side forces the bait back into the the middle of the two opposing currents. The bait stays in the tideline rather than being dispersed, and the salmon, also moved by the tide, are found with them trying to keep in contact with their natural food source. If you fish in or near a tideline, you will find that your chances of catching salmon are much higher than in the surrounding water, where there will be fewer fish.

How can you spot tidelines? In calm seas, they can be spotted by the naked eye two or three miles away as black lines running along the surface of the water. Up close, you will usually find a line of bubbles or scum in the water and also rafts of kelp and other debris brought there by the opposing streams of water. These long lines of debris persist for some time after the tideline peters out and still represent better-than-average fishing, even though the current may be imperceptible. In rougher seas, tidelines appear as either long dark patches on the water or flat white lines. The latter occurs when a tideline moves in the same direction as the wind while the water around it moves in another direction. A third clue for finding tidelines in rougher water is an area of choppy or standing waves breaking up the surrounding naturally flowing waves.

Tidelines are particularly important when fishing for certain species of salmon, such as coho, but are of less importance when fishing for sockeye and pink salmon. Coho swim in tidelines, actively feeding on baitfish, whereas sockeye and pink salmon are present primarily because the currents have carried them there. Chinook tend to swim deeper, so their association with surface tidelines is the most tenuous.

A current does not move forward as a vertical wall reaching from the bottom of the ocean to the surface. The various columns of water move at different speeds at different depths; depending on bottom contours, they may move in different directions. It is common in areas of tidal flow to notice your rod bend down and then rise for no apparent reason. This results from changes in water pressure under the surface that cannot be seen from the boat. In other words, under the surface tidelines may wander all over the place and are therefore more useful for locating fish in the top fifty feet of water rather than fish at deeper depths, such as chinook, which often run 100 feet down. Keeping this in mind, the rules about tidelines are:

+ *Fish tidelines when there are surface-running fish about, particularly coho.*
+ *Fish the moving side of tidelines.*

The second rule needs some explanation. In a usual tideline, one stream of water is pushing into the other side and moving it along. Bait being moved into the tideline, and also the salmon, are coming from the moving side. Accordingly, the chances of catching fish are greater on this side. The easiest way to spot the moving side of a tideline is to note which side has the debris in it. Fish that side. Care will be required, as snagging a reef of kelp can be extremely aggravating and a waste of time. Lines need to be checked for weeds more often, and using downriggers makes more sense than slip weights because weeds seldom slide past a downrigger clip. The same cannot be said of slip weights.

You may find it difficult to stay on the moving side of tidelines because they leave rather crooked paths on the surface. When this happens, it is much easier to keep your lure under the tideline for a greater amount of time by crossing back and forth over it rather than religiously going along one side. Gear will be fouled far more often, but far more strikes will result.

INTERPRETING CHARTS

Finding salmon presents a real challenge to even the most seasoned veteran. When you leave the dock, miles and miles of sea and shore stretch potential fishing spots out before you. Most of the vast wet spaces are devoid of fish, while a few highly localized areas consistently produce fish (and even these may produce for just one or two months of the year). How, then, does the fisher select a

likely spot? Local information is key but not always available. Besides
tidal movements, two other factors outweigh all other considerations
in locating salmon: land structures and salmon behaviour.

Land structures rising above the water—such as points, bays,
river mouths and islands—and those found below water—such as
reefs, drop-offs, shoals and mud flats—all influence the location of
salmon. Salmon tend to swim off points of land and above reefs
where water depth changes rapidly. Mud flats generally do not attract
salmon unless carpeted with needlefish and laced with troughs.
Sandy bottoms seldom attract much life of any kind. In conjunc-
tion with the tide, land concentrates fish in slower-moving water:

* *On the down-current side of land.*
* *Pushed up against indentations in the shore.*
* *On the down-current side of reefs or drop-offs.*
* *Off the end of islands.*
* *Before the entrance or after the exit of a channel.*
* *In tidelines.*
* *In whirlpools.*
* *Beside kelp beds.*

All of these structural elements in the fishy environment can be
studied on charts purchased from the Canadian Hydrographic Service, Ministry of Fisheries and Oceans. If you don't know an area,
and even if you can get local advice, charts can provide some of
the best clues to finding salmon when you go out. Charts also provide valuable information about the location of reefs that you might
just run into.

Take a good long look at Figure 1 (see page 46), a typical section of coast on southern Vancouver Island. Before examining
Figure 2 (page 46), try to determine where you would expect to
find salmon. The directions of flood (rising) tide and ebb (falling)
tide are noted to give you a hand. Look for areas where you think
the tide will move quickly, pushing bait and salmon right through.
Then find the calmer waters, the back eddies behind land masses,
where bait and salmon will end up when resting.

After giving it your best shot, look at Figure 2, which shows the
same section of coastline but with potential hot spots pencilled in.
These are not the actual hot spots for this area, but predictions
based on an understanding of how tides and land structures affect
fishing. Did your predictions agree with mine? I made mine based

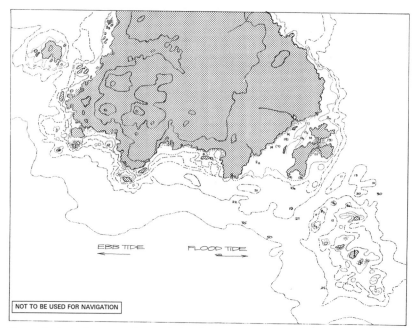

Figure 1: Typical section of coastal shoreline

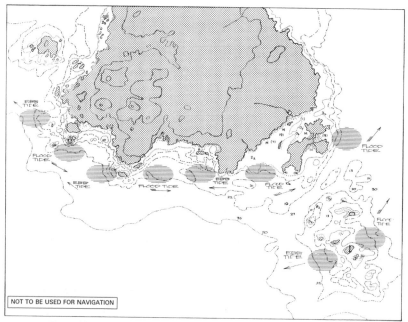

Figure 2: Typical section of coastline with predicted hotspots

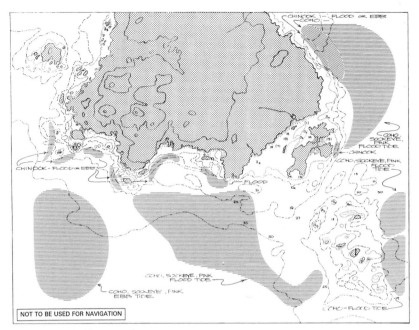

Figure 3: Actual hotspots by species in summer

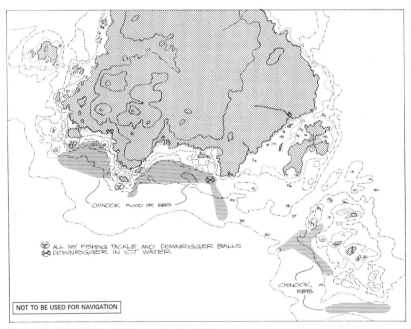

Figure 4: Actual hotspots by species in winter

solely on the information in the last few sections and did not take into account the behaviour of differing species or variations due to season. If your predictions did not agree with mine, go back and reread the past few sections until you are satisfied that my predictions seem reasonable.

The section of coastline reproduced in these figures corresponds to the southernmost tip of Vancouver Island, known locally as the Race Rocks area of Juan de Fuca Strait. These waters are well known for their strong currents, as well as tides, rough sea conditions, unpredictable winds and extreme variations in bottom terrain (including a few reefs that have ripped everything off my boat except the engine on the back end). Find the unhappy face for the location of a reef to avoid. "X" marks the spot where one of my downriggers sits in 107 feet of water, awaiting an intrepid diver.

Salmon could be found almost entirely by charts and depth sounders if other factors were not involved. Salmon would congregate with the bait around drop-offs and would behave virtually the same as trout in lakes. However, the tide affects fishing greatly, as does fish behaviour; salmon are found time and time again in highly localized areas. Chinook tend to swim close to and along shorelines, whereas the other salmon swim further offshore, quite often associated with tidelines. I mention this now in order to make Figure 3 and Figure 4 make sense. These figures list the hotspots where fish are actually caught year in and year out in the Race Rocks area. Most but not all the fish will be taken in these spots. Fish often do their best to confound the fishers by being caught in unexpected locations. For example, the occasional fifty-pound chinook bucks the trend and takes a route way out in the middle of the strait in the international shipping channels in over 600 feet of water.

Fishing patterns differ markedly from summer to winter; spawning fish have somewhat different behaviour than resident fish. Figure 3 lists summer hotspots, while Figure 4 lists winter hotspots. Note the differing species. Note also that actual fishing spots differ from predictions based on tides and charts, underlining the need for local information and meticulous logbooks.

FISHING DEPTH

Salmon have a strong tendency to swim at certain depths, and most fish caught on the same day will be caught at roughly the same depth. Given this, and keeping in mind the image of your lure as a kite in an empty sky, it makes sense to find the fish depth where the salmon will be cruising around looking for food. Depth preference is so strong that if you fish above or below the fish, little will be caught, even though the ocean may be oozing with eager, hungry fish. Finding the right depth, then, is part of the phrase "being in the right place."

For the moment, pick up a salmon and look it in the face. You will notice that its cheekbones are beneath its eyes. These cheekbones prevent the salmon from seeing down in the water, so they are more adapted to looking up. Since salmon swim horizontally, your lure has more chance of being seen if it is at their depth or slightly above, say five to ten feet. Having said this, I should add that one of the most common causes of coming home skunked is fishing too shallow, so try to determine exactly the right depth and concentrate your fishing there. When you wish to vary depth, do so in amounts of less than fifteen feet.

The depth at which salmon may be found depends on one or more of four factors:

- *water depth*
- *species of salmon*
- *season of the year*
- *light conditions*

Water depth effects are straightforward. If the water is shallow (50 feet or less), you can only fish down to that depth. Fish will be bunched up close to the boat. Quieter methods of fishing in shallow areas, such as drift-fishing or cutplug mooching, are often more productive, as boat noise tends to scare fish away. In deeper water, however, fish have more vertical height in which to swim. Finding the fish depth starts to depend more on understanding the behaviour of the different species of salmon than on anything else. Generally speaking, coho will be found in the top 50 feet of water, pink or sockeye salmon are seldom caught deeper than 60 feet, and chinook are the deepest-swimming salmon: I have caught them down at 250 feet.

It is worthwhile remembering that even though our waters reach depths of 750 feet or more, salmon are free-swimming fish associated more with the top layer near the baitfish (although down somewhat, out of direct sunlight). Fish depth can vary greatly from day to day, and a fishfinder depth sounder with a liquid crystal display can be a real help in eliminating the hit-and-miss method of locating them.

Seasonal variations in fishing depth occur in all coastal areas. Succeeding runs of salmon have marked variations in habits, so local information is your best clue to correct fishing depth; being out by even 20 vertical feet can spell the difference between success and being skunked. To confound what I have just mentioned, all around the coast there are runs of salmon that do not conform to the depths in the preceding paragraphs. There are, for instance, deep-running coho: winter bluebacks may be 100 to 150 feet down, and some summer runs can only be caught at depths of 250 feet. Even some earlier runs of spring salmon go against their usual pattern and are found in the top 50 feet of water. The changeover from summer to winter runs sometimes happens precisely from one October day to the next. One day you're fishing in the top 50 feet for summer chinook, and the next at 100 feet for the first incoming feeder chinook of the winter.

The fourth factor affecting fishing depth is light conditions. Salmon, and particularly chinook, have a strong daily pattern of moving deeper as sunlight penetrates the water, and then of ascending slowly through the night. One often hears the explanation that because they have no eyelids, salmon have no way to block the sun's rays and therefore move deeper to ease their sensitive eyes. Personally, I doubt they feel much pain on a sunny day and can't help thinking that many million years of evolution should have solved this problem for them. Regardless of the explanation, salmon descend and then ascend every day.

In the pitch-darkness in that long hour before dawn, salmon will be within 30 feet of the surface and will stay here for the first hour before they start descending. This is a beautiful, almost unreal time to be on the water. Herring swim to the surface and in dead-calm seas dimple the water like rain. In areas with shore lights, they become tiny points of light come to illuminate the dark water. Now and then, herring will come flying out of the water like confetti shot from a cannon. Even the most blasé of fishers can hardly restrain his or her feelings; herring only do this in desperation when chased by a salmon or ling cod. It's most enchanting to be 10 feet from a salmon made invisible by the dark, dark sea.

As the first hand of sun opens in the eastern sky, the dawn bite begins. Absolute first light can jolt fishers from dreams into a time of screamingly wild fishing, more Henry Miller adrenaline packed than any other bite of the day. And those fishers who stayed out late the night before drinking that last beer will be suffering a head hammering shortly, for which they'd better have brought along the Tylenol.

Within an hour, the dawn bite diminishes and both bait and

salmon begin descending. By noon they will have reached the depth at which they will remain for the rest of the day, and accordingly, your lines should be lengthened. In areas where fish descend to 150 feet, they may do so at a rate of 50 feet per hour, and your lines must follow. Once at their lowest depth, salmon remain deep for the rest of the day until about two hours before pitch-darkness, when in most waters there is another bite period. During these last hours, salmon move up slightly in the water column, and the fish found at 150 feet earlier may now be found at 100 feet. After dark, the salmon slowly rise until they are once again on the surface at first light.

Many factors influence the daily pattern. In summer, after very hot calm days or on full moons, salmon often remain deep overnight and will not be caught on the surface at first light. A deeper line needs to be put out almost right away to avoid missing the bite. In winter, chinook salmon, the usual quarry, do not rise to the surface and may remain at the same level twenty-four hours a day. Local information is required, as the crack-of-dawn depth in some areas can be as deep as 150 feet. On the other hand, rain and overcast skies often depress the rate at which salmon descend, and the depth at which they hold will be shallower.

Salmon do their best to create exceptions to the most general of rules. One bright, brittle November day, I was following my own advice and trolling at 125 feet when I spotted herring flying out of the water—something that ought not to have been happening. I reeled in my lines like a madman, changed to herring strip, extended the leader to thirty feet and crisscrossed back and forth over where the herring had been. In no time, we picked up five chinook salmon to twelve pounds. Be adaptable; salmon do not always do as they are told.

TEMPERATURE AND FISHING

Fish have definite preferences for water temperature. The warmer waters fifteen miles off our coasts tend to keep ocean-going fish—and this includes salmon—from crossing into the colder onshore waters. During spawning, salmon will hold offshore in the warmer waters until triggered to begin their spawning runs.

Freshwater fishers often make reference to water temperature to find fish. Temperature is highest at the surface and lowest at the bottom, and the gradient is referred to as the thermocline. Some fish—bass, for instance—can distinguish temperature differences of less than half a degree, and their daily and seasonal movements often depend more on water temperature than on light or other conditions in the small, warm bodies of water they frequent.

West coast commercial fishers do pay attention to water temperature, but it is seldom referred to by sportfishers. I am not sure why, but it may be because the ocean is virtually as frozen in the summer as the winter, deviating less than a couple of degrees. Added to this, the water is continually moving, so it doesn't have much time to be heated by the sun. And what little heat does get absorbed is quickly dispersed by the natural up-welling and mixing of colder, deeper waters.

RESIDENT VERSUS MIGRATORY SALMON

At some point in their life cycles, all five species of salmon move out into the open Pacific Ocean. Chinook and coho, however, spend part of their saltwater lives in the coastal waters of British Columbia and are referred to as resident fish during this period. Resident chinook are referred to as feeder chinook, and resident coho as bluebacks. Sockeye, chum and pink salmon, on the other hand, move offshore relatively soon after leaving their rivers of origin and are only caught by sportfishers on their return migration toward the spawning rivers in the summer months of May to October.

Resident salmon usually begin showing in local waters in late October and stay around until late April and early May, when they too move offshore. Resident fish, then, are the main quarry of sportfishers for the greater part of the year. They have different habits than migratory fish, even of the same species. Feeder chinook, for example, are generally deeper and more localized than migratory fish, including migratory chinook. Resident winter coho show as one-year-old one- to three-pound bluebacks and tend to swim in large schools within a larger but still localized area, and require more searching to be found. Once found, however, they are more eager than resident chinook, and far more of them will be caught in a day's trip. These fish can be among the most beautiful of the year, and are identifiable, even as they are being brought into the boat, by their distinctive greeny-blue colour. Varying runs of bluebacks frequent our waters from November to June.

Less is known about the life cycle of resident chinook, but it is clear that, because they range in size from two-pound two-year-old fish to +20-pound four-year-old fish, they may have a more unusual migration pattern than other salmonids. December to the end of March is the traditional time for feeder chinook. In some areas every fish caught will be a chinook. These fish take on a pronounced purple

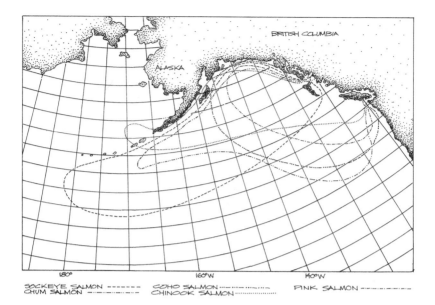

SOCKEYE SALMON -------   COHO SALMON ····················   PINK SALMON ---·---·---·---
CHUM SALMON --·---·---·---   CHINOOK SALMON ····················

tone to their otherwise green and black, spotted sides.

Not many British Columbians realize that for most of the year only two species of salmon are caught in coastal waters: coho and chinook. Sockeye are caught only on their return migration in the summer months, between mid-July and mid-September, and the annual run in any given area may last only four to six weeks of the year. Pinks return even more infrequently. On the southern coast, pink salmon return in odd-numbered years, and on the northern coast in even-numbered years. The pink run, then, returns through any given area only every second year and lasts six to eight weeks in a mid-July to mid-September period. The fifth species, chum, is seldom, if ever, caught. In nearly twenty years of fishing, I have never caught one, although millions swim through the straits from August to September en route to hundreds of spawning rivers on Vancouver Island and the mainland. Apparently, chum fishing is slightly more successful in the Queen Charlottes, but certainly not in the more frequented areas around Vancouver Island. One of the more frustrating sights in all of fishing is watching schools of 30-pound chum jump all over Cowichan Bay in October. Gluttons for punishment can be seen drift-fishing here and drift-fishing there. As literally hundreds of fish take to the air, they chase schools all over the bay all day long—and catch absolutely nothing.

Even though chum are not taken in any numbers, I expect that they and the other intermingling runs influence the fishing. Sometimes, all five species of salmon may be in your area and, strangely enough, this increases the chances of catching fish. Salmon compete for food, and if there are more fish in one area, they will be more voracious in snapping up a food resource that is just too small to support that many fish. I have often seen schools of trout in fresh water follow a hooked fish on a still-fishing setup that has multiple snelled hooks. Commonly this results in two or more fish on the line at the same time. Very odd behaviour.

In the ocean I have also spotted salmon following a hooked fish to the boat, presumably out of curiosity. My rather unsubstantiated explanation of such phenomena is that trout and salmon get excited by other fish, particularly those that are agitated, much the way that an entire hive of bees suddenly turns angry and, in this state, does things it would not do normally. Numerous times I have caught migratory chinook salmon on bright pink or orange hootchies when pink salmon are present. I have never ever caught a chinook salmon on such coloured hootchies unless in the presence of other species. The same may be said of coho, although to a lesser degree. Coho often prefer pink in a lure, but seldom bite a bright orange hootchie unless there are pinks or sockeye about. The few chum that are taken in the summer usually have bitten an anchovy—a food they do not eat, as they are strictly plankton-feeding fish. Perhaps they, too, are agitated by all the action. All this prelude to sex and death, the climax a salmon is aimed toward its entire life.

A BRIEF SALMON BIOLOGY LESSON

All five species of Pacific salmon—chinook, coho, pink, sockeye and chum—as well as steelhead, cutthroat trout and freshwater trout, belong to the osteicthyes class of higher bony fish and have similar physical characteristics. Salmon are swift, free-swimming, torpedo-shaped predators associated with upper- and middle-level waters. Their eyes, noses and mouths are located in the front of their heads. The position of the mouth is a key to their feeding habits, which involve cruising through the water looking for plankton or baitfish. This is in contrast to a fish like a halibut, which in its entire form is adapted to life on the bottom, i.e., a sedentary existence.

Salmon hearing is acute and located in the lateral line—the darkish line that runs along the side of the body as the faint border separating the darker dorsal half from the lighter ventral side. Typically, darker upper sides provide some evolutionary protection from predators above, who may fail to see the owner against the dark water below. Lighter bellies provide protection from predators beneath, who may not be able to distinguish the animal from the lighter colours of the sky.

The life cycle of all species of salmon is similar. All salmon breed in fresh water, spend a portion of their lives in salt water, then return to fresh water for breeding, at which time every salmon dies. At spawning, many males are bigger than females, which is surprising since females carry a greater load—thousands of eggs— and should require greater bulk for this purpose. I hate to say this, but males are less important than females. Males provide only sperm, and each individual is, therefore, less important than each individual female that carries eggs. After some months, the life cycle begins anew with alevins hatching from the gravel. After a period as fry in fresh water, the smolts make their way to the ocean for the maturation period of their lives. Salmon have incredible powers of smell, and, in returning to their river of origin, can not only distinguish these waters, but can return to the same 100-yard section of river from which they were hatched. Undoubtedly this helps to spread breeding pairs out along the limited space of the gravel beds. Salmon are so tuned in to their waters of origin that smolts reared in saltwater pens under piers will return there at the end of their lives and wait until they die rather than enter a local river to spawn.

SALMON SPECIES OF BRITISH COLUMBIA

Chinook

While found in smaller streams, greater numbers of chinook salmon begin their lives in major river systems, the most important being the Fraser and the Yukon rivers. Unlike other salmonids, newly hatched chinook fry spend varying lengths of time in fresh water, from a few months to a year. After leaving fresh water, chinook become the resident, year-round salmon in the coastal areas of British Columbia and may weigh, in their fourth year, more than twenty pounds. They do migrate vast distances into the Pacific Ocean during this portion of their lives as well, but little is known about the relationship between the portions of their life cycle spent as migratory and resident fish.

Normally spawning at four years of age, returning chinook can be from two to seven years old. Some of the older fish may reach weights in excess of seventy pounds, making chinook the largest of all salmon. In their first year, they will be less than 2 pounds and most will be shorter than the 45 cm (18 inches) size-restriction limit placed on southern waters. Toward the end of their second year, chinook may reach about 5 pounds, or slightly less than the Georgia Strait size restriction of 62 cm (24.5 inches). 10- to 15-pound chinook will most commonly be at least three years of age, and, of course, larger fish may be from four to seven years old. Variation in the year of spawning results in cross-fertilization of genetic traits from one brood year to another, and also minimizes the effects of years when few fish make it to the spawning beds. (This advantage is not shared by all species. Pink salmon, for example, return only as two-year-old fish, and this is why there is no even-numbered-year run for the Fraser River; it was wiped out in the 1920s and has never made a comeback.)

Chinook are among the easiest salmon to recognize. They have black mouths that are filled with razor-sharp teeth, which, though intended for ripping apart herring, do a good job on the hands of fishers as well. Seldom is there a time that I don't have a cut or two from chinook teeth on my hands. Chinook may be secondarily identified by the number of black spots on their backs, which extend into their tails. This, coupled with the large size of their scales, normally will distinguish them from other salmon. Another distinguishing characteristic, strangely enough, is their smell. No other fish in the sea smells like a chinook—a good thing, since they smell like a cross between a very new fish and a very old armpit. What they lack in odour, though, chinook make up for in looks; they are handsome fish with a black-spotted mid-green on their dorsal half, which has a lovely purple tinge in the winter and a blackish tinge in the summer. Chinook flesh is usually a darkish pink, somewhat closer to the lighter-coloured flesh of a pink salmon than the brighter orange of a sockeye; however, chinook is the only salmon with two genetically different stock—most have pinkish flesh, but a few have white meat.

Chinook behaviour is quite different from that of other salmon. They are the least tightly schooling salmon and tend to inhabit an area as they move, rather than swimming in the tight, coordinated formations of other salmon. On the other hand, as individuals they have a decided preference for hugging shoreline or specific offshore bottom features. They are found in more highly localized nooks and crannies than other salmon, particularly first thing in the morning; chinook tend to hole up right against underwater land structures overnight and seldom venture from these much, even in the day. In fact, chinook may be taken from shore all day long in many fishing areas.

In most areas, Chinook are the deepest swimming of the salmon. From the surface at the crack of dawn, they may descend as much as 250 feet in four or five hours. They are seldom caught offshore—that is, in a position unrelated to some bottom structure—unless the current pushes them there. These two characteristics influence fishing for chinook, and your fishing pattern for these fish should always take into account the terrain under your boat; move in and out from shore to match drop-offs and reefs. Where chinook venture away from a bottom structure, they have usually swum in a straight line while the shore has cut back to the inside.

Summer runs can be much shallower than winter runs. This makes for unusual fishing in October, when the last of the spawners are beetling for a river on the surface and the first of the incoming resident chinook are seeping in, as much as 100 feet below them. I find it fascinating that these two groups of fish will not intermingle at all.

Coho

Most British Columbia coho salmon begin life in one of nearly 800 streams. Unlike other salmon, coho spend at least a full year in fresh water before venturing into the sea. After leaving fresh water between April and July, coho move northward along the coast, then return to inland waters in winter as one- to three-pound bluebacks (which are, along with chinook, the resident salmon in these waters). In late spring, these fish again migrate northward into the Pacific Ocean, until dispersing later that year in late summer and fall for spawning. Most of their growth occurs in the last few months of their saltwater lives—as much as a pound per week—which accounts for their voracious habits when moving toward spawning rivers. Coho migration season is remarkable for the herring balls that endlessly form and reform as coho gorge themselves en route to the spawning dance.

Normally spawning at three years of age, returning coho can be either two or three years old. Some of the older fish reach weights of over twenty pounds, making coho the second largest of the sport-caught salmon. The size-restriction limit is 30 cm (12 inches),

and coho reach this length in their second year. Limited cross-fertilization from one brood year to another is a life-cycle feature shared
with chinook.

Sometimes mistaken for sockeye salmon, coho have a number
of identifying features. Although they are commonly described in
federal Fisheries and Oceans documents as having white jaws, the
upper jaw will most often be white while the lower jaw will be
black. Coho teeth are also the razor-sharp, pin-like projections
found in chinook; these teeth identify both species as the true carnivores of the salmon world. In colouration, coho are more greeny-
bluey-grey on the top, and much more silverish on the side than
chinook; hence they are called "silvers" in Washington State. Their
scales are roughly the same size as the chinook's, but are more
tightly packed. The main determining characteristic is that coho
have fewer or fainter spots on their sides and virtually none on
their tails, which are short and stubby and decidedly grey compared to a chinook's. In my opinion, a chinook is a better-looking
fish than a coho; side by side, a coho appears chunkier and slightly
dowdy in appearance. This is not true of younger coho, which are
usually a beautiful blue-green colour, and very bright fish indeed.
Coho flesh is bright red, almost magenta, and is closest to the
bright orange colour of sockeye. Coho are known for gorging themselves on euphasiid shrimp, and this food source is reputed to
account for their lovely bright flesh. This food source is undoubtedly the reason that coho prefer a bit of pink in a lure.

Behaviourally, coho are more similar to the three nonresident
species than to chinook. Coho are among the tightest schooling of
these salmon, with a school of mature fish seldom reaching fifty
feet across. (The same cannot be said of bluebacks, however, which
tend to disperse like a sneeze into a large area.) Many times I have
looked down into crystal-clear water while drift-fishing and seen a
school of coho drift by, perhaps fifty of them, so close as to be
almost touching one another. My lure flutters delicately, tastily.
Fifty salmon, some as large as 20 pounds, swim closer, then right
up to and around my stingsilda, which is practically screaming,
"Eat me!" But nary a one sees it, even though it is dripping down
their sides as they pass in a trance. Only in a bite period do they
seem to recognize it as food. Sights like this make you realize just
how many times fish must swim right by your lure without biting.
Another oddity is that this school passes in a completely horizontal
plane much like a squadron of airplanes going down a runway—a

behaviour that makes one appreciate the necessity for fishing at the correct depth.

The tight-schooling behaviour of coho affects your fishing. In order to reestablish contact with a school, you will have to be very precise in remembering the exact spot where you hooked (not landed) a fish. The need for precision is mitigated by the fact that, in any given area, there may be a number of different schools. This may give the impression that the fish are very spread out, when in fact you may be encountering a different school of fish each time you catch one.

Coho are most often found in the top 50 feet of water, making them easier to locate than chinook and also easier to spot as a school on a depth sounder. Occasionally taken by casters from land, coho are usually found one to three miles offshore, associated with a series of tidelines where shrimp and herring are being congregated. In contrast to chinook, coho seldom align themselves with bottom structures and tend to be found mid-channel or some distance away from land. In locations where coho buck this trend, they are usually as deep as chinook and may be fished in the same way.

One unusual aspect of migratory coho behaviour is their erratic bite periods. The bite period seems to come on and go off, and is not always associated with tide changes. A little light bulb switches on in their heads every now and then and they start to feed. Every hour or so, a 15-minute bite period will come on and every boat will seem to have one on the line, and then all will be quiet on the western front for another hour.

Blueback fishing differs slightly in that these fish are continually eager. Catching your limit is more related to cranking a tight turn and immediately going back over the exact spot where the school was last intercepted. Coho are excitable salmon and prefer shorter leaders—as short as 18 inches. If you get a fish on the line that is one second behind the boat, the next second in front of it and the next doing a cartwheel right over top of it, you likely have a coho on the line. They are the trapeze artists of the salmon world.

Pinks

The most abundant species of salmon, pinks spawn mainly in rivers and streams near the coast, although the Fraser River supports a large population in odd-numbered years. In mid-island areas, both odd- and even-year runs are recorded, while in northern areas—for example, in the Queen Charlottes—the run in even-numbered years vastly outnumbers that in odd-numbered years. Young pinks migrate to the sea soon after emerging from the gravel, and return as two-year-old fish, after an 18-month Pacific trek. A peculiarity of this species is its fixed 2-year life span; there is no overlapping of runs from one year to the next. This explains why the Fraser River even-year run, which was wiped out in the 1920s, has not returned.

Pink salmon are the easiest of the salmon to identify. Their most obvious characteristics are large, oval spots that flow into their tails, and tiny scales covering their bodies. Seldom larger than twelve pounds, pinks sport a nice, light-green colour. As plankton feeders, pinks have few teeth and the softest mouths of any species. Care is needed in landing them, as their mouths rip apart easily. Their flesh, the lightest sandy-pink colour of all species, also breaks down quickly after being caught. Male pinks are slightly larger than females and grow a decided hump on their backs, leading to their most common nickname of "humpies." Commercial fishers refer to them as "slimies" because, without a doubt, they are the slimiest salmon by far. It's not a bad idea to clean up your boat after every fish, or you may just join the rest of them in the drink.

True migratory salmon, pinks are caught only as mature spawning fish, during a few-weeks stretch in August and September. In other words, pink salmon are present only two months out of every twenty-four in most waters. At five to ten pounds, pinks are not large salmon, but it is rare to catch one smaller than the 30 cm (12 inch) size-restriction limit. But, ahh, when they are around, pinks make up for their size. Fishing for pinks can only be described as coho fishing at its finest—complete, utter, absolute, unending, indescribable, prozac-blandness-eradicating, napalm-rivalling-incandescent pandemonium. Pink salmon bite at the crack of dawn, an hour after the crack of dawn, on the tides and off the tides, an hour before lunch and an hour after lunch, at dusk and after dusk, and pretty well any old in-between time. Pinks swim in vast schools, right up by the rocks and every other place all the way to twelve miles out. They like shore. They like rocks. They like kelp and tidelines and every place else. They like bright orange hootchies and virtually any other lure you can throw out. I have had endless days of summer sun where we could have caught fifty of them if the limit allowed it.

If you can't catch a pink, it is time to give up. But before you give up, remember a few things to help you out. Pinks are the salmon of magpie-like behaviour. They are the salmon that will fin on dead-calm days, appearing as herds of teeny-weeny sticks. They will jump like dolphins one after the other. They are accommodating, and nearly always present themselves in the first sixty feet of water in depth sounder-spottable schools. If you see a herring ball, you are almost certain to pick up a pink. Generally plankton feeders, pinks will be caught oozing herring from their throats—they are the most omnivorous of all salmon. Pinks are completely moved by tides and can be found in the calmer waters behind land structures. On the other hand, some of the best bites I have ever had have come on the end of a long, slow-rising tide where increasing numbers of incoming pinks are slowly accumulating in front of a shallow (where, as you will recall, the current picks up speed much as it would at the tail end of a pool in a stream). I have had pink salmon jump out of the water and take a lure I was lifting into the boat.

After painting such a glowing picture, it has to be pointed out that on certain days the pinks seem to single you out for persecution. It is terribly frustrating when everyone other than you is catching them. I suggest that the ego beating isn't worth it and that you simply motor on until you find a more sympathetic school. I have had skunks turn into 10-fish days many times using this "trick".

Sockeye

Most sockeye begin their lives in one of the larger river systems in British Columbia, the more important being the Fraser, Skeena and Nass rivers, and those of Rivers and Smith inlets. All sockeye fry spend at least one year in freshwater lakes and may even stay for two or three years before migrating to the sea. Upon entering the sea, sockeye smolts immediately migrate to the Pacific Ocean, maturing across a huge range of water before returning to spawn in their third to fifth year as 6 to 12-pound fish, slightly larger than pink salmon. As with the other migratory fish, it is extremely rare to catch a sockeye smaller than the 30-cm (12-inch) size restriction. Although fertilization across brood years occurs, in many systems every fourth year brings a disproportionately larger return of sockeye.

To my mind, sockeye are the most difficult salmon to identify. Their most obvious physical features are their large, prominent eyes. If you can get close enough to see them without harming the fish, sockeye have the greatest number of gill rakers of any salmon, at 38 rakers per gill arch. A newly caught sockeye will be glassy smooth, as though it has been set in liquid plastic. They may or may not have spots, but are usually dark forest-green on top, changing at the lateral line to bright silver, and have large, evenly cross-hatched scales. Reputedly toothless plankton feeders, many sockeye nevertheless have stumpy teeth. Their flesh is day-glo orange and simply cannot be mistaken for any other type of salmon; this most likely reflects their food source. They are very handsome salmon. In the summer, if you find you cannot tell what kind of salmon you have caught—they sometimes look like a cross between a chinook and a coho—chances are it is a sockeye. Look for the baleful eye.

Sockeye behaviour approximates a professorial pink. Picture "Monday Night Football's" Frank Gifford as a sockeye salmon. Having said this, pound for pound sockeye and coho are among the best fighters in the sea. A 10-pound sockeye can be quite a battle. As with pinks, sockeye are usually only caught in a two-month period late in summer as they move from the high seas to the spawning rivers. Sockeye are also the salmon with mysterious behaviour. Many years ago, sockeye were about as catchable as sea anemones. Then for some we-don't-know-why-but-don't-care-as-long-as-it-continues reason, their behaviour changed. Initially they were only caught with red Krippled K spoons two feet behind a small dodger on a dead-slow troll. Over the years their bite index has risen, and today sockeye may also be caught on red or orange hootchies, red beads on a bare hook behind a flasher, a hook with a pink shank and so on. They will even snap at bait from time to time, perhaps because it represents a potential egg-rustling trout. My feeling is that all spawning fish are moodier than nonspawners and do more irrational things.

Territorially, sockeye travel with pinks. They are seldom seen on the surface (most are taken less than 60 feet down), although I've caught them as deep as 125 feet. They are definitely schooling fish, but do not swim as tightly packed as coho. So when you catch a sockeye, you are likely in a large, somewhat dispersed school that is single-mindedly heading for spawning. I have caught sockeye a stone's throw from shore and as much as ten miles out. Unlike chinook, they are not associated with bottom structures, but are found more often in a tideline regardless of its location. Sockeye are more likely to hit a lure when other species of salmon are present and also biting.

There are two secrets to catching sockeye. The first is to make sharp turns. I discovered this one day while cleaning out my front hold. Not watching where I was going, I glanced up to discover I was almost on the rocks and cranked a hard one. I immediately got a fish. I surmised that sockeye, even more than pinks, tend to follow a lure, mesmerized but not striking unless something changes its action. When you turn hard, the lure on the inside rod slows down and drops, while the lure on the outside rod rises in the water and picks up speed. Something about this change triggers a bite. The second secret is that sockeye prefer less rather than more when it comes to lures. When fishing with a hootchie, for instance, rip out a few of the fronds, and do not worry if the lure is unbalanced. Our killer hootchie was made by the kids; in trying to rip out one frond they ripped out a chunk of six, and it works like a charm. Do not cut off the tail ends of the fronds to catch a sockeye. Lure action stiffens and they do not seem to recognize the hootchie as food. If a smaller lure is needed, use a squirt or plankton squirt.

Chum

Most chum salmon are indigenous to one of the nearly 900 short, coastal streams of British Columbia, although some emerge from the gravel far from the coast. Yukon River chum, for instance, get their wake-up call nearly 2,000 miles from the ocean, and it takes months for them to wend their way to salt water. Coastal fry migrate within a day or two to the sea and can be identified from other salmonids in that they tend to spurt from the water in tiny leaps as the schools swim along the shores of protected rearing waters. Later in the fall, chum smolts move from the west coast and begin dispersing throughout the northern Pacific, where they spend two to three years. Some fertilization across brood years may result, as chum return to their rivers of origin as three- to five-year-old fish.

Chum salmon grow as large as 30 pounds, but, I'm sad to say, are seldomly caught by sportfishers. In southern waters, the few that are taken seem to snap in an irritated way at anchovy. As with other migratory salmon, it is rare to catch a chum under the 30-cm (12-inch) size restriction, as the fish are only present in local waters for a few weeks in the summer, as mature fish en route to spawning beds. Reports from the more northernly Queen Charlotte waters indicate better success; however, it is fair to say that chum, unlike the other four salmon species, are only of relevance to the commercial fishery.

Coastal chum present a pathetic and macabre sight on the spawning grounds. Barely a week or two before, these salmon were performing their characteristically unending series of leaps, their beautiful purple and yellow bars in the amber of afternoon. But as spawning approaches, chum become decidedly the blue-collar salmon. If sockeye can be described as professorial and shining, chum are the lunchbucket species, the Dan Dierdorfs of the salmon world. Their nickname is "dog salmon," perhaps from the hooked spawning snouts grown in their few remaining weeks. I believe in romance and prefer the alternative story—that the name has come down through the years from Native people. Whatever the source, these fish are almost disintegrating as they reach their destination, like mummies trying to keep their rotting wrappings from stripping off their bodies. Only miles from the sea among the cool, late-autumn, misty trees, they shiver in calm, clear pools surrounded by the rot of their own flesh, their fins like umbrella ribs without cloth, leprosied chunks hanging from their sides. These are not the sockeye who leap hundreds of miles upriver to spawn in the Addams River in their brilliant red and green masses. Sex and death and the Four Horsemen of the Apocalypse aptly summarize the mating ritual of coastal chum. Dismal. Depressing.

Just a short time before this, though, these chum are the salmon whose behaviour drives fishers crazy. As October closes, they ripen and leap everywhere. They swim in tight schools absolutely on the surface, erupting here, there and everywhere in a distinct behaviour no other salmon perform. Chum salmon launch themselves almost horizontally from the water, invariably falling lazily on their sides. The first leap is followed by another and then another until an individual fish has completed six to eight jumps, the line of which describes a gentle curve across the sea. There they are in their hundreds: huge, edible, uncatchable. You are more likely to catch one with your net on a long pole than with a lure. The uninitiated fishers can be seen having heart attacks when chum are about. The fish leaps; the adrenaline squirts; the fisher roars in hot pursuit; lures are jerked through the water. And then nothing. Then fifty yards away, the fish leaps; the adrenaline squirts . . . .

SEMI-PESKY ANIMALS AND OTHER BEASTS OF THE DEEP

Seagulls and Diving Birds

Most fishers believe that seagulls do precious little other than sit on their boats, digesting meals of clam shells and crab legs and then, when the sulphurous mass has worked its gaseous way through yards of intestines, doing their business all over the boat: on the bow, on the roof, on the canvas—even the ten-horsepower kicker innocently asleep on the back end. White piles of bones and shells and vertebrae.

Baked in by the sun, seagull droppings are next to impossible to get off the boat, and it's extremely embarrassing to pull up to a gas dock when your boat looks and smells like a Peruvian guano factory.

Hard as it may be to believe, though, seagulls do have their uses. They are excellent indicators of where the fish may be found, particularly in the summer. Seagulls spend a great deal of time crossing and recrossing the sea, patrolling for food. Seagulls tend to fly in straight lines, and, if you watch closely, they will—among the various individuals on the wing—cover every inch of water around you.

When one seagull spots food, it gives off an excited squawk recognized by other seagulls as meaning, "There's food here." Every seagull within squawking distance, some well over a mile away, come flying straight as arrows to settle in on the feast. The more seagulls that arrive and the greater the amount of food, the more noise they make, thus attracting even more birds. Most often, the seagulls will be feasting on a herring ball or the remains of one. As I've already mentioned, you can often hear the seagulls before you spot the herring ball. Salmon will be underneath, forcing the herring up (although from time to time it will be diving birds, or dogfish); the seagulls will be dive-bombing from above.

In approaching a herring ball, it's best not to charge right through the middle. This scares the salmon as well as the herring, and both will disperse. Instead, aim your boat to the side of the ball and cast across it or to the side. If you are trolling, also aim to the side of the ball. Once you pass the herring—and it's quite a moving sight, with all the activity and noise—turn toward the side that the herring ball was on, dragging your lure under it without disturbing the ball. Once you are clear of the ball, giving yourself just enough room to make a circle, turn and make another pass in the same way. Continue doing this until the herring ball dissipates. Remember, herring balls nearly always indicate salmon—feeding salmon—and therefore solve the problem of finding the fish. They should be fished thoroughly, before and after they dissipate.

Diving birds may also indicate the presence of salmon. Mures, guillemots, cormorants, grebes and the other diving birds feed on the baitfish that salmon feed on, so they are regularly found with one another. Diving birds, unlike seagulls, which can only penetrate the water a foot or two, dive to depths of over 100 feet. The longer a bird is under the water, the deeper the feed will be—an observation of great use in mooching and drift-fishing, where you are sitting in one place with enough time to count up the seconds that a bird is under the water. A whiskery, white mouth indicates a diving bird with herring struggling to get free. Keep your binoculars on diving birds to spot this clue to better fishing. They seem to come to the surface before swallowing bait, and they often sit for a minute, herring dripping out of their mouths. Seagulls are also looking for diving birds. When the two are seen together, the school of bait is usually just under the surface and either rising or descending. Diving birds on their own indicate a deeper concentration of bait.

Killer Whales

Nonfishers love killer whales. They are the embodiment of all that is wild and free and untamed in this polluted, old, arid, ozone-depleted planet of ours, tilting off in its unimportant corner of the sky. They stand for Canada, for everything we believe in and hold dear about our wild, beautiful country, as hauntingly alluring and remote as the call of the loon, which is our bush-mad national music, the music that means Canada.

Fishers hate killer whales; they mean a day of getting skunked. They are the kings of the sea, and every animal fears them. Their power is immense. One or two killer whales will enter a kelp bed and simply wipe it off the face of the earth with a bit of thrashing. The rest of the pod floats about the outside, leisurely plucking up anything that moves. And their effect on salmon is truly bizarre. Somehow salmon can feel the presence of killer whales even a mile away, and a circle of doom forms around the killer whales; fish seem to understand they are there, and go off the bite. Either the whales are vocalizing, a sound that salmon may fear instinctively, or, after contacting them, fish swim off in such agitation that they transmit this fear to other salmon they meet.

Over and over again, I have seen the fishing go off for the rest of the day when a pod of killer whales moves through. It slowly dwindles and then becomes nonexistent even before the whales get to you. My advice is to haul up your lines and call it a day. Alternatively, move to another spot, as far as ten miles in front of the killer whales.

My first brush with killer whales came as a close encounter of the extremely weird kind. I was new to the coast and to fishing and hardly knew what a killer whale was. I was trolling along, enjoying a cup of tea, when almost beside the boat this wet, glistening black obelisk rose from the sea, like something out of A Space Odyssey. Up and up it went, until it was standing six feet out of the water and all my hair was standing up at least as high. Then without a noise it slid back down and simply disappeared, leaving hardly a ripple.

After a minute or two it had not reappeared, and I began to think perhaps I had just been seeing things. I knew the cheese in my sandwich had been a little bit old, but hadn't seen any obvious signs of a strange ergot fungus. And then, even closer to the boat, the shape rose again, glistening, wet and black. I simply did not have a clue what was going on. There was no one else around and the eeriness and silence, the calmness of the sea, began to work on me. I started to wish I had worn my brown corduroy trousers rather than blue jeans.

The next time it came up, it became clear that what I was seeing was a dorsal fin connected to a body that was far longer than the boat, something I found extremely unnerving; however, I was so mesmerized by the beauty, the dream-like way in which the whale swam, undulating up and down, that I stayed trolling beside it on a perfectly calm and misty sea as the sun went down, feeling in perfect harmony with one of the elemental and divine forces of nature. I felt quite blessed, as though receiving the benediction of all of nature. And it did not matter that I caught nothing.

Sea Lions and Seals

Sea lions adversely affect the fishing, but not as badly as killer whales. When they move into an area, they set up a rookery as a base of operations, where they haul themselves out of the water to rest and sleep. Their presence can be detected from some distance away, as it is their habit to defecate where they lie and the smell can knock you over from 100 yards. From the rookery, sea lions comb the local area for fish, generally wiping out a great number in many species, including rockfish, before moving on a few weeks later. Consider a sea lion to be a small killer whale. Salmon are very frightened of them, but only in the very localized area where sea lions are swimming. The fishing declines rapidly when they appear, but resumes an hour or two later. If you encounter sea lions, it is probably best that you carry on until coming to an area where none are present. Porpoises, which are larger than sea lions, do not seem to affect fishing at all; perhaps they don't eat salmon.

I have been sorely vexed on many occasions by the presence of sea lions, both Steller's and Californian. With the burgeoning sea lion population on the Island coast, it is surprising that the federal government has not authorized a cull. Sea lions are reputed to eat as much as fifty pounds of food per day, and it makes little sense putting fish in the sea if one effect is to increase the population of their own predators.

After getting out of bed at three in the morning to be on the fishing grounds before dawn, it is frustrating to have the day ruined by sea lions. One morning about four o'clock, just as I'd gotten my lines in the water, a sea lion head rose directly in front of my boat. I was so ticked off at the prospect of getting skunked that I collected up all my weights, scrambled out on the bow of my boat and began pegging them one at a time at the sea lion. It was almost pitch dark, the boat was moving like a ghost through the water, lines out behind, and I was jumping up and down, yelling obscenities far more colourful than "Get the hell out of here," and "What the hell do you think you're doing out here screwing up the fishing?"

Then I heard a voice yelling out of the dark: "What the hell do you think I'm doing, you asshole?" I almost jumped off the boat, because for all I knew I was completely alone in the wilderness, and there shouldn't have been another human being for miles. Unfortunately for me, there was one lone fisher casting from shore not fifty feet away, who, from his angle, could not see the sea lion in front of me. I don't think I have ever been more embarrassed. I couldn't even think how to explain to the guy why I was standing like a raving lunatic on the bow of my boat. So I climbed back in the hatch without a word. I had thrown all my weights overboard, missed the sea lion and embarrassed myself—and I subsequently didn't catch a thing.

Seals are almost as bad as sea lions. They do not scare the fish, so you can continue fishing when they're around; however, they have one not-so-endearing habit. Seals must be able to sense the unusual vibrations made by a fish caught on a line. They are plenty lazy enough not to bother chasing a salmon if there are fishers around, and plenty smart enough not to get hooked as they neatly steal the fish from your line. Next they surface beside the boat and fling the salmon around to let you see how big it is, wolf it down and then descend and wait for you to get another one on the line.

The "bite" of a seal is easy to recognize. It is preceded by the tug of a five-pound salmon, which then changes instantly into a freight train. If you try to slow one down, it normally rips the hooks out of the fish, or snaps your line. If you are not so lucky, you receive a palm of bright pain where the single-action reel smokes your hand from fingertip to palm heel.

Seals have endless energy, and it's not that great a tactic to turn and follow one. The seal's likely to get the fish anyway, and you're likely to get your lines tangled in the chase. Only once did I get the salmon back from the seal. While reeling in a five-pounder, the line took off straight down, which is next to impossible when the boat is moving. The line then wound around one of the downriggers. About this time I realized I had a seal on the other end of the fish on the other end of the line. I took the rod and, leaning out one side of the boat, wound it around the downrigger. The seal then swam to the other side of the boat, necessitating my taking the canvas off the back end and passing the rod outside the stays to the other side, where the line then wound itself around the other downrigger and fishing line. Abrasion on the wire line sent shock waves up my arm.

I decided to persevere and passed the rod in a circle around both the downrigger and the fishing line. At this point, the line took off behind the boat and became tangled in my kicker, requiring me to lean out over the very cold water and get it off. Much to my chagrin, it become entangled in the leg as soon as it was free of the kicker. I took my coat off, reached my hand down and, shoulder-deep in the icy Pacific, managed to free the line. At this point, the line went dead, indicating, I thought, that the seal had won the battle. I reeled up a slightly heavy line and found a rather squished, tooth-marked, five-pound salmon on the other end. I can only surmise that the seal got bored or mistakenly let go. So on this occasion it was: man, one; seal, zero. Unfortunately, it seldom goes this way, and I suggest that when you get a seal, bear down on the line and rip the hooks out of the salmon's mouth. In this way, fishing time will not be wasted.

Ling Cod

Ling cod are the masters of the seabed and grow to 70 pounds. They sit on reefs like gargoyles, huge mouths opening and closing, waiting for hapless prey. In the blink of an eye, they snap out, gulp the meal in one bite, then settle once again like some beastie-muppet conceived by Jim Henson. Not often away from bottom or kelp, ling cod are sometimes caught swimming with salmon near rocky shores in the early dawn before they have hunkered down for the day.

There is one method of catching ling cod that is so easy it is hard to believe it works until it happens to you. First catch a rock cod on a drift-fishing lure, then lift it a couple of feet off the rocks and drift through an area of tidal flow. Raise and lower the rock cod to keep it in close contact with the rocky bottom. Ling cod, like all predators, are extremely good at sensing vibrations from an animal in distress, and a tiny rock cod is in extreme distress if it can't get back down to the safety of its rock.

When the rock cod comes within range of a ling, the ling lunges out and, faster than your eyes can see, sucks the smaller fish into its mouth. Your line will feel like you have bought a piece of the bottom. Ling cod are so sure of themselves as predators that they will refuse to let go of the rock cod and allow you to reel them up with steady pressure. They spread their gill covers and come up like pitbulls of the sea. They come right to the surface before taking any action, and it is an experience of the Jurassic Park variety to see a looming, prehistoric ling materializing from the depths, huge-eyed, brown-mottled green, yet absolutely still, as though some disembodied ghoul is rising to get you. The ling is normally not stuck on the hook, but won't, simply by sheer perverseness of will, release the rock cod, a characteristic that is its doom.

Netting a ling cod has its own berserk charm. Just as the ling nears the surface, very gently put the net under the water so as not to startle it and, as though a patch of swaying kelp, surround it completely. A partner can make all the difference in this subterfuge while you keep constant pressure on the rod. The ling is so used to getting its way that it will sit there until the net is completely around it. At this point all hell will break loose. A 30-pound ling that has come up without expending an ounce of energy has its full fury to release on you. Do not, whatever you do, bring the ling on board. Lean away and let it thrash itself to pieces in the net beside the boat before you attempt to bring it in. Ling cod of this size can destroy a net, something that is hard to accept until it is witnessed.

The other reason for not bringing an unsubdued ling on board is that it has large needle-sharp spines on its back and fins. A thrashing ling can easily puncture you many inches deep. These spines—all types of rock cod have them as well—leave very painful wounds, so be careful. They are reputed to be poisonous; however, the jabs I've received have caused nothing more than pain.

Dogfish

There are no "man-eating" sharks in these waters. Instead, there are bait-scarfing, line-slicing, fights-like-a-wet-leaf dogfish. These docile creatures grow to 6 feet and 30 pounds. As with most sharks, though, dogfish have very sharp teeth and are carnivores, feeding mostly on the same baitfish that salmon feed on. This is why they are often associated with one another in the summer months when dogfish are prevalent in these waters. Dogfish tend to be a shade higher in the water than salmon and can be so thick that it is impossible to get bait past them to the salmon.

The typical shark strike is quite recognizable: a mild hit followed by intermittent tugging that dies away to a wimpy sort of nothingness. Dogfish teeth are razor sharp and, unlike the pin-sharp spikes of a salmon, grow interlaced so that there are no gaps between them. Accordingly, bait that has been bitten by a shark is sliced cleanly from one side to the other as though chopped with a meat cleaver. A salmon bite, on the other hand, shreds the bait, and thus the bite pattern reveals whether a shark or salmon chomped your bait. Dogfish teeth are so sharp that they often sever your leader and take off a hook. If you haul up a line that is missing one hook, or there is no lure but the line has been severed at the hook end rather than the swivel end, a dogfish is the likely culprit.

After striking, sharks have an instinctive behaviour that also weakens your fishing line. Holding the prey in their mouths, sharks (and even animals as advanced as alligators) spin in circles. The water pressure is great enough that it helps the shark rip chunks out of the unfortunate animal. Dogfish exhibit the same behaviour and tend to roll up your line after biting. Shark skin is sandpaper rough, and really does a number on fishing line. Therefore, check the last ten feet of your line for nicks and cuts after catching one. In fact, this is just one reason for making it standard practice to strip off ten feet of line each day and retie the end swivel, and also a good reason to inspect leaders so that you don't get a break when a salmon bites.

When dealing with a dogfish, it is best to avoid bringing it on board. A dogfish has a spine on its lower back, and when out of water, snaps its body from side to side, making the spine a formidable weapon. Once the shark is at the side of the boat, take a pair of pliers and crunch down on its nose. Then cut your hook from its jaw with your gutting knife. Do not use your hand; the teeth are far too sharp. After getting your hook loose, or cutting it from the line, poke a few holes in the shark before dropping it back into the sea. This will release blood and attract other local dogfish to the wounded and dying shark, thus taking them away from the area in which you are fishing. Many nonfishers will object to killing sharks, and I apologize to them for suggesting it. However, to fishers, dogfish are nuisances; they ruin gear and eat bait that salmon would otherwise eat. I would happily bring back a shark that anyone wanted to eat.

Dogfish seldom bite any type of lure other than bait. This is because their sense of smell is so keen. If you are drift-fishing and keep getting bumps but are not hooking anything cleanly, it is likely that the bumps are dogfish. They are attracted by the visual and auditory impact of the lure, but can't catch it. Sharks are cumbersome, stiff animals and are not manoeuverable at close range. It is often said that they roll on their backs to feed, but I have seen no evidence of this. At any rate, they find if difficult to get a dropping drift-fishing lure in their mouths before it is yanked up, grazing their sides. This explains why you will often bring up dogfish that are hooked in their sides.

If you are having trouble—catching one dogfish after another—do one of the following:

+ *Do not use bait.*
+ *Use an artificial lure.*
+ *Speed up.*
+ *Check leaders and retie when nicked.*
+ *Move further forward in a tideline or move to faster water.*

I have mentioned that dogfish have an exceptionally good sense of smell. You may find it fascinating to prove this to yourself. Stand on a dock on a rising tide where you can see the bottom. Slowly drip blood into the water. In no time, the resident dogfish will come cruising out of the shadows, sending shivers down your spine, as they search the waters for injured prey.

Mackerel

Mackerel are not found in coastal British Columbian waters other than in a year of an El Niño current. These warm currents from South America raise the local water temperature just enough for mackerel to venture in from the high seas, something that is an unfortunate occurrence. Mackerel are voracious predators and, like hungry teenagers, devastate any food stocks in their paths. In inland waters, they gorge themselves on herring stocks and intercept salmon smolts on their way to the open sea.

Anyone who has encountered a school of mackerel knows that they can be caught one after the other and that they are so indiscriminate in their eating patterns that they will attack artificial lures—and probably Twinkies—as readily as bait. In fact, I suggest switching to artificial lures if there are mackerel present, as they will go through your entire stock of bait before you reach an area with salmon.

Mackerel abound in many oceans. I once hand-lined for them off the coast of Wales. We used stout cords attached to jigs, much like West Coast herring jigs, which were then attached to a two-pound ball. As the sailboat sailed we heaved the whole mess forward, tried to stay clear of the line snaking down and retrieved it as it sank. There were so many mackerel they lifted the two-pound ball until no weight was felt on the line. We caught 300 in one day. I was covered from head to toe in slime and mackerel poop, which was released the moment the mackerel cleared the gunwhales.

On the west coast of Canada, we do not hand-line for mackerel. We catch them incidentally while sportfishing for other species with only one lure per line. But that tale gives some indication of their vast numbers, particularly off a coast that has been so fished out for centuries that catching a skate or a tope—their version of our dogfish—is considered extremely good luck. Our sportfishing is so much better; we are lucky, indeed. One way of contributing to decent fishing would be to establish a commercial mackerel fishery on this coast. Perhaps the mackerel could be used for pet food or fertilizer. This would be a useful way of controlling this pest, and it would also protect the salmon stocks that we put into the oceans at great expense to ourselves, and support our commercial and sport fleets.

Parasites

Salmon have various parasites. All of them are somewhat disgusting, but none of them are dangerous as far as I know.

Sea lice are horseshoe crab-shaped crustaceans with small, string-like tails. They attach to salmon near their ventral openings, and feed by rasping holes through the scales and skin and eating the poor animals' blood. Sea lice must be able to swim quite quickly in order to catch salmon, and must swarm the sea in millions, as some salmon will have more than a dozen lice attached to them. Lice have a tenacious hold on their host, but may be removed by scraping with a gutting knife.

About half of all salmon have tapeworms in their stomachs. These are truly detestable-looking creatures. It is not my practice to pick them up with my hands, even though I doubt that this variety of tapeworm is dangerous to human beings. The reason I say this is that they are adapted to life in a cold-blooded animal, and it is highly unlikely that they would survive being warmed to the temperature of a mammal. I have never heard, for example, of sea lions being bothered by tapeworms, something that might be expected given their salmon-filled diet.

On rare occasions, you will spot worms spiralled up in cysts within the flesh of salmon. I inspect each fish I clean and simply cut out these disagreeable creatures when they are found.

There is also a skin infection, presumably a virus, that salmon sometimes get. It looks like pebbling under the surface and can distort the whole side of a fish. I have never known this to affect the taste of a salmon and assume that it is killed in cooking. If you catch an infected fish, it is safe to eat, but you may want to fillet off the infection if you feel so inclined.

After feeling squeamish about the various parasites of salmon for some years, I came face to face with a difficult decision one day. I arrived at the home of a Korean friend of mine for dinner and made a great show of handing across a fresh-from-the-water salmon I had caught that morning. The next thing I knew I was presented with a plate of very delicately sliced, very raw salmon sushi and some soy sauce dip. Blood drained from my face as I recalled all the tapeworms and other parasites twisting in their sickly, malevolent, infectious heaps. Despite all this, I was brave. I had a bite of raw fish and lived to tell the tale. May you be so lucky.

BOAT AND FISHING GEAR

Saltwater conditions can best be described as hostile to everything made by man. The sea, the sun and, above all else, the salt all act together to reduce boating and fishing gear to rubble in next to no time, and there is no satisfactory solution to this problem; however, your gear's lifespan can be considerably extended by buying good-quality products and taking care of them. For example, inboard marine engines on boats moored in seawater need to be replaced every seven years—an astonishing figure given their cost. This figure can be doubled to fourteen years if freshwater coolant is purchased. All that freshwater coolant does is isolate the engine block from salt water, and thus the effects of electrolysis. Extending the same simple procedure of rinsing the rest of your gear with fresh water each time you go out will similarly add years to its useful life.

Millions of dollars' worth of boating and fishing gear stares you in the face in tackle shops, marinas and boatyards, and it is sometimes difficult to decide what to buy. Generally speaking, the rule on ocean-going gear is to buy better-quality, sturdier, higher-priced goods. In addition to the adverse effects of salt, boat items are subject to sudden impacts, constant abrasion, exposure to water vapour and destruction by mildew. Materials that perform satisfactorily include stainless steel (the only metal that will not corrode or discolour), fiberglass, high-impact-resistant or high-flexibility plastic, plexiglass and graphite. Semi-resistant materials include nickel-, plastic- or enamel-coated metals, anodized aluminium, brass, high-oil-content woods like mahogany, and Naugahyde materials. Materials to avoid include porous fabrics and most woods. Most metals rust like crazy.

Other products to avoid include those made of more than one metal. Every metal has its own electrical potential, and together, two metals set up electrolysis between them. In no time, this will present you with a frozen piece of junk. For example, the motor mount for my secondary engine used two types of metal in the spring-loaded bushings. In the space of a couple of years, they became so frozen that it was impossible to raise or lower the small engine. The motor mount also used laminated plywood as backing material for mounting the engine. Over the years, water got into it and rotted it out, making the mount completely unsound. Neither of these problems was obvious to the eye, but both had the potential to be life-threatening if the main engine gave out in rough water, something that is not at all uncommon. So do yourself a favour: in buying your gear, lean toward the sturdier, more functional products. They may save your life.

<u>REELS</u>

In salmon fishing, two main types of reels are commonly encountered: single-action trolling reels and open-face casting reels. Prices vary considerably, but reels are one piece of equipment where the cheapest perform almost as well as their more expensive counterparts and represent good value for money in the early stages of one's fishing career, when the move to ball-bearinged graphite reels may seem too pricey. The cheap ones last for years and catch just as many fish.

Open-face casting reels are much less fun to use in playing salmon than single-action reels; however, they are useful in two circumstances: casting from shore or to rising salmon from a boat, and casting for spawning-bound herring with a herring jig. In purchasing a casting reel:

♦ *Get the biggest open-face reel you can find.*

The biggest reel with the biggest drum—not the most expensive—will cast much further than a smaller reel, a tremendous advantage when casting over kelp from a breakwater or casting into the sea from a high pier. It is also much easier to cast to a rising fish from a moving boat when you have extra range to play with. Having said this, accuracy of cast is critical, and I would recommend practicing in the backyard so that you can put a lure within a foot or two of where you want it. This will often spell the difference between spooking a fish and catching it.

While perfectly useful for casting, open-face reels are not very good choices for other methods of fishing. They are not strong enough, for example, to withstand the strain of reeling in line under constant pressure, as is the case in trolling. As line is wound around a reel under tension, the drum has to be strong enough to take the multiplying pressure; open-face reels are not really strong enough. On top of this limitation, their drum capacity is often too small for trolling. More importantly, because they use a drag system that is independent from the pressure of your hand on the drum, tension cannot be instantly adjusted when playing a fish. Thus, they are far less effective and fun than a single-action reel. It is an uncomfortable feeling, indeed, to be reeling in at the same time a fish is pulling line out—you can't tell when ground is being gained. Some fish will be lost because of the inherent weaknesses in these reels.

The second type of reel used in salmon fishing is the single-action reel, a simple but highly effective design. These reels are heavy-duty versions of fly reels used in fresh water. They owe their name to the action given to the line: either it can be pulled out or reeled in. And that's it. While these reels have a drag system, they really do not need it. The natural way of applying pressure to a fish is with the palm against the reel; if the fish runs, you keep pressure on the reel and let it go; when it stops you reel in; line is retrieved the same amount per revolution of the handle regardless of pressure. This is a much more effective system than an open-face reel. In addition, single-action reels are far, far more fun to fish with because you have the fish directly against the palm of your hand. The reel screams in your hand; your heart sings.

When purchasing a single-action reel, a number of considerations come to mind. The most important of these is a reel that will not corrode. Materials such as graphite, plastic, wood, stainless steel and brass fill this bill. Do not buy one with a drum of another metal, even if it is anodized aluminium or nickel-coated. Over time, these metals begin bubbling and corroding, requiring you to take the reel apart, sand it down and coat it with not very swish-looking rust-preventing primer. They also are notorious for rotting the handles right out of the reel. Pick up the reel and choose it based on how sturdy it looks in your hand and its absence of metal parts and gizmos. Longer handles are easier to use; shorter ones spin like crazy and love to take the skin off your knuckles if you miss them.

Spin the drum. The smoother it revolves, the better. The drum should have at least 300 yards' capacity of 25-pound test line. I recommend this greater capacity because sooner or later the reel will be subject to great gobs of twisted up and tangled line, which you have to cut off. Each time you cut the line, the amount on the drum is reduced. Therefore, you might as well start with as much as you can.

And remember that a fully loaded drum has a greater propensity to tangle, another reason to buy a larger reel.

Three variations on the single-action reel should be mentioned: wooden reels, fly-fishing reels and combination reels. The old standby six-inch wooden recorder reels are heavy gear, but in certain circumstances are the single-action reel of choice. When using two-pound balls or when using wire line, these reels are the only ones that can take the abuse day in and day out. They are also elegantly simple in their construction, and when taken apart can be easily cleaned and put back together in a few minutes. Wooden reels have a minimum of moving parts and are the classic coastal reel. On the other hand, they are rather sluggish in use and do not have the dynamic feel of the lighter graphite reels. In rare circumstances, salmon fishing is done with a fly rod. These reels are also single-actioned, although much more delicate than their saltwater cousins. One other unusual reel can be turned ninety degrees for use as a casting reel and then switched back for other uses.

Now that you have an armload of reels, I recommend taking a minimum of four with you when fishing from a boat: one open-face reel and three single-action graphite reels. The open-face reel is used for casting and should be kept at the ready with a 1.5-ounce drift-fishing lure on an 8½-foot rod dedicated solely for this use. Two single-action reels should be kept on the rods you normally use for trolling, and a third, with a full complement of new line, should be kept in the tackle box for the moment one of the other reels breaks down. There is no point having fewer reels than the number of rods in use, and most boats use two or three.

Generally speaking, backup gear will make you a happy person. There is no point breaking down on the water without a replacement, or wasting time untangling a more-tangled-than-a-magpie's-nest reel in the middle of the bite. Far better to swiftly mount up a standby and repair at your leisure. I carry a minimum of six reels on the boat: one open-face casting reel, four single-action graphite reels (I fish three rods) and one six-inch wooden recorder reel. In addition, I carry a seventh backup, an old single-action reel used only for making leaders. Backup gear saves much grief.

You will seldom find the American star-drag system reels favoured north of the border. These are non-single-action reels, and for that reason would not be my first choice. In addition, American fishing poles have rod guides going up the top side of the rod rather than underneath as we mount them. While used successfully as the gear of choice in the States for decades and decades, these systems have not caught on in the coastal British Columbia market. If you prefer them, by all means use them, but be advised that availability of parts may be as limited as hens' fins. Yes, you heard me, hens' fins.

FISHING RODS

Even more so than with fishing reels, a bundle of pointy sticks cannot be shaken at the number of fishing rods on the market. And, like reels, the absolute cheapest trolling rod will give many, many years of perfectly satisfactory use before more expensive, more specialized rods need to be purchased. When moving on to other rods, though, keep in mind the use to which they will be put. Consider the length needed, where the rod holders are situated, how flexible a tip you want and the method of fishing the rod is to perform. Today, almost all rods are made out of fiberglass or graphite. In the past, bamboo fly rods used to be the norm, as did solid-core fiberglass. Some old clunkers were made of metal, and probably functioned better as lightning rods than fishing rods.

A few characteristics are key. Purchase the lightest rod that you can find. Pick up the rod, put in a reel and "feel" whether an aura of comfort and lightness pervades. The balance point of the rod and reel should be comfortably ahead of the reel. Find the balance point by resting the rod on your forefinger. If this point does not correspond to the place you naturally put your hand while fishing, do not buy the rod. Comfort is particularly important for drift-fishing. If the rod imparts no comfort vibes in the store, it will not rest comfortably in your hand those many hours that you stare at the sea and lift the tip up then drop it down. Another important consideration is having six to twelve inches of rod butt behind the reel. This provides the weight to balance the rod, and also leverage when held against the forearm and elbow. More importantly, the rod butt wedges against your stomach when a fish is on the line and allows you a secure anchor from which to aim the rod tip high while cranking on the reel. You will tire much faster with a rod that has either too little or too much butt: too little and all the weight is on your arms, too much and your arms must be stretched to an uncomfortable, inefficient length. In addition, most rod holders will not hold a rod with a short butt; it will simply fall out and fall overboard. Finally, ceramic line guides are terrific for reducing friction in casting, but pop out in heavier use.

Moving on to rods for specific methods of fishing, trolling rods should be 7 to 8½ feet long. I prefer a softish tip for downriggers, as this gives more purchase when playing a fish. You will keep far more fish on the line if the rod gives a little more. After all, that is what a rod is for: to lessen shock. If you doubt this, hold the line in your hand the next time you hook a fish, and try to land it without the assistance of a rod. Nearly impossible. When using weights, utilize a stiffer 8½-foot rod to stand the strain of one- and two-pound balls.

My heavy roller-guided rods are also used with lead balls and in extremely turbulent water, but more often for wire line and planers. With rollers for line guides, these lines are locally made and repaired, and represent the heaviest gear on the market. They can lift the bottom of the ocean if desired. Hooks are easily bent and lures lifted from watery graves. These rods last for decades with virtually no maintenance; however, they have lost their following over the years to much lighter, more fun rods. The longer two-piece ones are best for two-pound balls and should be matched with the wooden reels already mentioned. The one-piece seven-foot rods are best for planers, the heaviest gear of all, because the two-piece ones sometimes break at the joint. I have had this happen and watched the top end of my rod disappear down the wire line, leaving me looking pretty stupid with a three-foot stick that looked more like a baseball bat than a fishing rod.

For the sake of sheer, unending, cartwheel-causing fun, buy yourself an inexpensive six-foot trout rod for salmon trolling. Trout rods can only be used in the middle of the boat as a shallow line, because they are too light to trip a downrigger or carry more than eight ounces of weight. I often use mine with one ounce of weight and without a flasher, if possible. A five-pounder seems like twenty.

For casting, get at least an 8½-foot rod, and move to a 10-foot rod where longer casts are required. Shorter rods can double as trolling rods. Longer rods whip the lure faster, snapping it much farther. Most of these rods have soft tips, which means they can serve double purpose as mooching rods.

As for mooching, use a rod up to ten feet long. This allows for spreading of rods and getting bait away from the boat. In addition, you want a very soft tip, one that will alert you to the teensiest strike when a salmon picks up the bait and rises slightly in the water. This miniscule bite makes the rod tip pop up as the weight is lifted by the rising fish, as opposed to the usual bite on any other gear where the rod tip suddenly bends down.

One final consideration: the longer the rod, the more difficult it is to net a fish. This is because you have to lift the rod tip higher and higher to get the line close to the boat. The problem becomes more acute when you are by yourself—form an image of yourself, one hand holding a rod way out to one side and the other leaning out the other direction, like you're doing semaphore in some fishing cartoon. If you fish alone regularly, it may be best to use shorter rods, no longer than 8 to 8½ feet (the rods you use for other forms of fishing). Even when fishing with others, longer rods cause problems. The person playing the fish has to back up inside the boat to bring the fish to the side of the boat for netting. If space is limited, that person may have no place to go.

Now that you have a fist full of rods, I recommend having at least four on board: two trolling rods, one backup trolling rod and one casting rod. As with reels, have at least one more rod than the number of rod holders on the boat. I carry a minimum of six rods: one short trout rod, two soft trolling rods, one stout trolling rod, one rigged-up casting rod and one heavy roller-guided rod.

LANDING NET

One time long ago, my brother-in-law decided to use my net when he went fishing and thoughtfully left me his trout net without saying anything. That morning, I dragged my nine-foot dinghy across the beach in the dark, and floated it out onto the water. I stood there in my hip waders, gloves and floater jacket, swiping frost off the seat, then putted off on my trusty, faded, 3½-horsepower Evinrude across the bay. At that point in my career, my rods were the cheapest on the market and the rod guides were affixed with black electrician's tape, the line opaque from use.

I landed two five-pound salmon in the near dark and a nice, juicy ling cod on a flat, almost empty sea. Then I hooked a 22-pound chinook and, in consternation, realized that my net just wasn't going to hold any more than that salmon's tail. Only one other boat was on the water. Risking losing the fish, I sped up and chased it down, my whale of a fish flopping along the surface as I steamed along at three miles per hour. When I finally caught the other boat, I weaved in among its many gleaming rods, picked up its net and veered off. I was lucky enough to land the fish, and then to weave back in without tangling myself in their four rods and downriggers and hand back the net. The boat was big, beautiful, fiberglass, and practically gleamed like the sun in the gloom. As I casually hoisted my fish, both fists stuffed in its bloody gills, it was truly enjoyable to see how far a set of jaws could drop.

There is another point to this story other than my semi-malicious good fortune in my rinky-dink little boat, and that is that the net I had was too small. My hope is that you will remember this as you stand in the store thinking, "Nah, there's no way a salmon can be bigger than this net I have in my hand. I shall save the ten bucks and not buy the bigger one." My own net, the one my brother-in-law borrowed, seemed huge in the store, yet on the water, even it cannot comfortably land a fish larger than 25 pounds. So the rule in landing nets is:

- *Buy the biggest net on the market.*

When you are leaning over the side of the boat struggling with a fish, you want the biggest possible space for it to fall into. So think huge in nets, both opening size and net depth; be sure the net is as deep as the Great Lakes, or you will lose fish after fish. Consider a longer pole if your fishing platform or transom is high off the water. For storage, a useful feature is a net that allows you to slide the handle up, thus reducing its overall length. Be sure, though, that the mechanism for tightening the net onto the pole is solid, or the net will twist when used, and the big fish you tried to net will be the one that got away. Another useful feature is a lighter aluminum net, one with a protective rust coating or baked-on enamel paint. It's a good idea to ask whether replacement netting is available, because, as I have mentioned, some fish, such as ling cod, thrash the living daylights out of a net.

TACKLE BOXES

Tackle boxes have their own mystique. They have certain habits. In due course they will slide off anything at all slippery, but only when the top is open. After being launched as Lethal Weapon 33⅔ as you fly off a wave, they will fracture against the hull behind your head. Left on the dock, tackle boxes allow themselves to be kicked open, spilling $500 of your treasures, which disappear into the ocean like Faggin's jewels in *Oliver Twist*. For these and other good, semi-plausible sounding reasons—and because I am a gear junkie—I have three tackle boxes. One I use strictly for trolling gear, one I use for drift-fishing, and one contains all those strange things I buy and never know quite what to do with when they don't work.

When buying a tackle box be sure that:

- *the box is made of high-impact plastic*
- *there is little or no metal in the box*

- *there is only one clasp and it has a fail-safe mechanism*
- *the box is bigger than you think necessary*
- *the tray divisions are large or can be removed and resituated as needed*

The best tackle boxes are made, strangely enough, of good old-fashioned high-impact plastic or flexible plastic. Wood will not stand up to the pounding, to the number of times the box is dropped. Metal is even less desirable; it will rust and ruin all your gear, particularly your bucktails and hootchies, by dulling them and covering them with reddish rust. The only place that metal is advisable in a box is in the hinges between the lid and box. This should be stainless steel or at the least a brass alloy. Plastic is not strong enough; I have had them break right off when in collision with the boat.

Tackle boxes that are simply sets of trays without outer shells and that open like accordions have their drawbacks. They have a terrible tendency to spill open at the wrong time. Due to the inherent lack of strength in the hinging system, these boxes tend not to last in the harsher marine environment. Regardless of box type, though, there is good reason to have a fail-safe mechanism in the clasp. If the clasp pops open but the fail-safe mechanism holds, the box will stay closed, keeping your gear inside while you scramble to grab it, something of much importance if the box is floating in the sea.

Purchase one of the larger tackle boxes. As you go along, the extra space will come in handy for pliers, hook sharpeners, sidecutters, hook removers, etc., etc. Give yourself extra space in the bottom of the box. I have, for example, at least ten flashers sitting in my tackle box. I want a good quantity of backup gear in the event of line breakage, but, more important, I need this many flashers due to my method of trolling. When changing gear, I attach a lure to a flasher, detach the existing flasher and lure from the line and then add the rigged-up flasher and lure. This saves fishing time.

Detachable divisions for tackle-box trays are also useful. These allow you to change the internal configuration of your box to suit the lengths and widths of your tackle. Most pre-moulded divisions are not long enough for rigged-up lures—extra space is needed for the leader and swivel. Some drift-fishing lures are too long for the divisions and some plugs are too wide. It always surprises me that manufacturers of saltwater gear fail to recognize that their tackle boxes are designed for smaller freshwater tackle rather than the much larger saltwater gear.

KNOTS

Many types of inventive knots fill large sections of sailboating and fly-fishing books. In practice, though, I seldom use more than two types: one to tie line to hooks and one to tie line to swivels. A third type, the palomar, will also be mentioned for tying line to hooks.

Knots are weaker than the rest of the line due to the heat and friction built up in tightening them. Thus most line breaks occur at knots. To lessen weakening, be sure that before tightening each and every knot you wet the line by putting it in your mouth. This will considerably strengthen the knot. After wetting the line, tighten the knot until you can't make it any tighter. Fish are often lost because knots unravel. This loses you a fish—which may die from dragging around all that tackle in its mouth—and as much as twenty dollars' worth of gear. So picture yourself as Arnold Schwarzenegger and tighten those knots ba-by.

Knots are also weakened any time a great stress is put on the line, such as getting stuck on the bottom, having a big fish on the line or getting hopelessly tangled in a raft of kelp. Get into the habit of retying knots frequently. If you are catching lots of fish—and let's hope you are—retie the knot on the main fishing line daily. When using slip weights, pull off six to ten feet of line and retie terminal knots every time out. This also applies after catching dogfish, whose sandpapery hides are very tough on line. As the line on your reel gets shorter over time, you may be tempted to reduce costs by tying new line to the end rather than installing a whole new line. This is not a good practice. Either the knot will bind in your rod or reel, resulting in a lost fish, or the line will break at the knot.

The diagrams that follow show how to tie the three knots that I use. You may find them easier to understand than the text descriptions that follow. If flummoxed, have someone show you how to tie the knots (especially the sliding knot, the most difficult of the three to do properly).

The clinch knot most commonly attaches line to swivels or drift-fishing lures.

1. *Take the line and pass it through the loop on the swivel, then loop around and pass it through the swivel again; the second "loop" provides the real strength.*

2. *Take the tail end, using at least six inches, and wind it a minimum of six times around the main piece of line (ie., the end that is heading back to the rod). My approach, instead of manually winding it, is to hold both pieces of line in one hand and twist the lure or swivel in a circle with the other hand.*

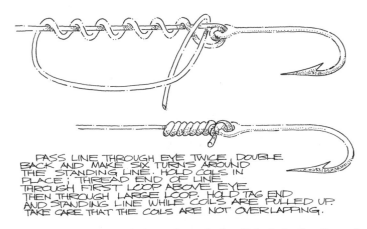

CLINCH KNOT

PASS LINE THROUGH EYE TWICE, DOUBLE
BACK AND MAKE SIX TURNS AROUND
THE STANDING LINE. HOLD COILS IN
PLACE ; THREAD END OF LINE
THROUGH FIRST LOOP ABOVE EYE.
THEN THROUGH LARGE LOOP. HOLD TAG END
AND STANDING LINE WHILE COILS ARE PULLED UP.
TAKE CARE THAT THE COILS ARE NOT OVERLAPPING.

3. *Take the free end and slip it through the slight hole that forms between the twisted line, just above the swivel, or lure, and then back through the loop that has just been formed in the free end.*

4. *Wet the knot and pull on the main line to snug the coils of line down upon the swivel.*

5. *Now tighten the bejesus out of it, making sure that the knot becomes uniform and handsome. As a quality check, pull on the main line to make sure the knot will hold.*

6. *Finally, take a pair of nail clippers and trim the free end close to the knot.*

The second knot, the sliding knot, is used to tie line to a single hook or two single hooks placed in tandem. This knot is far easier to learn in person than from a book, and you may wish to have someone demonstrate it.

1. *Slip a foot of line through the eye of the hook and down the shank. Make a loop in this free end, laying the end against the shank beside the beginning of the loop (ie., you will be holding two pieces of line against the shank).*

2. *Take the loop (with your other hand) and twist it around the shank so that it crosses over the two pieces of line. Wrap the loop at least six times around the shank, making sure—and this is important—to wrap each wrap up the shank toward the eye of the hook. The knot will not work if this is not done.*

3. *Moisten the line and pull on the loose end. A nice clean knot will tighten around the shank of the hook. This knot can be twisted around the shank—before it is tighened completely—to make the*

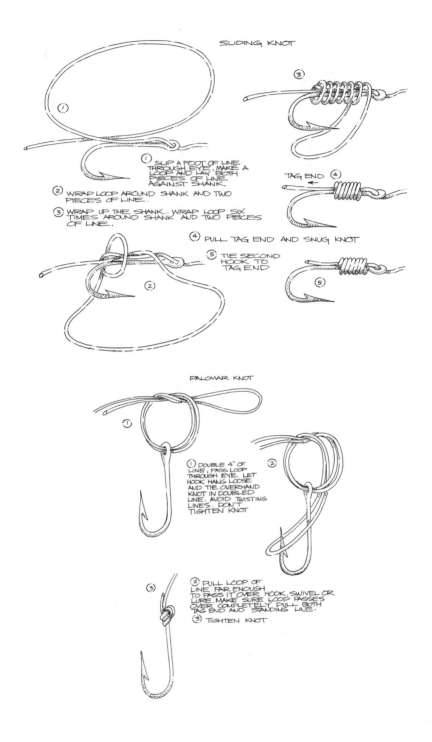

SLIDING KNOT

① SLIP A FOOT OF LINE THROUGH EYE, MAKE A LOOP AND LAY BOTH PIECES OF LINE AGAINST SHANK.

② WRAP LOOP AROUND SHANK AND TWO PIECES OF LINE.

③ WRAP UP THE SHANK... WRAP LOOP SIX TIMES AROUND SHANK AND TWO PIECES OF LINE.

④ PULL TAG END AND SNUG KNOT

⑤ TIE SECOND HOOK TO TAG END

TAG END

PALOMAR KNOT

① DOUBLE 4" OF LINE, PASS LOOP THROUGH EYE. LET HOOK HANG LOOSE AND TIE OVERHAND KNOT IN DOUBLED LINE. AVOID TWISTING LINES. DON'T TIGHTEN KNOT

② PULL LOOP OF LINE FAR ENOUGH TO PASS IT OVER HOOK, SWIVEL OR LURE. MAKE SURE LOOP PASSES OVER COMPLETELY. PULL BOTH TAG END AND STANDING LINE.

③ TIGHTEN KNOT

hook sit at any angle to the lure or bait that you prefer. Take the rest of the loop and tie the second hook in the same manner as the first. This knot is called a sliding knot because it can be slid up or down the shank of the hook. While this allows for setting the hooks naturally in the lure, the main purpose is extending the second hook behind the lure. You will find this knot invaluable on days when fish are tapping the lure without being caught. Once again, of course, trim extra line close to the shank.

The third knot is the palomar and replaces the first knot discussed above.

1. *Make a loop of line and pass it through the eye of the hook.*
2. *Tie a simple overhand knot loosely in the loop, leaving the hook— or swivel—to hang freely from the bottom of the loose knot.*
3. *Pass the remaining portion of the loop completely around the hook.*
4. *Moisten the line and pull both the loose end and main line to tighten. As with the other knots, trim the loose end.*

FISHING LINE AND LEADER

Fishing line attaches your rod to a salmon, and when a fish breaks off, it becomes crystal-clear that fishing line represents the most critical link in the great chain of becoming a successful fisher. It may seem odd, then, that I believe in purchasing the cheapest fishing line on the market.

In my opinion, more expensive monofilament lines do not perform well enough to warrant the extra outlay of cash. I can hear line manufacturers gasping, but that is my opinion, and I recommend spending extra dollars elsewhere. Cheaper line does have disadvantages, and you should be aware of them in case you would prefer to buy better line. Cheaper line:

- *is weaker and breaks more easily*
- *nicks more easily, leading to occasional breakage*
- *is often of greater diameter and thus causes more line drag (ie., your line rides higher in the water)*
- *is more visible to fish in the water*
- *stretches more, leading to weakening as well as to added pressure on reel drums*
- *retains a memory of line-twist and kinks*

More expensive line has its applications, particularly when subterfuge is required to entice spooky fish. In clear water or in other circumstances where fish get a really good look at your lure before biting, better line is preferred. Better line becomes the leader of choice, then, in drift-fishing and in mooching. It makes great sense to use better, thinner-diameter line if you regularly drift-fish deeper than eighty feet. As depth increases, line drag can strongly affect the action of drift-fishing lures, making them turn on end and spiral down rather than flutter sideways as intended.

Both types of line make decent leader material because the main consideration for leader does not depend on quality:

• *Leader should be a minimum 25-pound-test or greater for trolling.*

• *Leader should be a maximum of 20-pound-test in drift-fishing or mooching.*

Although at first glance it may seem strange to use heavier line for trolled lures (as high as 40-pound-test), there is a very good reason for using stiffer leader. The purpose of trolling leader is to attach the lure a set distance behind a flasher or dodger that moves in the water and imparts action to the lure. This movement is effectively dampened or eliminated by lighter line. Far fewer fish will be caught with lighter leader because the lure won't work properly. Cheaper line, being stiffer, has a slight edge in the leader department.

In mooching or drift-fishing, on the other hand, lighter leader results in more fish. Stealth and downright sneakiness become much more important in these methods of fishing. The lure essentially sits in one place and does not require the salmon to chase and catch it. Lures can be inspected much more closely, and leader invisibility really pays off. Do not be tempted, however, to create huge long invisible leaders. Six feet is long enough. Leaders of longer length, as mentioned, result in difficulty getting the fish close enough to the boat to net the beggar.

When you hit upon a lure-leader combination that works well, I recommend that you do not change it; of course, this suggests a use for superior-quality line. I have lures with leaders that have not been changed in years. That is because I do not want to lose the indefinable quality that makes one lure deadly and an identical lure as attractive as a smelly track shoe. Every now and then I lose a killer lure, but in the meantime I have caught dozens of fish. On the occasions when I change leaders, poorer luck normally results, so it may be best to change only if the leader appears obviously destined to break. I have some pretty funny-looking, beat-up, rust-covered, old setups, with opaque, grungy antideluvian line, knots and kinks so kinky nothing will unkink them, that consistently outfish all my flashy new lures. Ah, the mystery of fishing! Ah the feeling of having deadly lures in your—and nobody else's—tackle box!

HOOKS

While there are many styles of hooks on the market, three styles are used most of the time: triple hooks, curved single hooks and straight single hooks.

Triple hooks have three barbs and are the hook most often utilized with drift-fishing lures and certain bait setups. Theoretically, triple hooks offer three chances to hook a fish, and, therefore, improve the chances of turning nibbles into hooked and landed fish. In bait setups, one barb inserts into the flesh and helps establish a wounded baitfish action. In practice, single hooks can often provide a good alternative to triple hooks, even with drift-fishing lures. They hook more cleanly and hold more securely. In addition, three-barbed hooks are next to impossible to remove from fish to be released. By the time all three barbs come free, much damage has been done and the fish is often dead; it has been pointless going to the trouble of trying to release it. When fishing for rock fish, it may be best to file off all barbs, because most fish are small and better turfed back to grow. Kelp greenling, for instance, have small mouths, requiring much cutting to release all three barbs. Rock cod have such sharp spines that trying to get three barbs out while they wriggle like unimpressed gargoyles can become an act of bravery.

The second type of hook, the curved single, comes with a kirbed eye and is the one most often used in rigging up lures at home. Most packaged lures, such as hootchies, come rigged with this style of hook. The curved single has a bend or twist in the shank so that the point lies at an angle to the shank, presumably to hold more firmly once the hook point sets around the jaw-bone. Rarely will you find these hooks in stainless steel, which seems strange as they are the most common hook, so buy a whole bunch when stainless are found.

The third hook, the straight single, is made for plugs, spoons and other lures, such as the Apex, which need to ride straight and streamlined through the water. My hook of preference, straight singles are simple, clean and the most effective of all for hooking fish. My personal, completely fabricated belief is that they are effective because their point runs directly parallel to the shank. And those with the longest point are the easiest to sharpen.

As mentioned, try to purchase all hooks in stainless steel. Anything else and you will be constantly replacing rusty and decidedly less-than-fish-hooking hooks on your lures every time you go fishing, as well as having your gear covered with rust—a big expense with bucktail flies. Even nickel-plated hooks make a mess of your lures and tackle box in short order. Stainless hooks are also much

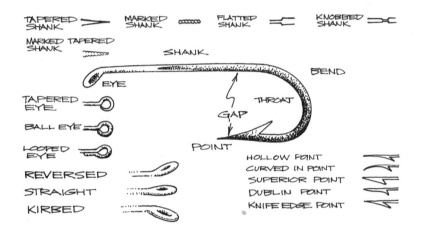

stronger than other materials and last for years.

Dull hooks will not hook fish properly. The second most important rule in all of fishing, right up there behind checking lure action in the water, is:

♦ *Never put a hook into the water until it has been sharpened.*

Test a hook by balancing the point on your thumbnail. If the hook slides off, it is not sharp enough. If the hook digs in or sticks, it is sharp enough. To sharpen a hook, first take a close look at the point and notice that it has two sides. Draw one side of the hook down a file in the direction of the point, then turn the hook over and draw the hook down the other side in the direction of the point. Keep testing sharpness on your thumbnail. If, after repeated sharpening, "stickiness" will not result, take another close look at the hook. Either the hook is old and/or rusty and should be discarded, or the point of the hook is coming down into a wedge rather than a point. When the point is a wedge, the inside front face (ie., the face closest to the shank of the hook) needs to be filed off until a sharper, needle-shaped point can be made. And remember to shine up the shank of your hooks by filing off any rust. This

makes them more presentable, and they w.
better at penetrating flesh.

There are many types of sharpeners on the n.
with grinding stones mounted above small engine.
however, in the excitement of the chase I have s.
broken every one I have ever owned, and for this reas
own any. Flat files with grooves in them do a reasonab   out
straight, flat, metal files are the simplest and best files on   .c market, despite their tendency to rust.

Finally, please remember that any hook sharp enough to catch a
fish is sharp enough to catch you, too. An almost eye-splittingly
painful chase occurs when you embed one hook in yourself while
another hook is embedded in a fish that is flopping around the
bottom of the boat. I have chased dozens of fish around my boat
this way over the years, and probably will chase dozens more. So
steer clear; hooks, not surprisingly, hurt like crazy.

GUTTING KNIFE

The first time I used my gutting knife I felt like one of those made-
for-television immortal beings whose broadswords are meant for
ceremoniously slicing off the heads of their rivals with a diagonal
slice so sharp that the very air splits in half, severing the neck in a
rush of St. Elmos' fire produced as only Hollywood can produce it. In
preparation, I swung my blade high into the sun, felt the glinting
strengthen my potentially immortal soul. Marvellous it was, how the
knife could slice already-sliced hairs; yet in my marvelling I reminded
myself—needlessly, I recall thinking—that the slippery sharpness
would just as expertly and indifferently slice me to pieces as the
salmon in my hand. I, of course, missed the salmon and cut my hand
right to the bone. I bled like a stuck pig until this door into my body
was closed with needles and thread pulled through my flesh.

Having cautioned you, I now have to recommend buying the
sharpest, best-quality stainless steel blade you can buy. Anything
less will not hold an edge and will rust in no time. Get a thin,
light, agile blade that can be sharpened easily. Also pick up a grinding rock and oil so you can do a proper job yourself. A sharp blade
makes neat work of slicing fillets off skin—a useful way of dealing
with rock cod. Scabbards are a must, because if you fall on a knife, it
will most certainly go right through you and kill you. If you are miles
from the marina and bleeding badly, you are, simply put, a goner.

Good gutting knives come with other features as well. The end opthe blade should end in a spoon. This is used for stripping the salmon's kidney, which lies right up under its backbone in a membrane-sealed pouch. A slice is made with the blade, the knife is rotated in the hand and the kidney is stripped with the spoon. The alternative is to stop with each fish, put down the knife, then pick up a spoon, something of difficulty on a slippery, blood-splattered, hose-washed gutting board. A floating knife comes in handy, as it is very easy in this gooshy environment to wash your tools into the sea. A less common but excellent feature in a gutting knife is a compass mounted in its handle. Not many knives have them, but it is foolhardy, indeed, to go out on a boat without one if not two compasses. Gutting-knife compasses can hardly be that accurate, but it doesn't matter; all you need to know when lost in fog is the general direction of land.

DEPTH SOUNDER

Like compasses, depth sounders are essential pieces of safety equipment. In foggy conditions, they give valuable locational clues, provided you have charts on board. In unfamiliar water, they can make the difference between running aground or hitting a reef. This scary prospect happened to me one day after crossing into the United States and unfamiliar water, far from help. I was bombing along on the other side of Deception Pass across the Skagit Bay flats, a broad shallow bay with only a narrow channel deep enough for passage. I missed one of the half-mile-apart marker buoys and became suspicious when another came at me on the wrong side of the boat. I was moving at full planing speed—three-foot chop hitting me directly sideways in the driver's window—trying to read unfamiliar charts. Then I discovered from the depth sounder that I was going full speed in less than five feet of water with my family on board, including my two young kids. My calculations were off by only fifty yards in a bay that was miles across, yet I could have killed all of us had I not had the depth sounder on and been thinking. This memory has scared me to death in many midnight moments, lying awake in bed thinking of close calls.

But, of course, the obvious, much less hair-raising use of a depth sounder is for finding and refinding those bottom contours that spell fish. In fact, as you get more and more familiar with the area that you fish and with your depth sounder's idiosyncracies, fishing can come to be done entirely by depth sounder, without reference to the shore at all. Added to this, many fishers will tell you where to fish based on following a certain fathom line, something you can't do without a depth sounder.

Depth sounders can tell a fisher many things. Most sounders can find the depth of the bait and also the fish. Paper recorders and liquid crystal display versions are sensitive enough to accurately find both fish and bait to considerable depths—well over 100 feet—and I suggest that you consider one of these before another type. My sounder is old-fashioned and has an "arm" that spins and flashes every time an echo is returned to the boat. Even with its limited abilities, I can determine the depth to 400 feet; double and triple readings; whether a bottom is flat or steep, or even a combination of contours; the presence of bait and individual large salmon to 75 feet; the depth of my downrigger balls to 60 feet; and false readings. Whichever style you prefer, be sure the sounder you get has a horn that you can set to sound in shallow water. This will save your bacon many times and help prevent loss of downrigger balls.

COMPASSES

My first rule of boating may seem odd:

+ *Do not go out in a boat unless it has a compass.*

Even a person with the best sense of direction will be completely lost in fog inside of five minutes. Yes, it is true that you can keep an eye on your depth sounder and follow bottom contours—sometimes—but fog is extremely disorienting. You have no idea how far you are moving in tidal flow and can be in a much different place than expected; reefs and islands you think you know by heart loom as complete surprises. Consider also that if you do not know which direction shore is, you do not know where to go if the wind blows up. In an offshore wind, for example, moving with the breeze—normally a sensible choice—takes you into rougher and rougher sea and, of course, much greater danger. I have already noted that I have been out in weather that went from flat calm to seven-foot waves in less than an hour. In some locations, there is the added danger of straying into shipping lanes. The hairs on your neck rise when the sound of a huge engine bears down but you can't tell where it is coming from or when it will appear.

It makes good sense to have two compasses. I was out one day in the fog when it dawned on me that whichever direction I turned, my compass said the boat was travelling east. I had no idea what was the matter, where I was or where the marina was. If someone had gotten hurt I would not have been able to get him or her to shore, because I had no idea where it was. When the fog lifted some time later, I was miles from my anticipated location. I also discovered why the compass had not been working. My sidecutters had been set down beside it and were magnetic, something I had not known. They had affected the compass enough that the needle was completely stuck. A second compass, left in the day pack used for all outdoor activities, can provide good insurance in this and any situation where the main compass fails. Hopefully you can refer to it before becoming lost. Some tackle boxes and gutting knives have built-in compasses, and of course, there are always inexpensive Boy Scout ones.

RADIOS

Communication with shore and other fishers can be accomplished by one of three methods: citizen band radios (CBs), very high frequency (VHF) radios and cellular telephones.

For the fisher, a CB is the most practical unit. It is cheap, easy to use and easily wired into the boat. Virtually all fishers use CBs, and you can get some pretty darn good information about fishing and water conditions. Guides often tell one another over their CBs what lures are currently successful. Tune the CB to channel 13 and leave it on. Channel 9 is the emergency channel.

For the boater more interested in cruising than fishing, a VHF is commonly preferred. It is standard practice to tune into channel 16 and then move to another channel once contact is made. Channel 16 is also the mayday channel, and consequently imparts a sense of safety to long-distance boaters. In any given area, two or three channels deliver twenty-four-hour weather updates. VHFs can be used to phone people as well. Fishers don't use VHFs that much, so there is no point buying one if your main interest is fishing. VHFs are more costly than CBs and slightly more difficult to use. You should be aware that to operate a VHF, a test must be taken and passed to receive certification. In addition, an annual licence fee is levied.

More recent inventions, cellular telephones can be carried anywhere and are unbeatable for making telephone calls when on the boat. Virtually all boating locations in the Vancouver Island area are within range of a cell, so you can speak with anyone as you would sitting in your own home. Cellular telephones are a very useful safety item; however, you cannot talk to your fellow boaters as you would over a CB or VHF. The temptation to use them for business purposes while fishing makes them seem less desirable to me; that use goes against the point of going fishing, which is to get away from work.

♦ 5 ♦
CATCHING SALMON:
HOOKING, PLAYING, NETTING AND CLEANING

THE THEORY OF THE BITE

The automaton cruises the ocean, twisting to the left and twisting to the right. Signals from its empty stomach glow in its pea-sized brain. From the distant green comes a flash and it snaps its tail, blasting through a cloud of parting squid. It slashes at a twirling shape and misses. Snout shaking, mouth widening, it closes in once more, chomping down on the hapless bright-red squid. Just now the rod jerks down and the reel begins to sing in your very own boat. You jump to the line and the fight is on.

If you think of a salmon as slightly smarter than a barnacle and much dumber than a seagull, you're in the right fishtank. Consider a salmon simply as an eating machine—a Pavlovian response, a slippery robot—that has little in the way of conscious thought, whose feeding is automatic; the stimulus is presented, the fish bites. And that's all there is to it. Unfortunately, while this understanding is essential, and the ethnocentric gloating almost unavoidable, knowing it doesn't make salmon any easier to catch. The reason is that they are extremely selective in what they will eat. On any given day, they may be feeding on only one thing and will simply pass right by everything else, even though it would satisfy their hunger.

The predatory salmon are chinook and coho (and also pink salmon to a lesser degree), whose main food is other fish. Carnivorous by nature, they actively seek out smaller animals, mostly baitfish, upon which to feed. As mentioned, though, they can be extremely selective, maybe taking a black Apex, a lure that does not even look like a food item found in nature; however, the action it displays extracts a feeding response. On the day a black Apex is preferred, it is common to find that none of the hundred other lures in your tackle box will catch a fish, and that includes another black Apex of a different size. Added to this selectivity is the common problem that salmon do not feed every day. I have caught empty-bellied salmon at all hours of the day from before first light to after last light. The interesting observation to be made is that the lure triggered a feeding response even though the salmon may have been swimming past natural food all day and all night.

The herbivorous salmon are sockeye and chum, whose food is plankton. These fish are taken on the same lures as the carnivores and omnivores but they bite for different reasons. Chum and sockeye are taken only on their spawning runs, a time when all salmon are understandably jumpy due to the hormonal changes associated with spawning—sex and all that. These salmon snap at lures that look like small egg-robbing fish, trout perhaps, and their aggression serves as a protection mechanism that ensures the survival of the next generation. It is significant that in the fall, orange and red become colours of choice for lures in many waters. As discussed in Chapter 3, this likely represents the colour of plankton, and may also be correlated with the infrared spectrum more prevalent in the autumn. Although salmon eggs are red, it is highly unlikely that a spawning salmon would snap at red lures because they represent eggs; most salmon do not feed once entering fresh water and, in any event, it makes no sense whatsoever to feed on one's own eggs.

Each salmon species has its own type of bite. Chinook have a tendency to take a lure and sometimes just sit there for a moment before moving off. When they do move, their brute muscle power is quite recognizable, particularly in larger fish: they imitate freight trains. You can expect to have to turn and chase the big ones because they are so powerful that they can take every last inch of your line and snap it off at the reel while you stare in dumb amazement. More than other salmon, chinook prefer to sound and stay deep. It may take some doing to get their snouts pointed up in order to gain any ground. Try plucking the line with a fingertip to get them moving.

Coho are much more excitable salmon than chinook and tend to smash a lure and zap off at full speed, sometimes hitting a lure while going full speed in the direction opposite to the boat. Accordingly, coho bites are usually more severe, and they veer off much more violently than chinook. Coho generally cover more space in less time than other species of salmon. If the fish on your line is here, there and everywhere, it is likely a coho, as is one that jumps repeatedly. When coho jump they tend to spin and flip around—a time of high tension, as great care must be taken to prevent the fish from throwing the hooks.

Pink salmon can provide heart-stopping action. Although not large, they also tend to zip around at great speed. Their bites come in bunches, so when you have one on the line be prepared for a double or triple header. Pinks are completely zany and unpredictable. You can be fishing along for hours, having not received a single bite at the crack of dawn or at a tide change and thinking there isn't a fish in the sea. All of a sudden the whole scene changes as though a light switch has been flicked, and the sea erupts with action for you and a hundred other boats around you. My suspicion in these circumstances is that you are encountering a school that is actively migrating past the spot you have been fishing, feeding as it goes; pinks are not resident fish and do not hole up for any length of time at all.

Pound for pound, sockeye salmon have a coho-like reputation for giving just about the best fight in the sea. They tend to follow a lure and just touch it. You will see your rod tip drop and then return as though nothing has happened. As mentioned in Chapter 3, try pulling some line and releasing it or turning sharp corners. Sharp corners in particular seem to entice a sockeye into biting, and you should always zigzag around when they are moving through. In fact, it's good fishing tactics to try this on all species other than resident chinook. Once hooked, sockeye walk on the surface like coho, or swim out to the side of the boat rather than behind it.

Chum are seldom caught, but when hooked have a deliberate, stubborn way of travelling.

KNOWING WHEN YOU DON'T HAVE A BITE

The rod bends down, the line screams and even the sleepiest novice knows that something quite fishy is up. This type of bite is obvious, but others are much more subtle or unusual, and their peculiar characteristics depend largely on the method of fishing being employed. Many times, however, it may be clear that something is happening, but the cause remains unclear. With experience, some of these bites or "non-bites" can be figured out quite quickly.

A fishing line that is caught on the bottom will not pull line from the reel if the boat is stationary. Drop the rod tip, and if the tension disappears, I'm afraid you have snagged a rock. Try backing the boat in the direction it has been drifting, and sometimes the hook can be freed. From a boat that is moving, the clue to a snagged line is the steadiness with which line moves from the reel. A fish, on the other hand, hardly ever stays directly behind the boat or moves in a straight line. If the line is not moving exactly in the direction your boat has come from and if your rod tip is bouncing up and down, chances are far greater that you have a fish.

A fishing line that becomes a heavy sodden mess is usually hung up on weed and should be checked. Similarly, if a rod's action changes, for instance, when the rhythmic up-and-down motion imparted by a flasher deadens out, most likely weed has been caught on the line as well. But this isn't always true. If the rhythmic action changes to a slight jerk every now and then, you probably have a shaker—a salmon less than twelve inches—on the line. Alternatively, you may have a small dogfish or a rock cod. If you haven't been watching for a while and the rod's action seems to have changed, more than likely there is a semi-conscious, all-played-out shaker on the other end—drowned, as the old-timers say, in the belief that when towed with an open mouth, a juvenile salmon's gill covers close; hence the fish cannot breathe.

Sometimes, no matter what you do, a fishing line cannot be stopped from moving away. Either you have a huge chinook or a seal on the other end. Normally, both animals will not be present at the same time, so it is easy to tell which is which. When both animals are in the area, however, a seal is just so powerful and so able to move at will anywhere around your boat that it is soon evident that one is on the line. In this case, I suggest you bear down and hope the hooks pull out of the salmon's mouth rather than attempt to wear the seal down. You will simply waste valuable fishing time doing this. Large halibut will also simply move away like undersea gods. The key to a halibut bite is line moving away but a refusal for the line to come away from the bottom. Patience, pressure and tweaking the line will usually move a stubborn fish. Another alternative is to clip a flasher on the line and let it work its way down to dangle in front of the halibut—very annoying.

It is extremely uncommon to catch a bird while fishing. Birds seem almost as smart as seals and are quite able to tell the difference between lures and the real thing. Perhaps both types of animals can see the line coming from the lure and know not to bite. This does not, however, stop a seagull swooping on a bait line that is being cranked into the boat. Crank quicker and hope for the best. If you do catch a bird, be very careful; they are wild animals and will do their best to hurt you. I suggest that at least two people take on one bird. One should hold its wings to its body and the other should carefully release the hook. And remember, your struggle may be embarrassing to you, but it is a source of much amusement to those in the boats around you.

When drift-fishing, it is not uncommon for the theme music from *Jaws* to be heard, followed by the entirely unintense, uncreepy feeling of an old sock on the line. You reel in your prize only to find that it is a sea cucumber. Look closely, and see if you agree that it seems completely implausible that sea cucumbers can swim, let alone be the carnivores of the sea. I've caught dozens of them, so they must be more stealthy than they appear. I can see it now: a rivetting new movie, *Revenge of the Sea Cucumbers*.

One day my drift-fishing lure was hanging straight down in the water, a position in which it should have had no action whatsoever. All of a sudden there was this teeniest of teeny tug and I leapt to the line. As I reeled, it was clear that there was something on the line, but not much. When I lifted the line into my canoe, there was an octopus, which should have known better but was caught by the edge of its apron. Imagine for yourself the next ten minutes of my life, trying to get it off the line. First it grasped my paddle and slithered out to the end like a mobile pile of jello, its great big eyes not for a moment looking away. Every time I reached out, it shrank away, and if one arm did not attach to something, another arm did. When I finally managed to grab it, its suckers attached themselves to my arm, an extremely unpleasant sensation. I ripped that arm away only to find another arm wrapping up my arm and the octopus sliding up my elbow en route to my face. In desperation, I grabbed it with my other hand again, and it succeeded in holding onto that one, too. It was like the old pratfall routine in movies where the Three Stooges have a piece of glued paper they can't seem to get rid of. Only this one had pincer-like teeth against my skin as I pushed and pushed it away. Fortunately, it was more frightened than I and finally plopped off my arms into the deep, never to be seen again.

THE BITE

Fifty percent of fish are lost on the bite. In other words, before you even get to the rod, half of the fish you might have caught have gotten free. Many days you will only get one or two bites, so trying to increase the percentage that stay on the line will dramatically improve the number of fish in the boat. Some of the ways to keep fish on the line during that short gap between the bite and the playing of them are as follows.

+ *Stare continually at your rod tip and grab the rod the second you get a bite.*
+ *Make sure hooks are sticky sharp.*
+ *Set hooks properly.*
+ *Pull hooks further back on the lure or mount a trailer hook on one barb of a triple hook.*
+ *Lengthen leaders. Quite often fish cannot grab a lure because it is moving from side to side too fast for them to catch.*
+ *Slow your boat down, or, alternatively, speed up.*
+ *Mount two single hooks in a sliding-hook arrangement instead of a triple hook. Pull the last hook so it protrudes beyond the tail of the lure.*
+ *Back off reel tension instantly so as to avoid fish breaking off. Use hand tension when possible.*
+ *Keep the rod tip high. Do not drop it to the water.*

I am such a wired-on-fishing type that nine times out of ten I catch the bite before my gear makes a noise. I have been known to scare the living daylights out of passengers as I explode toward the rod. Any poor soul who mistakenly stands between me and a rod is going to get straight-armed off the boat. When taking people out, I warn them not to stand in the doorway or I will go right through them on the way to the rod. And then I do, grabbing them by the shoulders and lifting them aside. The reason for this apparently rough behaviour is that you simply must get to the rod in the first few seconds or you will lose the fish. Once the rod is in your hands, the next steps are setting the hooks and playing the fish.

SETTING THE HOOKS

Once a fish has bitten on the lure, the hooks have to be driven home into the bony flesh of its mouth or throat so they catch and hold. Setting hooks is absolutely necessary in drift-fishing, casting and mooching, but seldom required in trolling; fish normally set the hooks themselves as they turn away from the spot where the lure was picked up. Fish instinctively move away from pain and this has a tendency to set hooks because trolled lures are to some extent anchored from moving. In fact, when trolling with wire line, setting hooks may have the opposite effect—it may rip them right out of a fish's mouth.

Setting hooks is accomplished by a single, sharp upward yank of the rod. In the split second before you yank up, quickly wind in any slack, then pull as hard and as high as possible. Be sure to rest one hand on the reel to prevent line from slipping out. This pull needs to be violent because monofilament line has plenty of stretch. If you have 100 feet out, for example, a 6-foot yank may only translate into a couple of feet at the lure end. And remember, you will only get one chance before the fish attempts to spit out the lure and melt back into the wide green sea.

PLAYING A SALMON

Fifty percent of hooked salmon are lost in the first few seconds that a rod is in a fisher's hands. A few simple techniques can eliminate this problem almost completely.

+ *Keep the rod tip high.*
+ *Keep tension on the fish at all times.*
+ *Let a fish take line when it wants to.*

Raising the tip as high as possible is the most important action you can take in playing a fish. The rod is allowed to perform its job, providing a safety spring, providing some give. Let the rod help you. Let it absorb the shock of runs. A rod pointed at the water cannot absorb tension, and many salmon will be lost. Keep your eye firmly on the tip, and if it rises, reel in. If slack appears, reel like crazy; the fish is likely headed directly at the boat.

The fish's head does not have to be ripped off, but pressure must be kept on it at all times. The purpose is twofold: to tire it out, and to keep the hook embedded in its flesh. As a fish fights, the hook opens up a wound, and if slack gets into the line the hook is allowed to drop back through it and out of the fish. A loose line nearly always means waving goodbye to dinner.

A fish can be hooked anywhere in its body. Very often a fish will be hooked in the side from thrashing at a bait and missing with its mouth—another reason for sharp hooks. A 5-pound fish that is foul-hooked weighs a ton and does a good imitation of a Mack truck. Its whole body mass is pulled against the water sideways. Many times I have had to stop my boat to bring in a 5-pounder, in order to avoid damaging my gear.

Tension can be exerted on the fish in a number of ways; the most obvious is by adjusting tension on the reel. Both casting and trolling reels have screws for adjusting tension. Tighten the screw just enough to prevent line from escaping when trolling. When drift-fishing, casting or mooching, be sure the tension is tight enough to set hooks, but loose enough to allow you to pull out line with moderate effort. Too much tension and hooks will rip out of fish; too little tension and hooks cannot be set.

Most experienced fishers, however, do not rely very much on the tension mechanisms built into reels. They do one of two other things:

* *Hold onto the line just above the reel with a forefinger.*
* *Apply pressure by keeping the heel of a palm against the drum of a single-action reel.*

The most accurate way of knowing instantly what is happening with a fish is by holding the line with the forefinger of the hand that normally holds the rod (for most people, the left hand). Tension from a fish is transmitted to your finger much more quickly than to the rod tip and you can begin adjusting even before your eye sees the rod tip dip. For example, if the line begins going slack, you can begin reeling that much sooner. On the other hand, if pressure is increasing, you can release your palm from the drum of the reel (for most people, the right hand). Whatever you do, though, do not wrap the line around your finger. A large fish will snap your finger off.

The best method of holding the reel drum is to cup your palm around its bottom third and apply an even pressure to slow the fish down. As the fish pulls, loosen pressure to avoid hooks being ripped out. Even a 5-pound fish can rip hooks from its mouth if the line is bound down completely. Many times I have had eight-pound fish break 25-pound-test line. And remember to keep your fingers out of the way of whizzing handles. Knuckle bashing is extremely painful. I have lost more skin to smoking fishing reels than to anything else on the boat. (This is saying a lot, because in my nearly insane adrenaline glee I have been known to repeatedly bash my hand silly trying to bonk a fish with my fish bonker.)

Now that you are watching the tip, feeling the pulse of the line, alternately reeling and holding the reel, you are playing the fish— the experience that is the whole point of fishing. If surrounded by other boats, you need to determine fairly quickly how big the fish is, something that only experience can tell you. Shout "Fish on" to nearby boats, and most reasonable people will stay out of your way. If the fish is large, which can be determined by the length of its runs, begin edging away from other boats so that you can fight the fish in clear, water where the chance of snagging another line is minimal.

Any fish over 15 pounds, or that can take 100 feet of line on a run, should be treated with such respect, and it may be better to employ other tactics. If you take the boat out of gear in good tidal flow, other boats will soon motor right on by. Have someone else bring up the other lines and downriggers, because a large fish has plenty of power, even when tired, to swim into them, get snagged and get off the line. When by yourself, stay moving, bring the gear in on one side of the boat and try to keep the fish on that side. This manoeuvre is easier said than done, and success is more likely when the boat is making a slow turn toward the side on which the fish is swimming. If the lines cannot be removed, be sure to play the fish a little bit more so that it tires before coming close to the lines. Take heart, though. In my many years of fishing, I have found that after the first thirty seconds, only a few fish are lost during the playing process—that is, unless they jump.

You are heartily advised to keep a fish (and this is next to impossible) from jumping. Fifty percent of all fish that jump get away. During jumping, hooks come free. When a fish comes flying out of the water, the pressure on the line suddenly drops, allowing the hook in its jaw to slip in the wound and fall out. Alternatively, when the fish falls and snaps the slack out of the line, the force of the sudden pull rips out the hooks. Fish are also able to use the sideways sheering pressure of a flasher in the water to rip hooks out of their mouths, particularly during aerial displays.

When a fish jumps clear of the water, immediately lift your rod tip as high as possible. If you have a flasher, dodger or planer on the line, allow it to rise to the surface, and the second it clears the water, reel in all slackness as fast as the handles can spin. Above all else, keep your rod tip high the whole time a fish is on the surface. You must keep all the line, and flasher, above water so the fish cannot build up any sheering pressure against the hooks.

Only one method helps to prevent a fish from jumping, and it does not work all the time: a fish that is played longer has less tendency to jump. When using 25-pound and higher test line, it is quite possible, provided that the hooks hold, to horse in even a large fish. I have seen 35-pound fish horsed in, so that they arrive at the boat completely unplayed and ready to run the moment the net comes over the gunwhales. This is not the best situation. The purpose in playing a fish is to use up energy on the way into the boat, rather than letting it go ballistic on the surface near the boat. Tire the fish by letting it take long runs right away. Keep a steady pressure on the reel and let it go rather than giving in to the excitement of yanking it in. Most of its fight will be dissipated before hitting the surface. Jumping takes tremendous energy, so it just may not jump. In practical circumstances, however, it is hard indeed to keep a fish from jumping. Once a fish jumps, give it more leeway and pay twice as much attention to technique; finesse it lovingly to the boat.

Not all fish that come to the surface are salmon about to take flight. Many other varieties of fish end up on the surface, usually in much more trouble than a salmon. A fish that rotates like a propeller behind the boat most often turns out to be a bass. Because of their round shape and because their mouths are not exactly in the midpoint of their faces, bass begin to spin when dragged along the surface. A fish that rides the surface like an orange balloon will be a red snapper. When retrieved from the bug-eyed depths, a snapper's swim bladder swells uncontrollably and finally protrudes from its mouth, incapacitating it completely. From this depth the fish simply lifts like a dirigible until it pops out on the surface. You will know a red snapper before it breaks the surface—its fight is replaced by a floating feeling as the fish begins rising helplessly, swim bladder ballooning with air. I suggest that you retain all red snappers, because a released red snapper floats helplessly on the surface until it dies.

A fish that appears to be a snake writhing on the surface will usually turn out to be a dogfish, its long tail waving. Similarly, if the fish comes in upside down, it is a dogfish. You will see its white belly and the dark cavity of its mouth, situated back from and below its snout on the ventral side of its body. If you see a phosphorescent green eye staring up, you are also hooked into a dogfish. Adapted to poor light, shark eyes are beautiful, prehistoric and eerie.

Once you have any type of fish close to the boat, try to determine whether it is well hooked and, therefore, easier to net. If lightly snagged or foul hooked, you will want to use more care; such fish have a much greater chance of getting away than mouth-hooked fish. Avoid lifting the fish's head during netting. Many times in the autumn, aggravated fish thrash clumsily around a lure, getting snagged somewhere other than the mouth. I have caught fish snagged in the gill, the eye, the back, the dorsal fin, the ventral fin and the tail. The fight of a tail-hooked fish can be truly wild because they don't have to turn against the line, only swim directly away from the pain of the hook.

Finally the moment of netting comes near. Instinctively, all fish attempt to swim upright. Even badly damaged or exhausted fish struggle endlessly to swim properly, so when a fish rolls on its back at the side of the boat, it must indeed be very tired. Your chances of netting it are far higher now. Watch for the white flash of a totally tuckered-out belly and get the net ready.

NETTING A FISH

If you have been following my math closely, you may be surprised to hear that there are any fish left on the line by the time netting arrives. And this is almost true. Far too many fish are lost between the bite and the inside of the boat. At the netting stage, I estimate that fifty percent of successfully played fish are lost. If the net is in the hands of a novice, this rises to eighty percent. This is why I recommend that the most experienced fisher net the fish.

In a perfect world, every fish is easily netted. The person holding the net places one hand high up the shaft of the net, and the other hand holds the loose netting against the shaft just above and behind the net opening, keeping it neat and out of the way. The tired fish lies on its side and the fisher gently leads it headfirst into the net, which is quietly dipped into the water to avoid scaring the fish into one last dash for freedom. The netter waits patiently for the fisher to lift the fish's head and, above all else, does not chase the fish. Fish are netted headfirst because they can only swim forward, not in reverse, so if the fish exerts a last gasp of effort it will only succeed in swimming even faster into the net. Finally, when the balance point of the fish passes the far rim of the net, the netting is released from the hand, causing the fish to slide forward and down into the net. Simultaneously the net is lifted, and voilà, the fish is safely in the net.

Having described netting in a perfect world, I should say that it seldom happens this way. Netting is indeed an art, a skill at which to marvel when performed consistently well. Netting from a moving boat, or when many lines are in the water, is difficult, and sometimes the best that can be achieved is dipping the net under the fish as it swims past the side of the boat. If you miss, it is far safer to regather the net, hold the netting against the shaft and try once more, rather than leaving the net in the water and hunting down the fish. Accordingly, two things should be avoided during netting:

 • *Do not let hooks get caught in the net. Virtually all salmon get away once a hook is caught fast.*
 • *Do not chase a salmon with a net.*

A chased salmon is usually a lost salmon. If you chase a salmon, you are trying to net it tail first, and it will simply swim away from the net. To a fish, this opening probably looks like a large mouth chasing after it. Even the most tired fish will try to escape certain death, such avoidance being the most basic instinct of any animal. In addition, it is very difficult to move a net through the water fast enough to scoop up a fish, because the water pressure is so great. Chased fish are usually lost, because in the confusion gear gets tangled in one thing or another and the hooks rip out.

Try to avoid netting a fish behind the boat. The engine creates a back eddy that draws the fish and your net toward it. You do not want to catch the net or fishing line in the propeller. Either they will be cut instantly or they will foul and stop the engine. I have broken the seals on my engine leg with fishing line, a very expensive mistake. An engine's strength can be witnessed when a fish goes through the propeller. The fish comes out sliced as cleanly as with a scalpel and the engine will not have missed a stroke.

Do not begin to feel like the Great White Hunter until the fish is safely inside the boat and bonked. Recently, I was holding a fish that I thought was well netted at the side of the boat. Quicker than I could react, it jumped like a trapeze artist directly from the bottom of the net up into the air and into the sea, never to be seen again. Don't count your fish before they've been bonked. Although you can purchase a bonker, one is easily made from a broom stick with a piece of pipe on the end. In a pinch, a hammer can double as a bonker. Please do a better job than I do keeping your fingers out of the way, and dispatch the fish with a good sharp whack to the head as soon as is practical. It is not fair to let the fish gag and asphyxiate, a death as gruesome as drowning is for a human being. Be sure the whack hits squarely on the top of the head or to the side right above the eye. Death is usually instantaneous, as every nerve fires at once and a great convulsion jolts through the fish's body.

A gaff is an alternative to a net. It has a sharp hook for impaling the fish, and then, while stunned, the fish is lifted smartly into the boat. Commonly used in commercial fishing, where losing a fish or two is less significant, gaffs are not used that often by sportfishers anymore. I surmise that people smack fish off the line more often than they catch them, and it is a sad sight indeed to see a fish swim off bloody and destined for death.

DOUBLE AND TRIPLE HEADERS
On those lucky days when God leans down benignly and touches

your forehead, as He did Michelangelo's Adam, you will be blessed with fish biting more than one line at the same time. This is the much-talked-about double and triple header. The successful landing of these fish is dependent on the speed with which you handle them, and on playing the largest fish first.

Quickly—and I mean within ten seconds—deal with all rods on which there is a fish. Grab one rod first, then adjust the tension on every rod with a fish. Set the tension high enough that the fish can only take out line when it runs. If line is pulled too easily, the tension will have to be tightened. Then play the fish on the rod in your hands. At the same time, keep an eye on the other rods, and if one of them seems to be stripping out a lot of line or the rod is bending almost double, it likely has the biggest fish. You want to be playing the biggest fish because that is the one with which most problems will arise and the one most likely to get off. While smaller fish are easier to handle, netting them first leads most often to sacrificing larger fish; smaller fish do not have the power that arises from turning a greater bulk against the water and ripping out hooks.

I also recommend keeping your boat moving or starting it moving if this can be managed easily. A good tidal flow may be enough help. The reason for keeping moving is that it keeps tension on the fish. If the boat is stationary and the fish swim toward it, the hook will come loose and be thrown.

One way of saving time is landing fish without using your net. If the fish is less than 7 pounds, is well hooked and is not a soft-mouthed pink, dispense with the net entirely. Quietly lean over, taking up as much slack line as possible and hold the line within 18 inches of the fish. Wait for the moment the fish becomes still at the side of the boat. In that instant, lift the fish in one smooth movement straight up and over the gunwhale. Drop it and get to the next line. Amazingly, you will land nearly every fish with which this procedure is attempted. The reason for taking up slack is to ensure that you get the fish over the gunwhale in one movement. Most fish will stay quiet for a smooth ride in mid-air, but if there is a "bump" this seems to alert them to the fact that something strange is happening; immediately, they begin squirming, and at least half of them will be lost. I do not suggest, however, lifting a fish of even 10 pounds into the boat. Their weight alone will rip out hooks, and sometimes the line will break.

If the net is required for more than one fish, take extra care. Try to keep the hooks from getting caught in the netting, and turn the net inside out to dump the fish. If worst comes to worst and you can't get a fish or a hook out of the net, do not waste time disentangling the hook. Bonk the fish a good one and net the next fish with the first one still in the net. If the fish in the net is large, cut the leader or unclip the flasher at the swivel to free it from the rod and net the next fish. May your God, whomever you may conceive of him to be, shine down on you during this wild time.

RELEASING UNWANTED FISH

Undersized salmon or other unwanted fish such as rock cod should be returned to the sea. The less they are touched and the sooner they are let go, the more likely it is that they will survive. Even fish that look fine when returned can be so traumatized by being caught that they soon turn belly up and expire. Try not to use your net or bring the fish in contact with boat parts, your pants or anything else; slime and scales can rub off, thus introducing diseases from the surfaces contacted, as well as providing an opening for the diseases present in salt water. A fish can swim off looking pink and healthy, then succumb in two or three weeks; some surprisingly disgusting infectious fungi lurk in the sea—an ugly death to be sure. So please:

♦ *Do not touch a fish you intend to release.*

When releasing a fish, lift the line with one hand, and with the other, slide up the line and grasp the hook firmly. Do not attempt to hold the fish in one hand and wiggle the hook free with the other hand. You will succeed only in squishing the fish to death trying to hold its slippery body, and make a bigger and bigger hole with the hook, damaging even more tissue and leaving the fish open to disease. Instead, with one hand firmly on the hook, turn it upside down and give a good swift snap with your hand. This will dislodge most fish directly back into the water. If the snap does not work, keep snapping until it does.

Even a foul-hooked fish is better dealt with this way. Attempting to take a hook out of a gill or eye or whatever is much more likely to result in a squished, asphyxiated fish that has lost more slime and scales than if it were snapped off. It also takes a lot more time away from fishing. There is, of course, the option of cutting the line and leaving the hook in the fish, but I think the chances of a young fish dying are great (and such an action may waste a killer lure). Reluctantly, I have come to conclude it is best just to snap a fish off and get on with fishing. My estimate is that less than 20 percent of fish die, a not unduly high proportion compared with the alternatives.

In order to conserve smaller fish, I seldom use triple hooks, but rig all my lures with one or two single hooks. Certainly, if you regularly use triple hooks and are out on a day when shakers abound, please consider—if only for that day—their conservation, and change to single hooks. In my experience, most small fish hooked with triple hooks die; as soon as you get one barb out, another seems to get stuck, even one that was not stuck in the first place. Very frustrating, and very hard on the fish. Personally, I'd like to see Fisheries and Oceans Canada outlaw hooks with more than one barb. There is not one lure on the market that cannot be rigged with single hooks. Thousands of salmon could be saved each year if this suggestion were implemented. It should be added that the only undersized salmon I have ever caught were coho and chinook—the species that sportfishers rely on the whole year round. Thus, we would be benefitting ourselves to make this change.

GETTING A FIX ON WHERE A FISH WAS CAUGHT

As discussed in Chapter 3, salmon tend to hang out in certain areas, and these can be extremely small pockets in very large tracts of ocean. Once a salmon is caught, one of the fundamental problems in fishing— being in the right place—is solved; where there is one salmon there are usually more. Accordingly, when you are in the boat take reference points as you go along, so that you know exactly where you are at all times. Even prior to getting a bite, you should know:

- *the distance to shore*
- *water depth and bottom contours*
- *the depth of your lines*
- *the direction of tidal flow*
- *the tidelines within a mile of your boat and their general pattern on flood and ebb tides*
- *the location of your boat in relationship to at least two bearings on shore*

Fish are localized in very specific areas related to tidelines or bottom contours. A school of coho drifts with the tide, while a school of chinook hovers over a structure. When you consider that a school of coho can be only fifty feet across, returning to the exact spot of hooking one takes much precision.

Make it a habit to assess exactly where you are every few minutes. Try to locate yourself within a few hundred yards. When you do hook a fish, take an immediate bearing (not when the fish is subsequently landed). This is the location of the school and where you wish to return. The landing location could be some miles from where the fish was originally hooked. Now that you know where the school is, return to that location and fish it again, being sure to fish through the area, moving in the same direction as before. I prefer, in all but the slowest water, to fish with the tide. Then I pick up the lines, bomb back and put them out again. Another small point to remember, if you are going to fish back to where the bite occurred, turn into the tide or wind rather than turning with it. You will be carried less distance from the spot you intend to fish.

Taking land bearings can be accomplished in more than one way. A precise triangulation method involves lining up a feature on shore—or a stationary feature in the water, such as a buoy—with another feature that is some distance behind it—for example, a building in the foreground and a mountain in the background. Then one turns ninety degrees and lines up two more features in the same way. Every time all four features line up, you are in the exact spot where you took the original bearings. I simplify this method by taking only one feature in either direction. I utilize a third triangulation method as well. In areas of well-defined bottom contours, I pore over charts and form a 3-D image of the bottom. Armed with the depth-sounder reading, which forms a straight line from the bottom to the boat, I then draw a second perpendicular—from the land to my captain's seat. Adding the two bearings together I can then return to the same spot. Of course, a loran or radar completely eliminates the need to look at land at all, but most sportfishers do not have these pricey but nifty bits of gadgetry.

There are other alternatives. As the day progresses, some species, particularly chinook, will be associated with a specific depth above a certain fathom line. Keeping an eye on your depth sounder, and without looking at shore, you can follow this fathom line and be in the best location for catching fish at all times. And there are other very simple methods for refinding the fish. For example, throw out a life jacket when you hook a fish, or a red crabtrap float or a four-litre jug half-filled with water. The lower a marker floats in the water, the less it will drift in the wind and the more accurately it will mark where the fish was hooked. Do remember to pick up these objects, because they are simply garbage when left in the water. If you have nothing to throw overboard, note your location in relation to something already in the water—diving birds or reefs of floating kelp, for instance, or a log; the bigger the object, the better. Carrying a few sticks to drop overboard isn't a bad idea, either.

Tidelines also mark the location of fish. One day during pink season we were catching nothing for what seemed like hours. The doldrums of "The Rhyme of the Ancient Mariner" had settled in; the vacant, deserted creak of wood, the jaded breeze, the yawning albatross... when all of a sudden we got a double header going through a tideline. By the time we got the fish into the boat, we were half a mile from the tideline and would have had to battle the tide to get back. We lifted the lines, went around the tideline and put the lines back in, then headed directly for the spot where we had caught the fish. We got another double header just as we went through the tideline. We caught seven salmon in less than an hour in exactly the same place, doing the same thing.

Remember that tidelines push fish along with them, so the hot location may move as well. On the day I have just described, the bite went off again and we milled around for an hour or so, trying to catch that eighth fish. Then we noticed that the tideline where we had been lucky had moved about a mile and a half. We headed for the spot where we reckoned the school would be, and in going through the tideline immediately got another double header. We landed both fish and then had to quit. This is well worth recalling when fish of other species—except for chinook—are migrating through in the top 50 feet of water. If the log you have caught fish by floats away and you are not catching anything, turn and follow the log. It just might mark the location of the fish.

Try, over the years, to get a feel for how the fish move around in the area you normally fish, and write your conclusions in your logbook for future reference. Then, the night before your fishing trip, pore over your logs and check the tide tables for the day you are fishing, as well as the previous day. These two sources of information will help you gain an understanding of where the fish should be as the day progresses. Patterns will emerge. As the years go by, the same spots will hold successive runs of salmon, because every fish moving through an area is affected the same way. Logs come to reveal species differences, seasonal variations and differences based on the tide patterns on any given day.

CHECK THE CONTENTS OF A SALMON'S BELLY

One way of improving your catch stats is to open a salmon as soon as it has been landed and see what it has been eating. The most common foods are herring, followed, in the case of coho, by euphasiid shrimp and then, distantly, anchovy and squid. Sometimes the feed is so recent that some is still wriggling. It is a marvellous, struggle-of-nature feeling to open a fish and have the contents tumble out shiny and iridescent, still flopping with life, a shiveringly elemental silver-of-the-moon feeling.

Depending on stomach contents, consider changing lures. If a fish is full of herring, you are advised to put on strip or anchovy. If it is full of shrimp, pink or red are colours of choice, and virtually all lure types come with some versions in these colours. An empty stomach tells you that what you have on looks pretty darn good. Regardless of stomach contents, file the information away in your logbook for future reference, particularly for your backup fishing plans. Correlate this information with fish species, as this will imply a clue either two, three or four years hence.

GUTTING A FISH

Now that you have a boatful of fish, the next step in the three-step process of catching them, cleaning them and cooking them is upon you. It is time to roll up your sleeves and clean and descale the fish. One of the important, not-to-be-overlooked aspects of cleaning fish is standing around on the dock getting as much adulation from other fishers as possible. I have, for instance, a Hemingway-esque hat for this purpose, and I generally swagger around as much as I can get away with. Wasps love fish blood more than anything in the world, and they will be your best buddies during the gutting process. You may want to sluice the table regularly as you work, ensuring that the drain for the table is smaller than the fish. I have lost many a fish to squirts of water that swept them right off the gutting table to seagulls waiting placidly and craftily on mud flats below. Keep your eye on your gutting knife as well.

For identification purposes and for proving that fish are of legal size, Fisheries and Oceans Canada requires that salmon heads be left on until the fish are taken home. This requirement complicates gutting to some extent. In my view, it would be better to return all offal to Mother Nature to be reprocessed, including the heads. However, I do understand Fisheries' difficulties. In circumstances in which fish can be processed without heads, gutting can be accomplished in three swift moves:

1. *Holding the fish by the tail, cut forward from anal vent to gills.*
2. *Turn the fish upright. Slice down behind the head and gills, but not all the way through.*

3. *Rip off the head by pulling down. The guts will come away attached to it.*

This is the best method of gutting a fish and can be accomplished in a matter of seconds, leaving a perfectly clean carcass. To satisfy the Fisheries Department, perform step one but alter step two; cut the small point where the gill arches join behind the gill covers, then cut back through the bony arches just beneath the backbone (the crescent-shaped plates upon which gills rest when closed). Then perform step three, in this case holding on to the cut-freed gills. Regardless of the method employed, finish up by running the blade of your knife along the inside of the backbone, and then the spoon end to remove the kidney. Wash all blood off and descale the fish.

Rotting fish entrails smell worse than anything in the world, and it would be nice to dispose of all excess body parts at source; however, this is not to be, so I suggest that you dig them deep into the garden, where they make tremendous fertilizer. If you throw them out, double-bag heads and tails before putting them in the garbage. Anything less is to risk killing the local garbage-loving raccoon population as well as everyone else in the neighbourhood. Fish guts are more lethal than chemical weapons.

DEFORMITIES, ABRASIONS, TEETH MARKS
AND MISSING ADIPOSE FINS

Many salmon have physical deformities that tell tales about their pasts. An incomplete jawbone or a dented face provides testimony to the successful release of juvenile salmon by sportfishers. Obviously, a great number of these fish survive into adulthood. Seldom seen, though, is a fish with opaqued eyes or missing gill tissue. My guess is that these types of hook-sustained injuries prove fatal—most likely the fish winds up in the teeth of predators. Many adult salmon are deformed by having been bitten early in their lives. The likely culprits are seals and killer whales; dogfish are probably too slow to catch young salmon.

Recent teeth marks can reveal salmon predators as well. If the marks are neat, much like the bite a child would take from a sandwich, the salmon was likely in the jaws of a seal or sea lion and managed to squirm free. If the wound is asymmetrical (ie., a straight line of grip marks on one side of the body while there are puncture wounds on the other), the salmon has been in the mouth of the strange-looking and rare daggertooth fish.

Other marks generally result from encounters with people. A

salmon with a puncture wound in its mouth or with a set of straight lines running back along its snout has been on another sportfishers's line in the not-too-distant past. Such marks may explain why some fish come up like rubber boots; it may just be that they really do not have any fight left. I have caught many fish with blunted noses, implying that they have run into something head-on, perhaps the back end of a boat when motoring right through propeller wash, even though not hooked. Sockeye have a reputation for such curiosity. I have never caught a salmon with another hook or line attached to it—although I have snagged a broken line, on the other end of which was a very unlucky salmon—so I must assume that the drag of a flasher wears a fish right out until killed. On the other hand, once the tackle is snagged on the bottom most salmon should be able to rip out the hooks. Open sores on the sides of fish and sections of scraped-off scales are evidence of close calls with a commercial netting.

A missing adipose fin, on the other hand, does not indicate a malevolent scenario at all. Right in front of the tail and anal peduncle, the adipose fin is a vestigal lump of boneless fat on a salmon's dorsal surface. When missing the fin, a fish has been marked by Fisheries: a tag was embedded in the skull during the fry stage. Very tiny and next to impossible to find, this tag should be returned for processing. Do not attempt to find the tag yourself. Check every salmon for missing adipose fins and leave the head of marked fish at a head collection depot. In due course you will receive a salmonid head recovery pin, a map of the province and statistical information about the salmon.

Marked fish heads are dissected by researchers to find the wire tags. Information encoded on tags identifies the river or hatchery of release, the brood year, species, size of run, etc. Movement patterns of individual runs can be very accurately determined, from the river of source to the high seas and back again. Tag information is very useful in conservation efforts and in negotiating fishing allocation agreements among the various user groups, as well as between Canada and the United States. Salmon runs from many rivers and from both nations intermingle throughout the year. Spot closures as well as timed commercial openings can, in theory, help to protect salmon stocks such as wild chinook strains originating from systems in the Gulf of Georgia.

WINNING FISHING DERBIES

Sooner or later the time comes, once you have caught a fish or two, to enter a fishing derby. In my first derby, I was the guide for my father and one of his friends. They grumbled about getting up before the crack of dawn when even the fish, they reasoned, were still asleep. We powered out in the dark to the steely terror of planing toward the moon through a bay full of logs, and set the lines in the dark. At first light we received one measly bite and landed a 5-pound chinook. I received great ribbing about how tiny this fish was for August, mistakenly having told tales the night before about 50-pound spawning chinook and almost mythically huge coho.

Sometime later we landed a coho of about 6 pounds and the ribbing decreased, but only for a while. It was a slow, slow rising tide, one of those days when even seagulls sprawl on the rocks in boredom and the sun becomes bologna in the sky. I knew I was doomed. Well, I fished here and I fished there, guided this way and that, hauled out my killer lures and generally wracked my brains to a background of criticism. I was told that "maybe we should be using these small ones for bait, ha ha," and "maybe we should have fished where everyone else is fishing," and "we could always stop at a seafood store on the way home, ho ho," etc., etc.

We fished like fiends for seven hours in sweltering heat. Finally, I couldn't take anymore, and rather than strangle them, I took them back to shore. I was far too embarrassed to go to the weigh-in and had to be dragged along kicking and howling.

When we got to the banquet, I unobtrusively became one with the background, trying to give the impression I had no connection with these interlopers from Alberta. After dinner I was a tad surprised when the three of us were called up to win a prize, something of real consequence, I figured, like a swivel or maybe even a bead chain. In complete surprise, we were handed a staggeringly heavy three-foot-high trophy for the largest fish in the derby. Then we were handed a two-foot one that looked an awful lot more like a cathedral than a trophy for the largest chinook, and then another two-foot-high trophy for the most fish in the boat. In addition, we were given a tackle box, a whole bunch of tackle and a brand-new expensive fishing reel.

It turned out that not one other salmon had been caught in the entire derby. In fact, only one other fish had been caught, a small ling cod. The next best "fish" was a starfish. A clam shell—admittedly a big one—claimed a prize, too. And that was it from the whole fleet. The moral of the story is that you can win fishing derbies with hardly any effort at all, so ignore the naysayers and get out there and win. And, of course, give them the raspberry when you do. Politely.

♦ 6 ♦

TROLLING

Generally speaking, trolling—pulling a lure through the water from a moving boat—will outfish other methods of fishing on a year-round basis. There are two main reasons for the success of trolling. First, one covers much more territory in a moving boat and, therefore, can search out the fish. Second, fish almost always set the hook when they strike a trolled lure, making it unnecessary for the fisher to do so.

Fish are spread out for most of the year, particularly in the winter when they are not actively migrating to spawning rivers, and it makes sense to try to find them rather than employing the hit-or-miss method of stopping in one spot to fish. Even in summer, salmon behaviour can influence the choice of fishing method. Migrating coho, for instance, bunch in very small schools, sometimes only twenty feet across, so one must actively search to find them. Trolling also imparts continuous action to a lure; thus the gear is fishing at all times, rather than only at the time one is actively fishing.

I can hear moochers groaning right now, so it's worthwhile pointing out that other methods can often outfish trolling. When fish are highly localized or squashed into very limited spaces by currents or land contours, or are influenced by other factors such as engine sound, other methods can be more productive. Wind will often push herring schools against shore and, of course, salmon follow into nooks and crannies where trolling is impractical.

DEMOCRATIC FISHING

Before getting into the nitty-gritty of trolling, I should say I have a couple of rules that I apply to make a day of trolling more enjoyable for all. My first rule is that the captain (that's me) gets the first fish. My kids only partly erroneously point out that this is not completely and utterly fair and that the rule actually demonstrates my basically greedy nature. I grudgingly agree that, at first glance, there is an appearance of greed, but add hastily that the rule stems from my altruistic nature.

I have learned from long experience how unwise it may be to hand over the lines to a less experienced fisher before at least one fish flops in the fishbox. My apparently "greedy" rule normally ensures that we won't get skunked. In addition, if only one fish glares balefully from the fishbox at the end of the day, I give it to the invited party, an option that would not exist had the fish not been caught in the first place.

Rule number two is that fishing should be democratic. Trolling is the only method of fishing in which any of the rods can be fished by any party on board, so set up an order for the people in the boat. The person at bat fishes all rods until he or she gets one in the boat. Then the next person in line fishes all lines until he or she has been successful, and so on. This rule prevents someone being left out. I have been out on numerous occasions in new areas with people who refused to give me an outside rod position or lend me gear which they knew was working and which I didn't have. On such occasions, I spent the day watching them catch fish. I might as well not have been there. So, in the interests of fairness, trolling should be democratic; let everyone have a chance. A secondary benefit of assigning an order is that it keeps people out of the way during the critical seconds just after a fish has bitten.

SETTING UP ROD HOLDERS AND DEALING WITH TANGLES

Most boats troll two to four rods. One rod holder will be mounted on either side of the boat, and if the transom is wide enough, two rod holders will be mounted on the stern. This usually gets reduced to one rod holder in the middle of the transom in boats with less than 8½ feet of beam. The rod holders on the sides of the boat are mounted at least 18 inches behind the downrigger mounting plates to provide clearance for the downrigger handles.

Typically, the lines off the side of the boat are attached to downriggers or fished more deeply in the water than the stern lines. (Sometimes stern lines are attached to downriggers and fished deeper than the side lines, but this is not commonly done.) The reason for this is that the closer any two or more lines come to one another, the greater the chance of tangles. This difficulty can be mitigated by using:

TWO ROD SETUP

THREE ROD SETUP

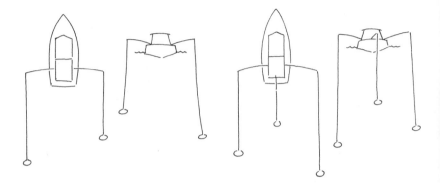

FOUR ROD SETUP

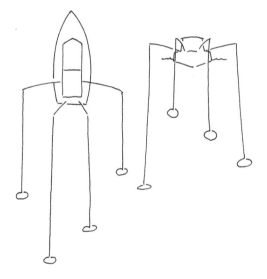

- *longer rods and weights*
- *planers on the sides*
- *one planer in the centre of the stern*
- *two rods per downrigger, 10 to 15 feet apart*
- *little or no weight on the centre line*

- *three fishing lines rather than four*
- *less line between the tackle and the downrigger release clip*
- *a heavy, displacement-hull boat that tracks true in the wind*
- *a line set-out method that does not place any line directly behind another line*
- *a gentler arc in boat turns*

While most boats will take a third or fourth rod over the stern, you are strongly advised to do this only in calm water or when your boat will troll in a fairly straight line. Tangling lines is a constant problem in trolling, either on turns or after a fish bites. Anything you can do to reduce the chances of inter-line contact will reduce the number of frustrating hang-ups. In areas where fish are deeper than 75 feet, it makes little sense to fish the surface, so a third or fourth rod is pointless unless each is attached to a downrigger. It sometimes pays off, though—there may be resident chinook below and blueback coho on the surface; thus one can be fishing two different runs separated by as much as 150 vertical feet, but this is rare.

FOUR ROD SETUP
FOR DOWNRIGGERS

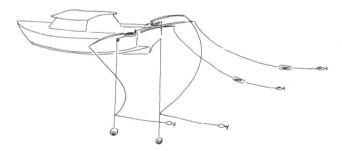

When you are fishing deeper than 75 feet, I do not recommend running three or more lines at the same time unless at least two are on one downrigger. Some people run three rods with two-pound balls or planers, but this is usually done from heavy, displacement-hull boats. I guarantee that you will spend your whole day cutting off tangles, most of which occur when a fish has been kind enough to attach itself to your line; fish have a penchant for swimming directly into other lines, particularly ones that are directly behind them.

Sometimes the unfortunate will happen and lines become tangled. In this unlucky occurrence, I suggest that you cut the line, attach new gear and get on with fishing. Do not waste time untangling tangled line unless you are using wire. Wire line is very expensive and it makes sense to cut away any monofilament and untangle the wire line. Another good reason for cutting off monofilament line is that it often has nicks. A healthy chop-off ensures that good, strong line is presented to the fish at all times.

Tangled lines often give the appearance of not being tangled at all: one rod zings away just like a big fish. Shortly, however, at least one other line will go wild, too. When you reel in the "fish," that second rod, and in the worst of all possible worlds, a third rod, will slowly go limp. Reduce line strain by reeling in all tangled lines at the same time, or taking the boat out of gear and reeling in. To resume fishing quickly:

1. *Pull everything into the boat.*
2. *Unclip the top end of the flasher/dodger from the line.*
3. *Cut lines above the tangle.*
4. *Cut line above the ball-bearing swivel and reattach it and the "red peg" to the fishing rod's line.*
5. *Attach the new flasher and lure (previously set aside for such an eventuality) to the reattached swivel.*
6. *Put the line back in the water.*
7. *At your leisure, tackle the tangle. Unclip the flasher from the leader, then hold on to the lure. Run your other hand down the leader. Sometimes the whole thing whizzes in circles until it comes free.*

DOWNRIGGER ASSEMBLY AND USE

From a moving boat, fishing tackle descends only when weighted in some way. There are three ways to achieve this: downriggers, lead weights and planers. Most common is the downrigger, a wire line onto which a fishing line clips until the moment of a strike. A handle allows the line, with a heavy 10-pound ball on one end, to be wound up and down in the water. The downrigger measures the length of line let out, and the ball can be set at any predetermined depth. Wire line does not stretch; thus the measured depth is true and, more important, can be reached accurately time and time again, a big advantage as salmon school at very precise depths. Furthermore, depth is instantly adjustable if the sounder indicates much shallower water is ahead. A ball of less than 10 pounds ought not to be used because the depth will not be accurate—current, speed and weed resistance lift lighter balls.

The purpose of a downrigger is to take a fishing line down easily to the fish via an attachment called a release clip, which, as its name suggests, releases the fishing line when the fish bites. Once the fishing line releases from the downrigger line, the fisher can play the fish without any other weight on the line. Understandably, downrigger fishing is far more exciting than heavy, draggy weights. Downriggers also have one distinct advantage: fishing lures pick up far less weed than with other weights.

Prior to use, a downrigger must be assembled and attached to the boat. To put your downrigger together, you will need wire line,

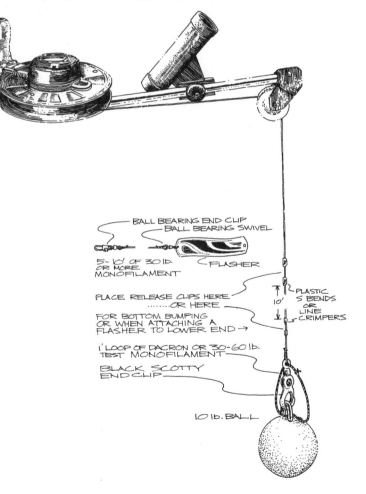

BALL BEARING END CLIP
BALL BEARING SWIVEL

5-10' OF 30 lb.
OR MORE
MONOFILAMENT

FLASHER

PLACE RELEASE CLIPS HERE
........OR HERE

FOR BOTTOM BUMPING
OR WHEN ATTACHING A
FLASHER TO LOWER END →

10'   PLASTIC
S BENDS
OR
LINE
CRIMPERS

1' LOOP OF DACRON OR 30-60 lb.
TEST MONOFILAMENT

BLACK SCOTTY
END CLIP

10 lb. BALL

line crimpers, an end clip and a downrigger ball.

I seldom recommend buying the best and most expensive item on the market; however, wire line is one of the few things that must be of superior quality. Specifically, buy line that is high-quality stainless steel, a minimum of 250 feet long, braided from strands, and the highest pound-test wire available. High-quality line lasts much longer than cheaper line and pays for itself many times over in saved downrigger balls and reduced levels of grief. I say this after losing dozens of balls over the years to cheap line.

Cheap wire line cannot stand the punishment dealt out by downrigger fishing. It rusts, frays and breaks. The frayed braids are very sharp, and I have impaled myself more times than I care to remember—very painful. Do not buy single-strand line to avoid fraying. Single strand line is more prone to kinking and, as a single strand, gives no indication of weakness until letting go. Cheaper lines also leap into big useless balls because they cannot handle the twist imparted by a spinning downrigger ball during fishing. Regardless of line quality, I normally buy 400-foot lengths because the end should be cut off periodically and the endclip reattached on sound line. Spray WD-40 on all wire lines to extend their lives, but to prevent the oily scent from impairing fishing success, use it only sparingly once a season.

Line crimpers are tiny metal tubes crimped onto wire line with pliers. They have three main uses: to secure a lead ball endclip, to join pieces of wire line and to provide stops for downrigger release clips. The third use allows one to fish more than one fishing line per downrigger. Though I use them from time to time, I do not recommend the plastic S-bends for securing release clips. In my experience, they cause wire line fraying and subsequent loss of all the end gear, including your downrigger ball and sometimes your tackle. It surprises me that manufacturers don't seem to recognize this problem and come up with a better product.

A lead ball endclip attaches a downrigger ball to the wire line. Make a loop of wire line at least 6 inches long; slide on two to three line crimpers, then the endclip. Slide the wire line's tag end through all the line crimpers, thus mounting the endclip in a loop of line. Tighten the crimpers until your hands fall off. If you don't, the crimpers will loosen and you can say goodbye to your downrigger balls. In this book, I steer clear of brand names when possible, but in my opinion there is only one good endclip on the market—the black one put out by Scotty. Please buy these ones for your own safety, and never, ever attach a downrigger ball directly to wire line. It is crucial for a ball to be able to break free. If you do not use a "breakable" endclip and then snag on the bottom, one of two things will happen. The current will move a smaller boat sideways until the downrigger side slips under the water, the boat fills with water and you all drown. (Always keep sidecutters on board in an easy-to-find place for such an emergency.) On a larger boat, the downrigger mounting platform will snap and your expensive downrigger will jump into the sea.

If you use any other type of endclip than the Scotty, you will lose downrigger balls. Dropping a ball even a few inches when putting it over the gunwhale can build enough force to snap other clips, sending your ball to the bottom. I have also lost balls simply lifting and dropping over waves. If you do use another type of endclip, the solution to premature breakoff—the safe solution—is to tie a loose loop of dacron line (or 60-pound monofilament) between the loop of downrigger line and the clip on the lead ball. Make the loop loose so that it comes into play only after the endclip has let go. The loop will save many downrigger balls while not causing a problem with snags— first the endclip lets go, then the dacron line breaks, rather than the two acting together, which results in the difficulties outlined above.

Many types of downrigger balls grace tackle shop shelves, from basic round lead balls to ones that look like and cost about the same as Trident submarines. I buy the cheap round ones because I can't stand losing expensive ones. Unfortunately, these balls twist in circles, adding kinks and frays to wire line. Solve this problem by putting WD-40 on the endclip or mounting a fin on the ball. The problem of line twist can also be solved by attaching a screw eye with a ball-bearing swivel into the side of the lead ball, then attaching a flasher on 10 to 20 feet of leader to the swivel. Although the main purpose of such an arrangement is to keep the weight of the flasher off your fishing line, it secondarily prevents twisting. The fishing line is attached 10 feet up the downrigger line between two line crimpers or plastic s-bends. Refer to the illustration of a fully rigged-up downrigger.

There are more types of release clips on the market than you can shake a school of fish at. I use two types: the old standby green plastic one with the red peg that attaches to the fishing line, and the black alligator-clip style that presses the line between two pads of silicone rubber. I use these varieties for two reasons. First, a release clip should let your line break free from the downrigger only when a fish bites. Second, if you do not spot a bite, valuable fishing time is wasted dragging around shredded bait and mussed-up lures. If the clip releases too easily, you spend your day reattaching your line to the downrigger, something that is extremely annoying and cuts into fish-catching time. If the clip does not release properly, fish are lost because the hooks rip out. Even a 5-pounder can build enough water pressure to achieve freedom.

Each type of release clip has its idiosyncracies. The trick to the old standby is determining how far to push the red peg into the hole in the green clip. Practice makes perfect. The problem with this style is that the peg sometimes pulls out of the clip when the downrigger is being let down. This requires bringing in the entire fishing line to retrieve the red peg before starting again. I should add that in the excitement of the chase I forget to put the red peg on the fishing line at least twenty-five percent of the time. This means I have to stop, then cut and retie the end swivel before I can fish. Also, the red pegs are next to impossible to see in low light. A bit more finicky, the alligator-clip style has a tremendous advantage in that it does not use a peg. One simply reattaches a popped-out fishing line while the tackle stays in the water twenty feet behind the boat. The downside to the alligator-clip type becomes apparent when line gets caught around the top end of the pad. There is no way in the world it will ever release, not for the biggest fish in the sea nor the biggest fisher in the boat.

Now that the downrigger is completely ready to go, it needs to be mounted to the boat. In addition to needing 18 inches of clearance from a rod holder, the downrigger should be mounted ahead of the rod or the two will tangle endlessly, until you reverse them. When using the downrigger, be sure to set the brake every time you stop turning the gurdy handle. If you don't, it will whiz around until you grab it or it stops itself, snapping your downrigger ball off the line on the beginning of a rocketlike freefall while you stand staring at the sky saying, "Why did I just do such a dumb thing?"

DOWNRIGGER FISHING

Now that all that dry and as-interesting-as-the-life-story-of-an-actuarial-table-algorithm assembly information has been digested and performed, fishing time arrives. To begin using a downrigger, first reduce tension on the fishing reel. Lay the rod inside the boat. Fishing rule number one will instantly leap into your mind: test lure action in the water beside the boat. Once the wonderfulness of its action brings tears to your eyes, attach the fishing line to the release clip. Let out 25 to 40 feet of line when fishing 0 to 30 feet deep. Let out 20 to 25 feet when fishing 30 to 70 feet, and 15 feet of line when fishing deeper than 70 feet. The reason for letting more line out when fishing close to the surface is to get the lure away from the sound and turbulence of the engine. Normally, fish swim away from the sound at right angles to the boat, then turn 180 degrees and swim back in some distance behind the boat. Spawners, on the other hand, seem excited by engines, and on many occasions I have had bites when lifting lures out of the water beside the boat.

Take care, though, when using more than 15 feet of line behind a downrigger: the greater the distance, the greater the chance of tangling lines when the boat turns. Solve this problem by letting out less line or by using less weight on the centre line so that it rides higher in the water. Alternatively, make longer, gentler turns with your boat. And don't cut too close behind another boat. It may be of some benefit to store away in your mind that less line, for some strange reason, can be let out in cold weather. This is also true on rough days and in greater tidal flow. Tidal flow muffles the sound of the engine or, at least, desensitizes the fish in some way.

When letting out downrigger line, stare bulgy-eyed at your gear to ensure that no weed or other contaminant fouls the line below the release clip. Fish will never, ever bite a fouled line. Let me repeat this. Fish will never, ever bite a fouled line. One of the great advantages of downriggers is that even when weeds choke the surface like moss on an unrolled stone, seldom will they get below the release clip to the lure. One can fish with confidence even when great wodges of weed slide down the fishing line from the surface.

Once the lure glides safely beneath the surface, pick up the rod and place it in the rod holder. Try not to let the line go slack or line twist will wind around the rod tip. Unless this is removed, the line will bind and then break free from the release clip and the attachment cycle must be repeated. The line will also pop out of a release clip if reel tension is too tight. My rod has been dragged over the edge of the boat for this reason, so put the rod in the rod holder for your own peace of mind. Assuming all goes well, as soon as your line has descended to the intended fishing depth, tighten reel tension until line will not stream out. But do not overtighten. The scream of the reel often alerts one to a bite; as mentioned in Chapter 5, it is most important to get to the rod as soon as the fish bites. Another reason for not over-tightening the reel becomes abundantly clear when a fish gets off or breaks the line. A fish as small as 8 pounds can snap 25-pound test line.

Once the lines are stowed in their rod holders, downrigger fishing begins. Except at the crack of dawn, when fish often school within 30 feet of the surface, separate each fishing line by 15 vertical feet. Reel one downrigger up and another downrigger down at 10-foot intervals during the first hour until the fish are located. Salmon change depth for no apparent reason sometimes—perhaps temperature has more effect in tidal areas than one would expect— and it's best to locate them if things go slow.

Remember to try all lures at a variety of depths and reduce experimentation time by getting local information. Fishing depth can change daily, so take a minute to find out current information. Many times, fish will descend 150 to 200 feet during the day, particularly in the summer. Try each lure at each depth and change it every fifteen minutes. When a fish is caught, bring all lines to roughly the same depth (ie., 5 to 10 feet apart). I don't use the same depth because I don't want my lures presenting themselves side by side. For the same reason, I use different lengths of line between tackle and release clip. If only one type of lure is working, switch all other lines to the same thing. The final thing to remember about depth, and this goes for all types of fishing, is that salmon see straight ahead and up. Accordingly, fishing lures should be presented at or slighly above the level where fish are expected.

When trolling, glance at the rod tip at least once a minute, if not continually. Try to catch each bite the moment it happens. With downriggers, the bite is first seen on the downrigger, which jiggles and then pops up. Second, the rod snaps up as the line breaks free from the release clip, and then down as the fish pulls. If your downrigger and rod keep jiggling, either the fish cannot break free or the ball is hitting bottom and ten feet of downrigger line should be reeled in pronto. If the rod and downrigger continue jiggling after reeling in, there will be a fish of 1 to 4 pounds on the line.

Watching the rod tip can, over the years, teach you a great deal about what is going on below the boat. The most obvious thing to note is whether you have had a bite. Small taps can be turned into hooked fish by employing one of the solutions suggested later in this chapter. Detecting bites is of great importance when fishing with bait. Bait should be checked after every bite; ruined bait will not catch fish. Line action also reveals whether a flasher or dodger is being used and working properly. Small rod-tip movements can also indicate undersized fish, large herring being hit by the line or schools of jellyfish. Hard as it may be to believe one can even determine the species of jellyfish. The large Man'o War jellyfish are encountered only in the summer months. They cause a slow deep bend in the rod. The rod then returns to its former position as the line cuts through their bodies. Check each line when these jellyfish are hit, because residue from their tentacles invariably slips down to the lure. Bright-purple slime is evidence of this species and should be handled with care. More will be said about these fire-breathers-from-hell at the end of the trolling section. As beautiful as the smaller white jellyfish are, I have never associated large schools of them with caught fish. And so I move on.

Continued appraisal of rod-tip action becomes doubly important when undersized fish are moving through. Small fish soon lose strength and get dragged along, causing imperceptible movement. Salmon will not bite a line on which a smaller fish dangles. Perhaps a ling cod will, but not a salmon. Small grilse salmon are detected by their tiny, intermittent, jerky tugs. Smooth repeated movements correspond to natural actions of the line, as do large movements that return the rod to its former position. Fishing through tidelines, for example, puts extra drag on lines, pulling rods down for a few seconds before they rise once again. When action goes dead, however, suspect a worn out fish or weed.

Check each rod at least once every 20 to 30 minutes. Reel in the line until taut and follow this with a good yank to release the line from the release clip. Then, most important, put the rod back in the rod holder, and reel in the downrigger. This allows the line to fish its way to the top. Every now and then you will get a bite. After releasing a line, wind the downrigger in so that the ball and fishing line get to the surface at about the same time. If a fish bites on the way up, its depth can be read on the downrigger. Readjust your lines to that depth. Make this standard procedure when fishing deeper than 30 feet. I seldomly release a line above 30 feet, as it takes less time to reel in both, check or change the lure and let the gear back down.

When trolling, one often follows a certain fathom line, particularly in winter when chinook are the main quarry. You may, for instance, be fishing 100 feet deep in 180 feet of water. The fish may not even know that a contour lurks below, but nevertheless swim along in a narrow strip of water far above the bottom. They may be in this band because the tide pushes them to the location or because feed congregates at this depth. This fathom line can be highly important when you fish in an area where there are not many fish or there are very definite reefs under the water. Remember my empty sky-and-kite metaphor. In the deep waters off Vancouver Island, salmon may often be found 100 to 150 feet deep in water as deep as

700 feet. This puts the need for precision in acute relief.

One final variety of downrigger fishing should be mentioned: bottom bumping. This method of fishing is utilized when fish are close to the bottom, feeding on needlefish. Normally, the bottom will be mud, or sand covered with eel grass. It will read as a narrow band on the depth sounder. The downrigger arm jiggles gently as the lead ball slides across the bottom. Be prepared for quick action, though. If the downrigger starts jumping wildly or making loud noises, the ball has likely hit rock, and ten feet had better be reeled in. Lead balls get wedged between rocks easily and this can cause serious problems in no time.

In bottom bumping, a line crimper, a swivel or two plastic s-bends are mounted 10 feet above the lead ball, and a release clip is added to the downrigger line at this point. The ten-foot distance keeps the flasher close to the bottom, allowing it to revolve without coming in contact with bottom weed. As you troll back and forth across the mud bottom, raise and lower the downrigger to keep the ball within 10 feet of the bottom. In bottom bumping, knowing the bottom contours is critical. For this you need charts. The fishing spot may be miles offshore and difficult to find even with a depth sounder.

Let me finish this section with two small practical considerations about boat turning and downrigger mounting brackets. During turns, the downrigger line on the outside of the turn swings in toward the engine. If you get wire line tangled in the engine, it can bind the engine to a standstill—an occurrence of great potential danger—or pop the seals, thus ruining the engine or requiring immediate salvaging. So be careful. Do not turn too tightly. I have shredded more than one propeller to Swiss cheese with wire line.

Turning to mounting brackets, make it standard practice to check them each day out. These brackets withstand a great deal of pressure, and weaken over time. As noted, I have had the bad luck of having a mounting bracket break, my downrigger sucked into the sea in front of my eyes before I could move. I have also had welds on mounting plates break in my hand.

TROLLING WITH WEIGHTS

Trolling with weights—either lead balls or sliding weights—has two advantages over downrigger fishing: weights are cheap, and on days when fish are finicky, they take lures further away from engine noise. This can make all the difference between catching fish and being skunked. Some days I don't use downriggers at all and just run weights.

SLIDING WEIGHT — 20 - 25' MAINLINE — BALL BEARING END CLIP — FLASHER — 3' — LURE

Let me deal first with sliding weights. These come in sizes from 1 ounce to 1 pound, and are attached 20 to 25 feet above the ball-bearing swivel on the end of the main line. Put the fishing line under the two hangers on the weight, then pull the line down through the loop on the front of the weight. The brass loop must face the fish end of the line. If the weights keep slipping down the line during fishing, wind the fishing line around the loop to add more tension. Alternatively, turn the loop to face the boat. To let your line out for fishing, peel off a set number of 2-foot pulls from the reel, usually between 30 and 50 pulls. Practice until you can get an exact pull every time. The point is to be able to duplicate the exact distance behind the boat; this determines your depth. "Pull" measurement will be discussed in the drift-fishing section of this chapter. Remember to check for weed fouling until the lure passes under the water's surface.

Depth is controlled by adding additional weights and letting out more line. One of the nice features about sliding weights is that depth can be increased while the line remains in the water fishing. Simply add another weight, usually one of 4 to 8 ounces. Slip the line under the hangers and let the second weight slide down to the weight already on the line. Keep an eye on the rod after the second weight hits the first. If it jars the first weight loose, both will migrate down to the swivel, resulting in what looks like a small strike followed by rod action going dead. Anytime this happens, bring in the line and check it. Weights at the tackle end deaden the action of the flasher or dodger and look very bulky. More important, fish will not bite the lure.

The use of sliding weights is only recommended when salmon are within 30 feet of the surface. One ounce of weight will take a light lure such as a spoon just beneath the surface. 4 to 8 ounces will take a flasher under the surface, but not much deeper than 5 feet. One pound of weight may take a line down 1 foot for every 3 to 4 feet of line pulled from the reel. Past 80 feet of mainline, do not count on any further depth. Line drag may be further overcome by utilizing 2 pounds of sliding weight. Line descends perhaps 1 foot for every 2 to 3 feet pulled from the reel and may reach a maximum depth at 100 feet of mainline. If lead balls are available, I do not use sliding weights to reach deeper trolling depths. They can be used in a pinch, but downriggers and lead balls are far better alternatives. Note also that it is illegal to fish with more than 1 kilogram (2.2 pounds) of weight on a fishing line. See the illustrations of rigged-up sliding and lead ball weights.

Sliding weights do have some downsides of which you should be aware. As the name suggests, they are intended to release when a fish bites and slide down to the end swivel. In my experience, they rarely do this, requiring one to hand-release them as the line is brought in. Take care and be quick so that the fish does not get a good pull when the line is in your hands—nine times out of ten the hooks rip free and the salmon swims away, proving my contention that it is a rod's give that holds most fish on the line. Releasing sliding weights is far easier with two people. A second problem arises because the brass loops are hard on fishing line. Line gets crimped in the loops, causing nicks that soon lead to breakage. To avoid this, cut 6 feet of line and retie the end swivel every day you go out. Sliding weights also damage the knot at the end swivel. After releasing, they smack the top side of the swivel and over time cause the knot to break. Remember, too, that when you put on more weights, a stronger rod will be needed. Carry a stout rod on board even if it is not used very often. The cheapest rod on the market serves this purpose well.

The second type of lead weight, the lead ball, is rigged up differently than sliding weights. These balls look like small downrigger balls and come in 1- to 2-pound sizes. As with sliding weights, lead balls are attached 20 to 25 feet above the end swivel. The line is cut and a bead swivel inserted. The lead ball attaches to a 2-foot piece of dacron line, on the other end of which is tied a section of bent coathanger or a large single hook, barb removed. The coathanger or hook then slips over the beads or through the top loop of the bead swivel and line is let out. The best rods for lead balls are the heavy roller-guided rods. These 6-inch wood reels have counters, and greatly simplify letting out an accurate length of line.

Lead ball weights may be used effectively to about 100 feet. One-pound lead balls reach the depths listed above for 2 pounds of sliding weights. 2-pound balls descend about 1 foot for every 2 feet of line pulled from the reel until about 100 feet of mainline is reached. This ratio slowly changes, and by the time 250 feet of mainline has been reached, the weight will be about 100 to 110 feet deep. Past this distance, line drag prevents much deeper depths from being reached.

When a great deal of line has been let out, be sure to give other boats plenty of room, most obviously other boats using heavy

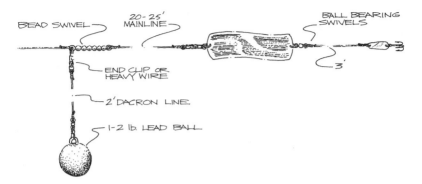

weights. Evidence of heavy weight setups, as well as planers, includes stout rods, the lack of downriggers, and bells on rod tips. In addition, to avoid tangling your own line, turns must be made sweepingly. One interesting aspect of note is that when you turn, the inside weight drops in the water and slows down. I have often found this a good recipe for catching bass and enticing the occasional salmon to bite. The downside is that you sometimes snag bottom.

Fish playing has its own little idiosyncracies when lead balls are used. When taking off a lead ball, lift the ball into the boat with the rod and quickly slip the hook from the bead swivel. Keep tension on the fish and play it a bit more before attempting to reel in the bead swivel. Every time the swivel goes through the rod guides it has the potential to snag. This presents a real possibility of losing many fish, especially the big ones. There are two solutions:

+ *Tire the fish thoroughly before bringing the swivel through the line guides.*
+ *If a fish takes a run after the bead swivel is through the guides, point the rod tip at the fish to allow the swivel easier return passage. If the swivel gets caught, immediately snap the rod tip hard and give the line a short, quick tug.*

Bead swivels cause real damage to rod guides and can snag coming out of reels. If your rods have ceramic line guide liners, do not use lead balls; bead swivels will knock them out in short order. The solution in this situation, although a poor one, is to tie a loop in the line at 20 to 25 feet rather than inserting a bead swivel. At the end of the day, cut the line above this knot because it will have weakened tremendously, even more if you have caught fish over 10 pounds.

As with other forms of trolling, it is important to watch the rod tip. Bait can be shredded by the lightest snap. If the tip keeps jumping up and then pulling down but no fish appears, the flasher is hitting the surface, then being dragged under. This occurs in high waves and in high current. The answer is to use more weights, either sliding or ball ones. Check your line, though; anytime it hits the surface, weed could be picked up.

There is one important advantage in using weights over other methods of trolling. I have already mentioned it, but it's worth saying again. If you are using hootchies and spot the occasional tap, pull two feet of line from the last line guide, hold it a second and then let go. From a fish's point of view, this looks like the hootchie has stopped, puffed out right in its face and shot away in fright. I have been out on days where this corny old technique has resulted in eight fish for our boat. This works especially well on pinks and sockeye. If you get a fish doing this and it weighs a ton but does not seem to be fighting, usually it has been hooked in the side rather than the mouth.

And, of course, lead balls have their downsides, too. They are so heavy that they reduce the enjoyment of playing a fish. They weigh an absolute ton to bring in from 250 feet, covered in weed. Furthermore, a lot of time is wasted letting them out and bringing them in. I don't use them often. But I carry them for use on days that fish are spooked or my other gear breaks.

PLANER FISHING

Planers are the heaviest gear used in fishing. They truly do work like upside-down kites; the water presses against that broad plastic surface and pushes it down. When a fish bites, however, the planer trips, allowing you to fight the fish rather than the planer. During fishing, on the other hand, they exert so much pressure that a novice fisher can get yanked out of the boat trying to hold onto the rod. I have broken my heaviest rods many times because of the pressure. Getting a weed-fouled planer up from 350 feet from a moving boat is a feat for the Terminator.

Planers do have their advantages, though. They get the line further away from the boat than downriggers, and this can translate into huge numbers of extra fish in calm water or any location where resident fish are fussy. Properly functioning, planers are much lighter to retrieve than heavy weights. They also track around corners at the same depth rather than sinking like the much heavier lead balls they replace. This means that they also stay at roughly the same speed all the time, an important consideration in bait fishing.

Planers have one unusual advantage. When a fish taps the lure and trips the planer but does not hook itself, the planer begins migrating to the surface. This appears to the fish as if the lure is dashing for freedom and, of course, the salmon follows in hot pursuit. What you see is a double-strike effect on the rod. Another useful feature of planers is that they release when hitting bottom. As a result, they come up without snagging—much more frequently than weights. Bottom weed usually drapes the planer, rather than the lure, proof that the rod has taken evasive action on its own rather than waiting for you to see the problem.

Two styles of planers may be purchased: the lighter, Deep Six or Pink Lady style can be used to about 75 feet on 150 feet of line (see the package for a depth-versus-line-length guide), and the heavier rectangular type can reach about 150 feet on 350 feet of wire line.

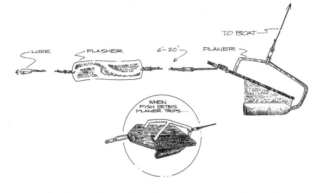

Deep Six/Pink Lady-style planers are much easier to use than their plexiglass counterparts. Use at least 30-pound-test mainline, and attach the line directly to the swivel on the top of the planer. Even heavier mainline should not be ruled out; light line stretches too much for you to trip the planer from the boat. In addition, the pressure exerted by a planer is so great it weakens light line quickly. As with the other style of planer, attach a ball-bearing swivel to the bottom of the planer, add 25 feet of 25-pound-test leader, a ball-bearing end swivel and then your tackle. I will describe later how to make the rectangular planer removable from the line, thus avoiding a fish-losing hand-over-hand retrieve of the leader. Some people get around this problem by attaching their lure to the planer with a 6-foot leader, but this should only be used for a lure that does not need a flasher or dodger. I must admit that I have never found this style of planer that effective. They don't go much below 75 feet and don't work anywhere near as well as the rectangular type. But lots of people use them, particularly in areas of Washington.

The second type of planer finds much more common usage in coastal British Columbia and can be the gear of choice in calm areas such as the fjordlike waters of Saanich Inlet. The big rectangular paravane-style planers are the heaviest fishing gear, requiring baseball-bat stout Peetz rods with rollers instead of line guides, six-inch wooden reels and 600 to 900 feet of wire line. I have even broken these rods, so do not use anything lighter. The rod must have rollers because wire line chews holes through other types. Oil sparingly, and wipe off excess; even rollers get eaten by wire line. In addition, do not fish the same rod on the same side of the boat all the time or the top roller will get a cut. Once a cut forms, the wire line starts to fray, leading to replacement of a very expensive item. Wire line is required because monofilament stretches too much to trip the planer and simply hasn't the strength to take the pounding.

Before fishing with these plexiglass planers, they must be installed. To rig up the planer, you will need: 2 line crimpers, 2 bead swivels, 7 feet of dacron line, 2 heavy-duty end changers, 1 quick changer, 2 feet of surgical rubber tubing and 2 common swivels. I apologize for the arcaneness of the following instructions, and refer you to the following illustration should the text become impossible to decipher.

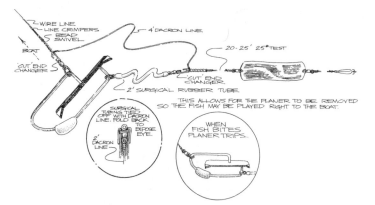

First deal with the rod's wire line.

1. *Put 2 line crimpers on the end.*

2. *Add a bead swivel that is small enough to pass through the rod guides.*

3. *Make a loop in the wire line and pass the tag end back through the line crimpers.*

4. *Crimp on the bead swivel, ensuring that one line crimper covers the end of the wire line. This helps it pass through the rod guides without snagging.*

5. *Attach 4 feet of 60-pound test monofilament or dacron line to the bottom end of the bead swivel.*

6. *To the top split ring on the planer, attach a heavy-duty end changer, the clasp of which has been previously cut off (or a piece of coathanger that has been bent for easy removal).*

7. *Attach the end changer to the bottom of the bead swivel where the dacron line is also attached.*

Next a snubber must be made. Made of highly stretchable rubber, a snubber provides the only give in the system and is vital for preventing fish from ripping out hooks.

1. *Take one of the common swivels and tie 3 feet of dacron to it.*

2. *Thread the dacron through the surgical tubing— no easy feat.*

3. *Push the swivel completely into one end of the tubing and tie a piece of dacron around the middle of the swivel.*

4. *The next manoeuvre is really hard: fold the end of the tubing back over the dacron tied around the tubing, thus exposing half the swivel.*

5. *Take the other end of the dacron (ie., the end threaded through the tubing) and tie it to the second common swivel.*

6. *Push the swivel into that end of the tubing, tie it off and repeat the difficult manoeuvre.*

7. *Voilà. Now you have a snubber. Attach it to the bottom split ring on the planer rail.*

Finally, the bottom end of the planer apparatus must be assembled.

1. *To the free end of the snubber attach a quick changer and the second heavy-duty end changer (which has also had its clasp cut off).*

2. *To the free end of the 4-foot piece of dacron (or 60-pound-test monofilament) attach the second bead swivel.*

3. *Slip the heavy-duty end changer into the top swivel on the bead swivel.*

4. *To the fishing end of the bead swivel, tie 25 feet of 25- to 30-pound-test leader.*

5. *Tie a ball-bearing end changer at the tackle end of the leader.*

If you have followed this obscure explanation, give yourself a pat on the back. You have a functioning planer on your rod. The planer can be removed, thus allowing you to play a fish right into the boat rather than be yarded in hand over hand once the planer is reached. Put a bell on the end of your rod and it will ring out the instant you have a bite.

After all this assembly, you are actually ready to get the line in the water. Avoiding tangles, carefully let out the 25 feet of leader, pick up the rod and lower the planer into the water. This type of planer is set by slowly moving the rod tip to the rear of the boat so that the split ring travels up the planer railing to the top position. In this position, the planer descends like a rock—a far simpler, far more effective system than the other style of planer. This same slow movement can be used when the planer needs to be reset even 250 feet from the boat. Pull the rod forward, slowly move the tip to the rear of the boat and the planer will set. This can prove necessary when checking for small fish without bringing the entire line in or when the planer trips inadvertently.

A planer can also be tripped from the boat. Starting with the tip high, drop the rod smartly. Just as the slack goes completely out of the line, snap the rod tip up, tripping the planer for easy retrieval. If the planer will not trip, weed fouls the top of it. Unlucky you. You will now spend ten minutes grimacing like a World Wrestling Federation tag team member, trying to bring it in. In the other extreme when the planer continually trips on its own, flasher drag is the usual culprit. Put a downward bend in the middle of the top half of the planer rail so the split ring cannot slide past it and trip the planer.

Wooden recorder reels help determine fishing depth. Planers descend 1 foot for every 2 feet of wire line until 150 feet of line has been let out (ie., 75 feet of depth). After this length of line, planers descend 1 foot for every subsequent 3 feet of wire line until 350 feet of line has been let out. For example, at 350 feet of wire line, lure depth will be 75 + (350−150) /3 = 142 feet deep. If you don't have a recorder reel, assume 1 foot per revolution. And in either case, do not let out more than 350 feet of line; line drag prevents further depth.

Planer fishing can produce spectacular results in calm water, especially when filled with resident salmon. Planers outfish other trolling gear 2:1 to 3:1 up to 142 feet deep. The reason is not hard to fathom. A planer that is 142 feet deep will be 350 feet from engine noises, whereas a downrigger is 142 feet away. This is a trememdous advantage when fish are spooked or nonmigratory. Past 142 feet, however, a planer will not outfish a downrigger and you might as well switch over.

The strike on a planer rod is the most exciting in all of fishing. Take your Valium. (Or is that Prozac in contemporary-speak?) These rods snap up at least 3 feet, causing heart attacks. Then they snap back almost into the water when the fish takes its first run. This all takes a millisecond and is accompanied by rattling and bell dinging. Because the reel has been tightened off completely due to the pressure, you had better be in flight between the steering wheel and rod, because you have that millisecond to loosen the tension before the fish breaks loose. Wire line has not 1 inch of give in 350 feet, and releasing the reel's tension has to be accomplished immediately if not sooner.

When the fish runs, it seems to do so much faster than with monofilament line. Keep your fingers out of the way of the handles or they will get bashed to pieces. The unstretchable nature of wire line makes the jolt of a big fish feel as though it's pulling directly on your arm. Ah, what fun. After minding your knuckles, be ultra-careful playing a fish because the wire line will not help you. Be careful about sideways shear as well, especially when the planer rises to the surface and the fish pulls at right angles to the boat. As soon as the sideways stress has stopped, lift the rod tip so the planer completely clears the surface. And be sure to play a fish completely before bringing it in, particularly if you have not made a removable planer.

Best of luck with planer fishing. It takes real skill. Remember, too, that with 350 feet of line you must make corners slowly. If you tangle wire line it takes ages to untangle, and once kinked might as well be cut off—very expensive. Another way to avoid tangles is to set the planer so it will fish further out from the side of the boat. This can be accomplished by bending the weight on the bottom of the planer rail toward the side of the boat on which it will be fished. Once in the water, the planer tilts away from the boat, thus taking it out a bit from the side of the boat. Recall, as well, that many people do not realize how far a planer can be let out as they cross behind you with their downriggers. This can result in a pretty ugly mess, a waste of time and frayed nerves all around. I switch to downriggers in areas of heavy tidal flow, partly for this reason, but also because planers go wild, threatening at any second to snap the rod in half or rip it right off the boat.

I fish both downriggers and planers at the same time to gain the advantages of each. First thing in the morning, a downrigger will catch fish at the same rate as a planer, and I start with a planer on one side and a downrigger on the other. This helps, incidentally, to avoid tangles on turns. Then, until the fish descend from the surface to 150 feet around noon, most bites occur on the planer. At

150 feet deep, I put away my planers and fish downriggers on both sides until later in the afternoon when the fish begin rising once again in the water. At this point I remove one downrigger and put out a planer in its place until last light.

Now that the real technical stuff has been dealt with, let's move on to more interesting material: factors affecting success, and lure types.

FACTORS AFFECTING TROLLING SUCCESS

Binoculars

On days when you are catching a fat lot of nothing and others all around you are gleefully bringing them in by the bucketsful, do not become veiny-eyed despondent. Try to determine what they are doing, and copy it. If you can get close enough, ask other fishers about their lures, fishing depth and, if there's time, leader length. Then thank them; they may have changed your luck for the better. On days that you can't sidle close enough, binoculars become vital for examining tackle from afar. Scrutinize rods on which a fish is being played—it may be the only tackle on the boat that is working. Consider the following:

+ *Is a dodger being used? This implies bait, usually anchovy.*
+ *Is a flasher being used? Hootchies or strip are the likely lures.*
+ *If there is no dodger or flasher, the lure is likely a plug.*
+ *Determine leader length. 4 to 6 feet implies bait, probably strip, 2 to 3 feet, and the lure is likely a hootchie.*
+ *Check lure colour. Silver usually means bait, other colours suggest hootchies and, less often, Apexes or spoons.*
+ *Sliding weights imply 1 ounce to 1 pound and a depth of 0 to 25 feet. Lead balls suggest a 20- to 50-foot depth, unless you know the fish to be deeper.*
+ *When tackle returns to the water, check depth by counting pulls at 1½–2 feet per pull, or downrigger turns at 1–1½ feet per revolution.*

In determining a course of action, mix the clues together; sometimes the information coalesces when pondering the bits and pieces. In your speculations, also consider the boat's fishing pattern. Is it in a tideline or a back eddy? Is it facing into the tide or travelling with it? Is there a reef under the boat? Is it fishing a set fathom line in a straight line? Are fish being caught all around you or only in a certain area or in one direction? Follow someone who is having luck.

Speed

Boat speed can have dramatic effects on fishing success and is, in my opinion, one of the factors to which too few fishers pay enough attention. Fundamentally, speed affects how well a trolled lure works and, indeed, whether it works at all. Even when a lure works properly, its speed can tantalize fish into biting or send them into delirious boredom. A high trolling speed lifts tackle from correct fishing depth and causes gear strain and breakage, while a low speed allows tackle to drop in the water.

Unfortunately, improper boat speed can be one of the more annoying problems to overcome in trolling. Boat idles vary from day to day and it is good practice to assess speed daily throughout a fishing trip. In measuring, do not judge speed in relation to land; it is how fast the fish want your lure to move in the water—which itself may be moving—that counts. There are places on the coast where you may be carried ten miles while staying in contact with a school of fish. Many times you will be whizzing by land but moving too slowly in the water to elicit a strike. Sometimes the boat will be moving backwards in relation to the land, but will be presenting your tackle in the right direction, sending fish to eating nirvana as they swim into the current toward it. Test water speed by:

* *Spitting or throwing a toothpick into the water and noticing how quickly the object recedes from the boat.*
* *Judging how fast waves pass the boat.*
* *Judging speed in relationship to floating objects such as logs or other boats.*

Fishing speed is a personal thing, and you should get to know precisely the speed at which you are most successful. Be aware that speed has an intimate relationship with leader length and the bait action you prefer. Generally speaking, I fish slower in still water and faster in tidal flow; however, I always consider the speed of boats that are catching fish.

One important law should be observed: every time speed is changed, all lines, particularly bait lines, must be checked to ensure that they are working properly. When you slow down, flashers can stop spinning and bait can stop revolving. If you seem to be moving too slowly, this is easily altered by applying more throttle. As speed increases, though, bait begins whizzing in circles and Apex action can go bizarre. No fish will bite such a lure even if it can catch it, so every time you change speed, bring in the bait and check to be sure it is still exhibiting the fish-catching spiral that you prefer.

The slower you move, the shorter your leaders should be. Faster speed calls for longer leaders. My standard length is 36 inches for chinook and about 30 inches for coho. Somedays I shorten leaders all the way down to 20 inches for coho and pink. Sockeye take variable lengths, but tend more often to be enticed by slower, less erratic lures: a longer leader is better. Chinook sometimes take bait rigs on dodgers with up to 6 feet of leader.

If you're fishing the same gear as successful boats but you are catching zilch, compare boat speed. Do you catch up to or fall behind successful boats? If you need to slow down, there are a number of tricks you can try even if your boat won't run more slowly.

- *Lower the engine's idle, if possible. Idle screws are adjustable in seconds. But don't lose the engine cover or get salt water on the engine interior.*
- *Tie a five-gallon bucket to 20 feet of line and run it directly astern of the boat.*
- *Use the kicker engine.*
- *Mount a baffle behind the propeller.*
- *Change propeller pitch.*
- *When using lead weights, pull two feet of line from the last rod guide, wait and then let go.*
- *Take your boat out of gear, then put it back in. Lures will follow in an enticing crest and trough curve, changing speed as they go. Yummy.*
- *Fish across tidal flow rather than with or against it.*
- *Zigzag back and forth across tidelines rather than following them.*
- *Lower leader test from 25 to 30 pounds to 15 to 20 pounds.*
- *Lengthen leaders.*
- *Change from flashers to dodgers.*

Speed changes affect dodger and flasher action. As I have stated, dodgers sway from side to side like hula skirts while flashers rotate in circles; each is used to impart a set type of action to a lure. If that action changes, lure action changes and will not perform correctly. Hootchies, for example, are meant to be towed behind flashers. A hootchie makes a circle or figure eight at fishing speed. If the boat slows, the flasher stops revolving and takes on dodger action, swaying from side to side. This completely eliminates proper hootchie action, which should be the jerky asymmetrical fish-escaping pattern established by a flasher.

This is another reason for using a leader in the 30- to 40-pound test range: flasher and dodger action transmits more smartly to the lure. Increased speed causes other problems, too. More gear foul-ups result because fast circular motion gets the better of even ball-bearing swivels. Lifted clear of the water, line winds up on itself, and anything else within reach, like an amphetamined snake. Increased speed also turns dodger action into flasher action, thereby ruining bait action.

Even if lure action is maintained, faster-spinning bait often leads to fewer bites. The only salmon that regularly prefer a faster, tighter roll are coho. (This is achieved with shorter leaders or by speeding up the boat.) Coho tend to bite and veer off at high speed, so the bite can come as the delightful shock of a screaming reel.

Having tried to convince you to regulate speed, I have to add that there is good reason to vary speed. Fish sometimes prefer a lure travelling at a speed different than expected. Fishing is very precise on any given day and every day can be different, so on slow days, make speed one of the alterable variables. If anything characterizes summer trolling, for instance, it is variation or—to coin a *Monday Night Football*-ism—erraticism. The fish are swilled with hormones, thinking of sex, preparing for a battle upstream. Famished as libidinous teenagers, they snap at anything that gets in their way. With all five species beetling back to their rivers of origin, summer action in August, September and October can be wildly unpredictable. Change speeds if things aren't working out, particularly during periods of intermingling runs. When four or five species lumber through, my experience is that each becomes much more bite-crazy, sensitized to the mass hysteria of it all. In contrast, resident winter chinook and bluebacks seem far more rational and predictable.

And remember that each species does have its preferred speed. Fish at slow speed for sockeye, slow to medium speed for chum and chinook, slow to fast for pink, and medium to fast for coho. I have seen people fish coho almost at planing speed, lines churning in the wake, but have seldom seen them catch anything. Note well, though, that in such a circumstance, were a coho to bite, it would simply scream off. A most satisfying jolt!

TROLLING PATTERN

Now that you are trolling along, alert as an eagle to the minutiae of salmon-catching success, consider that your fishing plan should contain a strategy for covering the watery terrain around you. In slow water, fishing into the tide usually produces more fish. Fish swim into the tide; therefore, your lure is in front of them longer than if it were going in the opposite direction. This is not true in faster water. Commercial trollers fish with the tide. They put their gear in above where they intend to fish, fish through the area, then pull their lines and motor back. Thus they cover more ground in less time and have confidence that their tackle is performing as expected. This makes good sense for sportfishers, too, especially when fishing alone. Boats spin when going into the tide, and it's much easier putting out rods when the boat will track straight (ie., when moving with the tide). In fishing areas with good tidal flow, virtually all boats end up bunched together, facing into the tide, covering a fraction of the territory they could cover fishing in the opposite direction. They zip down with the tide, turn and then inch back to where they started. There is simply no point wasting this time, or worrying about your gear whizzing like a windmill; if the tackle won't work as intended, it has as much chance of catching a fish as if it hadn't been put out.

Another important decision is whether to fish with, across or against the fishing pattern of other boats. If you fish in the same direction as other boats, often you will get stuck moving along packed in a row with little chance of getting out; you may not be able to fish the pattern that you expect will produce the most fish. Furthermore, as noted in the last chapter, problems steering clear of others can arise when a large fish is hooked. On the other hand, if you choose to fish against the pattern of other boats (ie., fishing down or across the tide), you will be threading between the boats coming toward you; however, some latitude is afforded for picking your way around the fishing grounds because there will be few boats moving in the same direction.

My recommendation is to choose a fishing pattern that increases your chances of catching fish. Before going out, I decide the pattern I will utilize and stick with it. This means that I seldom fish with reference to other boats. Instead, I pick and thread my way through the pack, doing what I think is best. Quite often I fish across the normal fishing pattern, at 90 degrees to other boats. In my "plane" there are no other fishers, and this gives me much more steering freedom. Some days this can make for hairy fishing, but in the long run, I am convinced that more fish will be caught. Learn how long it will take you to cover a certain distance. If it looks as though you will cross another boat's path or be in the same place at the same time, turn a circle to burn up a few minutes, then continue unimpeded in the intended direction. This is a useful technique when catching up to or being caught by another boat, as well as in areas where the productive fishing pattern is specific and well known. I don't like boat noise scaring the fish near my tackle, so in fishing my chosen pattern I try to leave room around my boat at all times.

Why do I go to this trouble? After studying the area, its tides and currents, I decide where success most likely will be found and fish the fish, not other boats. Most people head over to other boats and throw out their lines. It makes more sense to head to the fish and throw out your lines. Once the lines are down, get out your binoculars and determine whether other boats are catching the fish. If they are, abandon your plan for the moment. Turn and move toward the fishy area, your gear already in the water and working properly.

Let me illustrate my point with an example. Let's say that the other boats are putting along half a mile from shore, catching nothing. Doesn't it stand to reason that the fish are not in this little ribbon of water? And doesn't it seem a reasonable plan to fish in the water surrounding the other boats until you pick up something? If you see the bite come on for those other boats, you can always mosey over towards them. You will, over the years, catch far more fish if you decide on a plan and go with it. The reason for this is that you are actively trying to figure something out, rather than passively doing what the rest of the crowd does. The more you figure out, the more you will be rewarded for making that effort. Success will follow you to more and more fishing locales and into times when the fishing gets tough. It is no accident that the same people come in with fish in both the good and bad times. Much has been said in Chapters 3 and 5 about fishing in the right spot, and I suggest that you reread that information.

One final thing to be passed on concerns the general rule for turning while trolling: turn into the current or into the wind. When both conditions are encountered simultaneously, turning into the wind is normally the better choice.

The reason for turning into the current is that you will be carried by the tide a much shorter distance than you will if you turn with the tide. Turning 180 degrees takes the same length of time no matter which way you turn. Accordingly, if you turn with the tide it will carry you much further from where you started, and thus as much as half a mile from where you want to end up. In some areas, it may take 30 minutes to remake this distance, if indeed it can be regained at all.

Turning into the wind presents a dicier proposition; however, as with turning into the current, you will be carried less distance from your intended destination. When by yourself, though, it can be next to impossible to accomplish. At the point where your bow crosses the wind, it will swing wildly, resulting quite often in crossed and tangled lines behind the boat. Even for an experienced boat handler, it is far less hairy to turn with the wind, an action that has the added benefit of turning the boat in the same direction as the waves. Unless your boat tracks very true, it may be wiser to turn with the wind. Regardless of which direction you choose, there comes an uncomfortable point where the boat is completely broadside to the wind and waves, and is pushed sideways strongly. Lengthen out this portion of the turn to lessen the chance of your lines tangling on the inside of the turn. It's also a good idea to fish with the wind on a brisk day, even more so when on your own. Travel past the far end of the fishing grounds, turn and put in the lines. Then fish in comfort until through the area, pull the lines and go back.

ALWAYS CHECK LURE ACTION

A lure that does not have fish-catching action might as well be a tennis racquet; salmon will not recognize it as food. I hate to be a nag, but never, ever put a lure in the water without first checking its action. And once you are satisfied, never change trolling speed without rechecking lure action.

Check lure action at normal trolling speed. Establish trolling speed for a minute, then gently lower the lure beside the boat. Stick the dodger or flasher down into the water to ensure that the lure will be performing below the surface and scrutinize it carefully. A 2-foot stick notched at one end makes a fine alternative to a flasher. Slip the notch down the line until the lure is pulled under-water. Close examination may reveal that the hootchie tails that appeared to be moving freely above water do not, in fact, float freely underwater—hook fouling is the common problem. Or it may be that the perfect-looking anchovy does not spiral in the water, or rotates in an unintended direction. It may be that that nifty plug veers to one side because the leader has not been attached to the top of the lure eye. Or you may be using an Apex—a lure that is ultra-sensitive to speed—and it is rotating rather than tail-wiggling, because the boat is going that smidgeon too fast. Take care not to check action while the boat is turning or being pushed diagonally by the wind. The boat needs to be moving at actual trolling speed (ie., tracking in a straight line).

It may seem rather obvious to point out that the lure must be attached to the mainline before checking action. But anyone who fishes with me knows that I fish entirely wired. It's like sitting next to a gambling addict who is sure his luck's about to change. I have been known to do all sorts of fish-catching stuff, such as trimming knots, sharpening hooks, examining action, replacing leaders, etc., only to let the leader slip through my hands, reach for the rod and find that I have not attached the flasher to the ball-bearing swivel. So to prevent this, take a pill, leave me on shore and attach the tackle to the mainline. After checking action, carefully let the 20 or so feet slide through your hands before weights, planer or downrigger are attached. Letting it slide against tension prevents hooks from swinging back and becoming tangled in the line, or other deleterious outcomes, such as hootchie fronds becoming stuck. Watch your gear until it is underwater. One molecule of weed will persuade a fish that a lure is not a tasty treat.

FLASHERS AND DODGERS

Flashers and dodgers have been mentioned in passing numerous times in this book. Now is the time to say a bit more. Both flashers and dodgers have the purpose of attracting fish. They do this by periodically reflecting sunlight and by imparting action to a lure. The flash of light is seen by Mr. Salmon, and his natural curiosity makes him swim closer until the lure is seen and he snaps at it. The theoretical canon also includes the suggestion that the flash represents a salmon streaking through a herring ball to grab a meal. In other words, the flash triggers an eating response in salmon, much as seagull squawking draws a crowd of a hundred seagulls in no time flat.

I am not convinced that it is simply the flash of light that attracts salmon. I have some very beat-up flashers that hardly reflect light—that have tape stripping off in chunks—yet are every bit as good at attracting fish as any other flasher in my tackle box. In fact (and this may just be a peculiarity of my own mind), I think some flashers get better as they age; newer ones need a bit of skuffing-up before being completely seasoned. Call me a superstitious fool. My flasher-dodger theory includes the assumption that they vibrate and the fish are attracted from some distance away. Fish are regularly caught deeper than 150 feet, where there can be very little sun, and yet a flasher or dodger can be critical to catching fish. In murky water the same results can hold true.

Sometimes dodgers and flashers do not produce bites. In calm water, a four-inch bait on its own often far outfishes one with a dodger or flasher. Alternatively, a long leader of 4 to 6 feet may be required to move the lure away from the flasher. Generally speaking, smaller fish are more susceptible to dodgers and flashers than larger fish. This may be because the younger fish that prefer a flash get caught young, and only those that do not prefer a flash live longer. Perhaps. It is certainly true that larger chinook are less excitable, slower moving and more particular. They are more likely to take larger, slower moving, less adorned gear.

Before moving on to specifics, let me say that you should buy quality dodgers and flashers. Expect a good-quality chrome finish on dodgers and, if you can get them, buy only brands that utilize ball-bearing swivels on the top and the bottom. Flasher swivels should be anchored by metal grommets, or the plastic may break. If the unit offers a quick changer on the bottom, you might as well have that, too. Be sure you have both dodgers and flashers in your tackle box. Ask for local information each time you fish in a new locale. Find out which is preferred and whether there is a brand of choice. Hard as it may be to believe, the same fish can swim ten to fifteen miles and want a different brand in a new location.

A flasher is designed to turn a circle when towed behind the boat. This circle is 2 to 4 feet in diameter and carries the lure behind it in roughly the same diameter circle. If action is not imparted completely, the lure moves in a rough figure eight. Either of these actions is acceptable. Flashers come in different colours, the most common being red, green and blue. I think colour matters little. (However, the day that I get skunked and some lucky swine comes staggering up the dock with fish and a flasher of a colour I don't have, you can bet your last rupee that the next time I go fishing I will have bought at least two.)

Flashers are usually made of plastic and have mirrorlike, sun-reflecting metal tape on both sides. Plastic flashers are much lighter than metal dodgers. They do not drop as deep as metal blades, either when the boat is travelling in a straight line or turning, thus they do not snag the bottom before your depth sounder says they should. In addition, they do not have the drag of metal on your gear or when a fish is pulling against them, so knots do not pop as easily.

Strangely enough, plastic flashers are more durable than metal, because their metal fittings are stainless steel and need less servicing.

Dodgers are usually made out of a metal that has been chromed to improve reflectivity. Dodgers do not have to be made from metal and it makes much more sense to make them from plastic due to the advantages listed in the last paragraph. On the other hand, the greater weight of metal makes dodgers more deliberate in the water. The top end stays more or less still while the bottom end swings back and forth. Accordingly, the lure sways back and forth in front of the fish. Since this lure action— and dodgers are used mostly with bait—is more subtle than that imparted by a flasher, stiffer leader proves beneficial for transmitting dodger action.

A dodger is really a flasher that does not spin in a circle. There is no other significant difference between the two. You can easily change a metal dodger into a flasher and back again: either speed up the boat or bend the dodger. The here-I-am-fellas-and-you'd-better-come-and-get-me-before-I-get-away sway of a dodger becomes a circle if you put a more pronounced "S" bend in its tail half. The longer and springier the dodger, the better that bending will work. Put the dodger over your knee and bend it down just above the halfway point. Flip the dodger over and bend down the tail end. Then put the dodger in the water and see if it rotates like a flasher. If it does not, make the lower bend more pronounced. The greater the bend, the faster the spin.

LEADERS

A leader is simply a short piece of fishing line that attaches a lure to the mainline via a swivel, weight, dodger-type device or planer. In trolling, action is more important than subterfuge; fish spend less time examining the gear and more time worrying about the tasty treat of your lure getting away. For this reason, the pound test is higher than in other forms of fishing. In addition, leader stiffness (ie., 25 to 40 pounds) is essential for transferring action from flashers and dodgers to lures. Rig up a hootchie with 15-pound test to prove this to yourself. Note that flasher action is dampened along the line and the hootchie tends to spin in the middle of the much wider arc of the flasher. With higher-pound test, action is passed along smartly.

Leader length is an imprecise art, and giving general advice is difficult. Plenty of local variation exists. For instance, one year I caught oodles of fish on an 18-inch leader in an area where I was assured that the leader standard was 4 to 6 feet behind a flasher or dodger blade. In subsequent years, I caught nothing and reluctantly moved to

longer leaders. I have written the short leaders into my logs, however, and test a short leader every fall when fishing in the same
place. Some indications of leader length can be given, though.
Chinook prefer a 36-inch leader; coho one of 20 to 36 inches; pink
like a 24- to 36-inch leader; sockeye one of 30 to 36 inches; and
chum, if they have a preference at all, will be in the 36-inch range.

Two other considerations should help guide your choice of
leader line. Use different-coloured line for leaders and mainline. This
helps in sorting out tangles. If you can see which line is which, it's
much easier to know which one to cut. In fact, it's not a bad idea
to pack different-coloured line on different reels for the same reason. I
have already said that I use less expensive line for my mainline. It
makes more sense to use better line for leaders. Leaders are not
replaced anywhere near as often as the end of the mainline is cut
off, so it's worthwhile using quality line that can stand up to getting nicked and opaqued over the years.

TROLLING LURES

All trolling lures are meant to imitate some sort of feed swimming
through the water. The more common types include bait rigs,
hootchies, plugs and spoons. As suggested in the introduction, buy
two of everything. Most days, salmon will bite on only one lure,
and you will catch many more fish if you have at least two of each
lure to throw out. Also, if you lose the hot lure, it's unlikely that
you will catch anything else unless you have a backup. I have half a
dozen of some lures, each with a different leader length, hook setup
or other minor modification. I simply reach into the tackle box for the
thing I need without wasting fishing time to rig it up. My tackle box
has about 50 hootchies and squirts, for example, and I buy the bright
blue-green-combination hootchies by the half-dozen.

Over the years, some individual lures turn into pure dynamite.
They outfish your other lures many times over, even though they
seem the same. Treat them like gold, and I guarantee you that no
matter how old, how rust-covered, how downright yucky they look,
they will continue catching fish forever. I have some antediluvian
squirts that are covered in mildew picked up on Noah's Ark. They
have lost most of their fronds and still outfish virtually all of my
other squirts. Any such lure ought not to have its leader changed.
The leader is part of its mystical fish-catching chemistry, and retying the leader is like cutting off Samson's hair. The magic leaks
away. I once stepped on a strip head and cracked it. Until it broke

sometime later, it consistently outfished all my other baitheads. So reuse anything that works, no matter how odd it looks.

After buying everything on the market, you will end up with some stuff that will not work. If the lure is just too wild, throw it away. For example, I once bought a drift-fishing lure that was two pieces of diamond-shaped lead. They clacked together as the lure dropped in the water. Seemed a good idea in the store. Over time it seemed about as sexy as a breadboard, and so I turfed it. On the other hand, I have purchased some unusual bait-holder arrangements that I am convinced will catch at least one fish before I die. Relegate such lures to the third tackle box and clean them from time to time.

HOOTCHIES, SQUIRTS AND PLANKTON SQUIRTS

All of these lures simulate a squid, and on many winter days can be the most productive lure in your tackle box. Squid is probably the food of choice on the high seas, and coastal salmon likely bite these lures due to genetic predisposition. The soft tails are the strike trigger. On occasions when I have snipped the fronds to imitate a smaller bait, I have not caught a thing. Perhaps the shorter fronds are stiff. When selecting these lures, be sure that the fronds are long, delicate and slightly curled.

These lures come in a hundred different colour combinations. Local information will suggest the current preference. My former wife used the if-I-were-a-fish-I-would-like-this-colour approach to buying them, and I have some nifty-looking purple and yellow ones that have never caught a fish. Current all-the-rage colour combinations include the army-truck and peanut-butter patterns. They don't look fishy to me, but they work. Get two of each in the most productive colours and get backups in squirts. Squirts are smaller versions of hootchies, and on some days will far outfish hootchies of identical colour pattern.

You will find it cheaper and, as my kids say, "funner" to rig up your own hootchies. Take a trip to your local tackle shop and pick up swivels, spacer beads, the rubber bibs, hooks, mylar tails and leader. Tie two hooks in a sliding hook arrangement or attach a single straight hook—known as a Siwash hook—to a small swivel and then to a leader. Single straight hooks are far superior; they do not get mixed in the fronds and, in my opinion, hook salmon more securely than sliding hook types which curve down the shank. I am a maverick when it comes to trolling hooks. I use the largest hooks

I can get away with. Sneakiness is irrelevant in trolling, and the larger the hooks, the better. I use 5/0 and 6/0 hooks, which, by some people's standards, are rather large.

The critical point in rigging up hootchies is getting the hook absolutely at the end of the fronds. Rigged this way a fish will close on the hook, rather than closing on the fronds and just enough hook-scratch to scare it off. There is nothing more frustrating than watching your rod dip all morning long without hooking a single fish. Spacer beads inserted on the leader under the hootchie bib will put the hook at the right place. If hooking fish is still a problem, mount the hooks sticking out behind the fronds, or hold the rod in your hands and set the hooks manually. Alternatively, change to lead weights and perform the corny old pull-two-feet-of-line-and-let-it-go trick; this works better with hootchie-style lures than any other.

Mylar twinkle skirts may be added above the hooks and before the rubber bib. Mylar skirts are silver fronds that catch the sun like fish scales. Unfortunately, they are difficult to keep straight, and getting a hootchie working in the water becomes a task of some frustration. After a fish has bitten, mylar becomes even more difficult to straighten. Unless a lure comes rigged with a skirt, I do not use them anymore. I also feel they seldom produce more fish, so why use them?

Hootchies, squirts and plankton squirts are always used in combination with a device that gives them action. Most commonly, flashers are used. The revolving action makes the lure almost irresistible. I'd bite it myself. Action can also be provided by insertable butterfly heads, which look much like small shovels and give the lure a side-to-side, pluglike wobble. When using these heads, be sure to assess lure action. Higher speeds make them spin in a decidedly unfishy circle. Another variation is to cut a hole in the side of the hootchie head and push the leader through it. This imparts a wounded action. There are pre-rigged versions of hootchies on the market incorporating this feature. (I've not found them that successful, but they're worth a try on a day so slow that even slugs and snails are bored.)

Hootchie colour is crucial. On any given day, usually only one colour and one size will work. The standard colours, in addition to the two mentioned above, include white, green, green and white, blue and green, blue and white, and pink. I am painfully aware of how short this list is. There are seasonal variations and variations based on salmon species.

For example, sockeye prefer pink and bright red to other colours, as do pink salmon. Pinks, however, are the least discriminating of the salmon and will bite a broad range of colours. Coho like pink and red later in the summer and when euphasiid shrimp abound. Coho and chinook are most commonly taken on green-and-white and green-and-blue variations in the winter. A colour chart is offered a little later in the chapter, although local information is far more accurate than any table can be. You will note that chinook don't have much of a fancy for pink; however, when there are intermingling summer runs, they go just as bonkers over a pink hootchie as any other species.

The most important comment to be made about hootchies is that one should spend as much time perfecting their action at the side of the boat as one would spend on bait. Hootchie fronds get caught in the hooks or bent back into the head; so operating, a lure will catch nary a limpet. The last thing you should do is throw a hootchie out of the boat and crank it down a downrigger. It will foul every time. Even a lure that hangs freely in the air should be checked in the water. Hooks often rotate and bind some of the fronds. Every time you put a hootchie in the water, let the mainline slide back through your hand. After attaching the line to a downrigger, I pull the line in hand over hand if I have any suspicion of fouling. Adjusting and readjusting those fronds is the key to hootchie-style lures.

One of these days, some smart cookie will come out with a new lure that will rival the hootchie in appeal. In drift-fishing for bottom fish, there are many lures made of that super-wiggly rubber stuff attached to a lead weight. Well, one of these days someone will make that material into a fish-shaped lure for trolling that is just as successful as hootchies. Think of the hundreds of colour combinations! It makes your head reel with visions of money.

PLUGS

Plugs are the most ingeniously effective yet underused type of trolling lure on the market. They are simple to use and have an enticing action: a tail-wagging wobble with a side-to-side dart thrown in—the cleanest lure you can buy. Plugs come in hundreds of different colours and, as with other lures, only one of these will work on any given day. Good tackle stores have colour charts indicating the combinations for certain areas and for different seasons. My recommendation is to buy only those plugs—some brands come identified by number—specified by a local who is in the know.

The action of a plug is very delicate. Plugs are fish-shaped with a shovel on the front end. The shovel catches water, thus pointing the lure slightly down and giving it a characteristic tail-wagging swim. These are the only trolling lures on which I use lighter leader; this enhances the action rather than dampening it. I use 15-pound test and a softer, better-quality line. I also use one of those lines that changes colour in the water so that the plug's presentation is as unobtrusive as possible. Action is further enhanced by the use of a large straight single hook (ie., the Siwash variety), which allows the lure to ride truer in the water. A longer hook has the added advantage of travelling well down the salmon's throat by the time the plug is contacted. Plugs are also the easiest lure to remove from a fish. Turn the hook upside down and the fish flops into the fishbox.

Plugs are the only trolling lures that are consistently used without a flasher. This makes them more enjoyable to use, simpler to rig and far more fun when playing a fish; there's no drag other than this teeny-weeny lure with its very large fish-securing hook. Rig a plug on a 4- to 6-foot leader. I use a ball-bearing swivel, not because the lure rotates—which it must not—but because it stays clean and shiny and in good condition so much longer. Rotation results nearly all the time from trolling too fast, and you must slow down to get the plug to dart from side to side. If you do use a plug with a flasher or dodger, check its action, as this other tackle may induce a roll.

The most important aspect of rigging plugs is attaching the leader. The newer-style plug comes with a small loop embedded in the front edge of the shovel. After tying an absolutely 100-percent-sure, tight, clean, handsome knot, push the knot to the top of the loop. Look down the lure from the front end, making sure that the line is perfectly centred and vertical. If it is not, the lure will not dart properly—it will ride over to one side and stay there, limp, dead and decidedly unfishy. The older-style plug comes with a bead swivel that slides through the plug and attaches to the line. For this reason, it cannot be secured so that the plug head points down during trolling. The trick is to take along a supply of very small rubber bands. Once the lure is attached to the leader, slip a rubber band over the front of the plug, pinning the line to the lure. Again, ensure that the line rises from the rubber band vertically and centred to the lure. Recheck this each time you put the lure back out.

APEX LURES

Apex lures are closely related to plugs. They have the same side-to-side darting action and are also clean, simple lures in use. Each comes ready-made with a quality straight Siwash hook, and most have reflective tape to attract fish. The hook rides well behind the lure, so once again the fish has the hook firmly in its mouth by the time it clamps down on the lure.

Like plugs, Apexes do not work well if the action they exhibit is circular. Promotional information sometimes suggests that rotation is okay, but in my experience such motion is the kiss of death. In addition, I have also noticed that Apexes are much more likely to spin than plugs. Accordingly, check action closely. These lures sometimes are not well enough balanced to overcome this problem. I discard ones that don't work and buy new ones. One alternative is to shave down one side of the front face so that it presents less resistance and does not overpower the lure into a spin. Another alternative is to slow down the boat. Unlike plugs, Apexes may be fished quite successfully with flashers or dodgers. They come with a good long leader and this can be shortened to taste. Seek out local information regarding proper length.

SPOONS

Spoons, like plugs, are underrated lures. Usually made of chromed metal, spoons are ribbon- or tear-shaped. Molded plastic ones tend to be chunkier. The most commonly used brands include the Krippled K, Tom Mack and Pt. Defiance spoons. Use stiffer leader in the 30-pound range because spoons are nearly always fished behind a flasher and can use the extra kick of action transmission, but are too light to take heavier line. These lures come ready-made with Siwash hooks and have that satisfying ability to hook fish cleanly. Spoons are rather old-fashioned gear, and this, I think, is why few people use them; however, they can be just as effective on the right day as any other lure.

The trick to the spoon, if it is thin and made of metal, is customization with a slight bend so that it looks like it ought to be thrown out. Bend the lure in its latter half, not exactly at right angles to the length of the lure, but on a slight diagonal. This adds an injured, erratic little tinkle of movement that makes all the difference between dry gulch and a boatful of fish. Buy a few spoons and bend each one a bit differently. I guarantee you that one will outperform the others. Take a close look at it and rebend the others in the same way. And, above all else, if you get a lure that works, do not change it in any way. It will continue to work even after all the colour has worn off and the lure looks like a refugee from a chrome factory. I have one ancient, crummy-looking Krippled K that has a bent-open split ring, vague remnants of colour like Napoleon's rag-tag army retreating from a frigid and forbidding Russia, and a hook that has been sharpened so many times it hardly has a barb. The leader has long since turned white, has more bends and kinks than the tortuous route legislation takes through Parliament, and one little knot. The brass swivel looks like it came to Vancouver Island with Captain Cook a couple of centuries ago. And yet it catches fish far better than any other spoon in my overflowing tackle box.

Many fishers do not have confidence in a spoon's ability to attract fish on its own, and use it only with a flasher. Some days, I find spoons to be far more effective without anything in front to attract fish. In the fall, troll the centre line just below the surface in the wake of the boat. Use 60 to 80 feet of line and 1 to 8 ounces of weight. Try red spoons in summer and fall; green ones are better in the winter. (Of course, you will be fishing deeper, most likely for chinook, and a flasher makes sense in the deeper, dimmer waters that they frequent.)

One of the lure combinations that you can "invent" for yourself is a double-spoon arrangement. Take the hook off one spoon and use a small split ring to attach the bottom of this spoon to the top of the second spoon. Leave the hook of the second spoon sharpened and ready to snag the first foolish fish. Adapt this rig by bending or hammering the spoons into curves. My inclination is to bend the trailing spoon. This arrangement can be fished on its own or with a flasher. The green and silver ones are best for this purpose, and you will find them more effective in the winter. My experience is that the Krippled K works best, but you can decide this for yourself.

TROLLING WITH BAIT

Bait fishing is the most productive yet most exacting form of trolling. Bait must be adjusted absolutely precisely to perform as intended, and, being soft tissue, it disintegrates during fishing. It shreds easily and should be pulled in for a check every twenty minutes. The care taken in handling, rigging and checking action will result in a spectacular difference in the number of fish caught.

There are three types of bait: whole herring, whole anchovy and strip. Each of these comes in different sizes so that natural feed size may be matched. Check with the marina for current size. Remember always that smaller bait will catch more but smaller fish, while larger bait will catch fewer but larger fish. A slower roll and a slower troll will also catch larger fish, and vice versa.

All trolling bait comes frozen. Inspect each package before purchasing. If there are a great number of ice crystals inside, or if the ice surrounding the strip is eroding, do not buy that package. Whole anchovy and herring come in trays, each fish frozen in a layer of ice to prevent freezer damage. If the snouts of the fish look brown or the fins are ragged, do not buy the bait. Freezer-burned bait does not perform well in the water and does not have that nice fish-attracting shine of a newly injured baitfish. It also has a characteristic freezer-damaged smell. Fish have extraordinary nasal abilities, so give them good-quality bait.

Once on the boat, keep whole bait out of direct sunlight and strip in a bucket of water. Whole anchovy and herring become soft in water. Keep them wrapped in paper or in a thermal container on ice. Any bait put in water should be put in salt water, not fresh water. Fresh water breaks down bait, making it shred in use. This includes bait that you refreeze. Bait refrozen in fresh water is too soft to use. One variation for onboard storage, and in contradiction to what I have said, is laying bait out in the sun, sometimes on the engine cover. This warm surface dries a curve into the bait. This approach mitigates bait disintegration and imparts a built-in curve to enhance the roll you will be seeking when fishing. In my opinion, however, dried-out bait is less effective. It goes hard and shrivels. The shininess of the scales decreases markedly.

While fishing, make sure that the stomachs of whole bait do not swell. Swelled bait has begun rotting. You will have trouble rigging such bait, as it will fall apart in your hands. Furthermore, the bait, once rigged, does not have the strength to stay together when pulled through the water behind a flasher or dodger. If you bring in an anchovy or herring and part of its gut is sticking through the stomach wall—usually looking like a brown worm—the bait is too soft and likely all of your bait is useless. The solution is to buy and use only good-quality bait. Inspect bait before you are miles out on the water.

At the end of the day, some bait can be refrozen for reuse. Keep the strip container and some salt water. Refreeze as soon as you get home. Refreeze whole bait in the tray in which it came with a plastic bag around it. Be careful not to squash or bend the bait. Refreezing bait allows ice crystals to build up in the flesh. This rips the cells apart. The tensile strength of the bait breaks down and it will not roll properly in the water. Always recall that refrozen bait is far more susceptible to freezer burn than when first bought, so check refrozen bait thoroughly. If it looks bad don't use it. Buy new bait. Fishing success depends on bait quality, so don't save a dollar's worth of rotten bait and ruin a whole day's fishing. Again, smell bait before reuse and discard any with that eau-de-rotten-poisson-distilled-until-it-repells-even-a- garbage-loving-bear odour.

Don't restore bait for very long. Refrozen bait should be thrown out after three weeks. Alternatively, make up a brine solution and store bait in the fridge. A brine solution can be made by mixing one cup of pickling salt with one quart of water. This is a better way to store used bait than in the freezer. It firms the bait and maintains colour. Brined bait can be kept at least three weeks in the fridge. Use a sealable jar that fits comfortably in your tackle box. The firmness of brine-stored bait really enhances action. I know super fishers who immediately unfreeze just-purchased bait and make up a brine solution. In other words, the bait is put in brine before fishing rather than after.

TROLLING WITH HERRING STRIP

Rigging Up

Herring strip that you purchase precut is a precise slice comprising one side of a large herring. During fishing, it presents one meat side and one scale side that is dark on the top and silver on the bottom. Commercial strip is cut to fit plastic baitheads, of which there are many brands on the market. Some spread open, then pinch to hold the bait, while others hold the bait with a toothpick. The most common holder is made by Rhys Davis, and virtually all tackle shops carry this variety either ready-rigged or for self-assembly.

I recommend rigging all strip holders yourself. It is far cheaper and allows for customization. Ball-bearing swivels are a must with every trolled bait to prevent line twist. The other two aspects over which one has control are leaders and hooks. I have already suggested leader lengths for different species. These distances are measured from the top of the swivel to the tail end of the last hook. For chinook, I hold the swivel to the middle of my chest and the hook with my other arm stretched out, a distance of exactly 36 inches. I prerig strip-holders as short as 18 inches and as long as 6 feet. Ready to be snapped on and off the mainline, they wait eagerly in my tackle box. The short ones are for fall-run coho; the longer ones are used when a flasher or dodger is intended to provide a visual attractant but not action. The shorter the leader, the snappier the action, and the longer the leader, the slower the action.

Longer leaders have a second application: use without a flasher or dodger. In this circumstance, the ball-bearing swivel on the leader attaches to the ball-bearing end changer on the mainline. This lump of metal should be as far from the strip as possible, so it does not attract the fish's attention. Some of the taps received in fishing probably come from salmon biting the nice, shiny swivels rather than the bait. I certainly have had fish bite swivels beside the boat. Modifications can be made to the hook presentation as well. Strip holders come rigged with treble hooks, and, as mentioned, I do not like using treble hooks where possible. Single hooks are perfectly secure. Either a single hook may be used or a tandem sliding hook arrangement. Specific instructions may be found in the next section.

Remember to shove a toothpick in the tiny blister on the side of the strip head. This tightens against the line, allowing the hooks to be slid toward or away from the baithead. Hooks positioned closer to the head result in a faster spinning bait, while hooks further back slow bait action. See the illustration for an example of each type of bait setup.

Three sizes of strip holder may be purchased. The large size is for large strip and the even larger tyee strip. The super-strip size is for super strip, also the same size as large strip. Do not use super strip in any other type of holder. Super strip is cut from the other side of the herring than large strip. In use, it spins in the opposite direction; hence, the super-strip holder has been adapted for this purpose. The third size is the tiny teaser for narrow, tiny strip. This strip simulates needlefish rather than herring.

Each locale has its preferred bait size. Sidney, for instance, has great clouds of needlefish on its various mudbottom fishing spots and the tiny teaser is used more frequently. Tyee holders can be used in front of Victoria, or anywhere large spawning herring hold in the middle of the winter.

CONVENTIONAL STRIP RIGGING AND DENNIS' APPROACH

Many minor modifications can be introduced in bait fishing. In conventional rigging, the treble hook is pulled back one half to two thirds of the way along the strip and a neat hole pressed through with one barb. This barb inserts cleanly and the other two barbs smooth against the meat side, presenting a streamlined bait in the water. The leader pulls snug and straight from the hook eye through the baitholder blister. If action is unsatisfactory, the fisher holds the

STRIP... CONVENTIONAL APPROACH

TREBLE HOOK
BALL BEARING SWIVEL
BAITHEAD
STRIP
2'-6'
TOOTHPICK (TRIM ENDS CLOSE.)

ONE BARB OF TREBLE HOOK GOES THROUGH ⅔ OF THE WAY BACK AND EXITS ON THE SCALE SIDE. JUST WHERE THE WHITE BELLY TURNS TO THE DARKER DORSAL SIDE.
TAKE UP SLACK BY PULLING LINE GENTLY. THIS PRODUCES THE WOUNDED BAITFISH SPIRAL.

STRIP... DENNIS' APPROACH

BALL BEARINGS SWIVEL
BAITHEAD
2'-6'
BEND
BLISTER

USE A SLIDING HOOK ARRANGEMENT. TRAILING HOOK EXTENDS PAST TAIL END OF STRIP. HOOKS SHOULD RIDE STRAIGHT UP AND DOWN, NOT AT AN ANGLE TO THE BAIT. BEND PLASTIC TAB TO INCREASE SPEED OF SPIRAL.

ANCHOVY.... CONVENTIONAL APPROACH

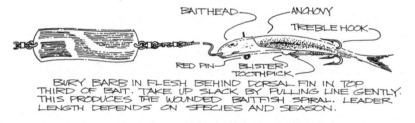

BAITHEAD
ANCHOVY
TREBLE HOOK
RED PIN
BLISTER
TOOTHPICK

BURY BARB IN FLESH BEHIND DORSAL FIN IN TOP THIRD OF BAIT. TAKE UP SLACK BY PULLING LINE GENTLY. THIS PRODUCES THE WOUNDED BAITFISH SPIRAL. LEADER LENGTH DEPENDS ON SPECIES AND SEASON.

ANCHOVY.... DENNIS' APPROACH

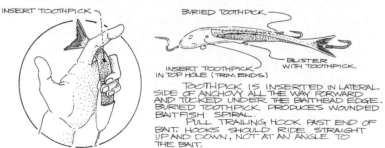

INSERT TOOTHPICK
BURIED TOOTHPICK
INSERT TOOTHPICK IN TOP HOLE (TRIM ENDS)
BLISTER WITH TOOTHPICK

TOOTHPICK IS INSERTED IN LATERAL SIDE OF ANCHOVY ALL THE WAY FORWARD AND TUCKED UNDER THE BAITHEAD EDGE. BURIED TOOTHPICK PRODUCES WOUNDED BAITFISH SPIRAL.
PULL TRAILING HOOK PAST END OF BAIT. HOOKS SHOULD RIDE STRAIGHT UP AND DOWN, NOT AT AN ANGLE TO THE BAIT.

holder in one hand, and with his other hand holds the leader between thumb and forefinger against the head where line exits from its top. By turning the thumb and forefinger down, a small bit of leader is pulled through the baithead. Because the hook is embedded in the strip, extra curve and hence faster roll results.

I have a different approach. No doubt it will leave manufacturers shaking their heads. I always use a double sliding hook arrangement with strip holders. The advantage in my setup is that I can pull the last hook out behind the tail end of the strip. The hook passes down the fish's throat before it closes on the bait and gets hooked more cleanly than with the conventional hookup. And, of course, small fish are released easier. This setup is particularly useful on days when plenty of bites occur but the only action is the tail end of the bait getting shredded. Moving the hooks back can make the difference between fish-filled smiley faces and owly-eyed skunked ones.

Care must be taken in my setup to establish bait action while maintaining the streamlined image of the conventional setup. Much more will be said about strip action in the next section, but to state it briefly, greater roll is achieved by bending the baitholder tab out at 90 degrees to the bait. The greater the bend, the quicker the bait will roll. The alternative, in the conventional approach, is to mount a single hook on one of the treble hook's barbs. If you prefer a sliding hook setup, simply insert the upper hook in the bait and produce a curve as described above without bending the baithead tab at all.

Let me back up one step and discuss insertion of strip into the baithead. When inserting the strip, push it, scale side up, all the way to the top, leaving no space or air bubble. The bait must come out the bottom end of the holder in a neat, straight line. In pressure-fit versions, spread the head, insert the bait and let go when the bait exits nice and straight. In the teaser-type holder, insert a toothpick through the head to anchor bait in the holder. Push the toothpick through the strip from the meat side and out the hole on the other side of the head. Continue pushing the toothpick until it wedges tight, then trim both loose ends with nail clippers. Do not leave bits hanging out; they influence strip action and also catch weed, not to mention looking odd—not too many fish are used to eating feed with wood sticking out like Frankenstein's neck bolts.

The final thing to remember is that the hooks need to lie straight along the bait rather than in a wodge, sticking out at different angles. The smoother they lie along the bait, the more it will spiral like a wounded baitfish. Hooks hanging out at angles slow bait roll and the bait appears less natural. This problem is easily overcome. Twist the leader in the baithead blister so the top hook lies along the bait. Then twist the sliding knot around the shank of the lower hook. These two adjustments allow you to rotate the hooks so that both hooks point either exactly straight up or straight down, or one points up and one down.

STRIP ACTION

Perfecting bait action takes years. During those years of trial and error, the mystique of trolling reveals itself. Bait may cover you with slime and make you smell so fishy that your partner points you to the shower when you get home. But it's a wonderful feeling to savour on weekend mornings, a dimension removed from the exhaust and speed of the weekday world: the perfect fish-catching roll of a well-hung piece of bait.

All trolled bait needs to rotate in a spiral when towed behind the boat. The intention is to imitate a wounded or dying baitfish at which a salmon has just slashed. Chapter 3 notes that wounded baitfish have great difficulty maintaining vertical stability. They slowly turn on their sides and, in an effort to right themselves, swim harder and harder. This effort turns them in a spiral as they swim through the water. Duplicate the motion and your strip, herring or anchovy will fire dazzlingly incandescent hunger pangs in the brains of your quarry, the salmon.

Schooling herring exhibit one specific behaviour that salmon must recognize as well. Every now and then one zags off like a zombie in a tight spiral, as if on some strange drug. On each revolution, sun flashes on its side, making it appear like a strip of neon lights zapping through Las Vegas. Why herring do this I do not know. I do know that it is much like the action put into trolled bait and must spell FOOD to salmon.

Properly rigged, bait spirals in a corkscrew-like pattern. The baitholder actually leads the bait in a spiral about 6 inches across, and the bait follows its lead. The important word to remember is spiral. Bait should not flail behind a spinning strip head. The tail must follow within the arc of a spiral, not out from it. If anything, the spiral of the tail should be less in diameter than the spiral of the bait head. Viewed from directly above, and ignoring the depth of the spiral, the bait pattern looks like a zigzag about 6 inches across. I hope this explanation is intelligible. Let me repeat myself: the bait must follow the head around in a spiral, not spin around behind it. Not a single fish will bite such a bait. Tiny teaser bait, properly rigged, will arc in a much tighter spiral, perhaps 2½ inches across.

As already discussed, spiral action is achieved in one of two ways. Conventional technique embeds the hook in the meat side and out the scale side where the light half melts into the dark half. As slack is taken up on the leader, a faster and faster roll results. In contrast, I produce rotation by bending the plastic tab at right angles from the baitholder: the more the tab is bent, the more the strip will roll. My technique uses freely floating hooks which are not anchored to the strip. Care must be taken to ensure a streamlined bait. When neither approach will do the trick, try changing the bait. Occasionally, bait is not cut properly and will not line up in the baithead. It exits at an angle and will catch an enormous amount of nothing. Take it off and try another piece. Be very choosy in assessing bait action. It should be exactly as you want it to be and should not exhibit any variation. This variation will only increase under the water. Cranking up and down on a downrigger can change the action of delicately adjusted bait; aim for action that is solid and easily reproducible.

How much rotation is enough? This is a hard question to answer. Each fisher has his or her own theories, and each fishes in a slightly different way, including boat speed, which is the most important determinant of bait roll. Generally speaking, though, tiny teasers should roll quickly, as should bait rigged up for coho. Chinook like a slower roll, and the larger the chinook, the slower the roll. Pink salmon are indiscriminate, and I use a chinook roll so as to appeal to more than one species. Slower than slow entices the sockeye. My bait rotates just a shade quicker than once a second. I do, however, try a lot of different speeds and often speed up the roll when the doldrums arrive. Bait roll is an art, not a science. You will become better and better the more you use it; perfect your own style.

I know many good fishers who do not believe in the slower rolls that I utilize. They have become successful with some other combination of the basic elements. For example, they may use a faster roll but a longer leader behind a flasher, or they may use a dodger where I use a flasher. Alternatively, their boat may be faster or they fish in an area of greater tidal flow. I like to fish across the tide, and this slows down my action. Some excellent fishers believe in even slower rolls than I do, so slow and tantalizing, in fact, that the bait hesitates at the top, then flops over as if in the swan song of a gasp before twitching to death centre stage on a Shakespearean set. I do not prefer a hesitating roll because the slightest alteration in any of the other variables—for example, boat or current speed—eliminates the roll entirely, and thus the bait ceases to work.

You can also change the spiral by drilling new exit holes for the leader in the top end of the baithead. The closer the hole is to the leading edge, the tighter the strip will roll. This also allows you to fish these lures at a faster troll, while the strip will still roll at about the same rate, a good tactic for summer and fall coho. The further away from the leading edge, the wider the diameter of the spiral, and, hence, a slower roll can be expected. Experiment with this parameter until you find an exit-hole position that favours your style.

Strip holders come in different colours. The standard is the green head, which for some reason catches way more fish than clear ones. In recent years, much more work has been done on introducing different-coloured strip holders. The new blue heads are proving quite effective on coho. Newest on the market are glow-in-the-dark heads, a really good improvement. When you consider that light is very scarce in deeper waters, anything that glows on its own will attract attention and, once attracted, the bait is spotted. Whammo.

I have noted that boat speed affects bait action. The faster one moves, the faster bait spins, and vice versa. And, of course, action should be checked every time speed changes. This is particularly important when you slow down: a bait that stops spinning stops fishing. On the other hand, a bait that rolls quicker will catch fewer fish, but is still fishing. In other words, speeding up is less detrimental than slowing down. A subtle decrease in speed is experienced as more and more gear gets put in the water. I fish with two downriggers and three fishing rods for a total of five lines in the water. This drag slows the boat. Make it a habit to check bait lines once everything is in the water.

After a salmon has been landed, reuse the piece of strip if it's still in good shape. Over and over again I have found that the tiny, elusive factor that makes one bait sparkle while another elicts a whole lot of ho-hum-nothing can be used to your advantage. If the bait has not been cut off or shredded, recheck its action and get it right back down there. I have often caught my limit of four fish on one piece of bait on a day when not as much as a sniff was recorded on anything else, including other pieces of strip I tried. You will find, however, that whole herring or anchovy cannot be reused.

They are too soft to survive a strike. Either they shred or the action goes off, and a spiral cannot be reproduced. Replace these baits after every strike.

WHOLE HERRING AND ANCHOVY

In many coastal British Columbia waters, whole herring and whole anchovy are the most commonly used baits. More effort is required to rig them and produce satisfactory action; however, they will often outfish strip, presumably because the salmon is presented with a whole, intact, sparkling fish rather than a one-sided slice, sans fins, sans eyes, sans everything else, too.

Virtually everything that has been said about strip is applicable to whole baits, and I suggest you reread the strip sections when gathering tips for whole-bait fishing. Consider purchasing one or more of the Charlie White underwater videos as well. These graphically demonstrate bait action and, more important, how a fish approaches a lure and bites. A salmon looks like a wasp in the wind, zeroing in on something tasty. The fish will follow the bait around in a circle or from side to side until that little light goes on in its head and it lunges in for the kill. It is surprising how many times a fish will miss, a frequency that increases with the speed and action of the bait. This may explain the need for either the longer leaders used in whole-bait fishing or the use of a dodger.

Herring and anchovy bait holders are larger and more rigid than strip holders; bait-fitting technique thus differs slightly. As with strip holders, the green whole-bait holders produce more steadily, but there are other colours on the market, and you may wish to try them. Dodgers are used more commonly than flashers. Dodgers are heavier and their slow sashay seems to match the needs of whole baits for action. I surmise that a flasher provides too much action, so a fish does not feel comfortable catching the bait. The usual setup is a Pal No. 3 dodger, 3 to 6 feet of leader and a whole bait in a baithead. I have successfully used shorter leaders, though, and one year consistently outfished even the guides with an 18-inch leader, something they said would not work. And although not commonly done, there is no reason why a whole bait cannot be fished by itself and catch fish.

The two important aspects of rigging whole bait are: anchoring bait securely in the bait holder and perfecting action. I will describe these with respect to anchovy, but all instructions apply to herring as well. Refer back to the illustration for a finished rig.

Bait anchoring is performed once the anchovy head lies neatly within the holder. Insert the anchovy's snout into the bait holder, checking first that the bait holder is indeed right way up: the leader comes out of the top front edge of the bait holder. Squeeze bigger anchovies behind the eyeballs to squash the head bones enough for the heads to slip comfortably into the holders. Once the anchovy has been slid completely to the front of the holder, turn the holder and anchovy over in one hand. In the other hand, take the red pin, which has been placed on the leader between the exit blister and the front-end leader hole, and push it through the hole in the side of the holder. This pin must pass directly through the anchovy and out the hole in the other side of the holder. If you have difficulty doing this, push the red pin first into one hole and then into the other so as to make a hole in the bait. Once the pin is inserted, twist it so that the leader passes in a straight line from the exit blister to the front-end leader hole. This makes for a cleaner, more streamlined bait.

Now the bait is anchored. The holder has a small hole on the top and a small hole on the bottom. Drill these holes if the brand you have bought does not have them. Jam a toothpick through each opening into the anchovy's head, thus preventing it from slipping back. The red pins are intended to anchor the bait; during fishing, however, the hole they make in the anchovy enlarges, allowing it to slide back. When this happens, the bait takes on a right angle halfway down its body. Even if spiral action can be maintained, the bait ceases to look like food and a salmon simply will not bite it. Anchoring bait is critical, and I am surprised how many fishers overlook it.

The next step, of course, concerns producing the much-debated fish-tantalizing roll. Whole-bait roll has an elegance and purity far exceeding that of strip, but is harder to achieve. There are many ways to establish action. Conventional canon includes inserting the provided treble hook one half to two thirds along the bait (ie., behind the dorsal fin), at the lateral line. The lateral line may be found at the boundary between shiny belly and darker dorsal surface. One barb passes cleanly into the bait and the other two prongs lie smooth along the flank. When bait is small, pass the first barb right through and out the other side. Roll is established, as in the conventional strip setup, by shortening the leader between the hook and the exit blister on the bait holder. Hold the bait holder in one hand, and leader in the thumb and forefinger of the other hand. Twist the leader hand down a tiny bit at a time to take up slack. Don't overdo it or the hook will rip out of the bait. A smooth curve is best; abrupt bends do not entice fish a jot.

I establish roll another way. I use a sliding hook setup, but do not insert either hook into the bait. Thus the roll has to be produced by other means. Hold the rigged-up bait—snout toward you—in one hand, placing a forefinger over the bait. Push a toothpick into the lateral line behind the dorsal fin and pass it forward inside the body of the bait so that the end tucks in under the bait-holder head, still inside the bait. This stabilizes the arrangement. My approach is the old-fashioned way of doing things. I utilize it on days when bites are frequent and the necessity exists to get gear back in the water quickly. Days when bites are as few as blue moons, it is far better to use the conventional method of establishing action, and this is what I usually do. The roll is easier to impart and, without a doubt, will result in more bites.

There are two alternatives to my approach. You may use a straightened paper clip or, preferably, a wire to establish spiral action. Once the wire has been inserted, roll can be adjusted by bending the bait, something that becomes easier if it has been stored in brine and is thus a little stiffer. When adjusting roll with a toothpick, the toothpick has to be removed from the bait and pushed back in at a slightly different angle, something that if done too many times renders the bait useless. In the second option, a wire attaches to the trailing edge of the bait holder. During bait insertion, run the wire down inside the body of the bait, keeping it completely out of sight, then bend the bait to achieve the roll that you prefer. Works like a charm.

The reason for using a nonconventional method of bait attachment is to turn snaps into hooked fish. The salmon takes a tentative touch at the tail, missing the hook that sits at least an inch in front of the tail. One can go through two packages of bait some days and end up with nothing in the boat. Extremely frustrating. The double sliding hook arrangement solves this problem because the hooks are extended out behind the bait where, as previously noted, they will be the first thing the fish hits. Alternatively, mount a single Siwash hook on one of the two barbs of the treble hook lying along the body of the bait. A further alternative is to make a sliding hook setup: the upper hook, a treble; the trailer, a single. As for hook size, the usual trolling trebles are the 2 and 3, and, in curved singles, purchase 4/0 - 6/0. 2/0 Siwash hooks are in the ball park, too.

Refer back to the strip section for bait action. Whole-bait action should also be a nice, even spiral, perhaps 4 to 6 inches in diameter. You will spend many productive years establishing the pattern that works best for you. Consider taking a seminar, because the intricacies of bait fishing are, to say the least, complex. The comments I have made in the strip section about various species also hold for whole-bait fishing. It goes without saying that action must be checked every time a bait goes in the water. And be careful sending whole bait down and bringing it up— the extra pressure of moving through the water often makes it sag and lose action. Watch the bait like a hawk until it descends beneath the surface. If it changes action or picks up weed, bring it back in to reestablish that intermediate roll of a bit more than one per second.

WHAT YOUR BAIT IS TRYING TO TELL YOU

Whole-bait success depends to some extent on constantly reassessing the bait. Stare tirelessly at your rod tip. When a bite occurs, bring the bait up right away. A bite invariably shreds whole bait, making it useless or, at the very least, diminishing fish-catching action drastically. Take a close look at the bait. It is trying to tell you something. If the bait has been shredded or jaggedly severed, a salmon likely made the marks. Tiny scrape marks mean that a very fussy salmon has touched the bait in a lazy way and then let go. It may also be the sign of a sockeye. They have very gummy jaws, not the shredding teeth of coho and chinook. There are a number of solutions to this problem, and you may refer to previous sections for others.

+ *Lengthen leaders.*
+ *Move from a flasher to a dodger or dispense with them altogether.*
+ *Slow down the boat.*
+ *Use larger hooks or larger bait to deter smaller fish.*
+ *Sharpen hooks.*
+ *Use artificial bait.*
+ *Use a lure that rotates like bait.*
+ *Fish across the tide.*

If the bait has been neatly sliced in half, the guilty party is a shark. Check the line for nicks and abrasions—particularly the short piece of leader between the hooks of a sliding hook arrangement, or just above a single hook. Sharks have razor-sharp teeth without gaps between them, unlike salmon teeth, which are more like a set of pins in a jawbone. Refer to Chapter 3 for ways to deal with and avoid sharks; the best is to stop fishing with bait.

BUCKTAILING

A form of salmon fishing with a long tradition, bucktailing is freshwater fly-fishing adapted to trolling in the saltchuck. Bucktails are large flies made from essentially the same materials used for fresh water, except that the hooks dwarf those of their cousins. Fur or thread wraps a saltwater hook to form a body, foil mylar adds sparkle and an outer coating of hair streams back from the eye. As with most trolling lures, simply hundreds of colours of bucktails salute you from the shelves of well-stocked tackle shops. While the variations march on seemingly without end, the minimum purchase should include a white bucktail, a Grey Ghost, a light green as well as a dark green bucktail, a blue and ones that mix green and white or blue and white. Pink, and versions with red, such as the Coronation, will normally provide greater success in the fall. In the dim light of early morning, lighter-coloured bucktails catch more fish. As the sun rises higher—producing a lighter-coloured background to the water—darker bucktails are better.

Polar-bear-hair bucktails catch far more fish than bucktails and flashtails made of other materials—poor old polar bears. Their rangy fur waves slightly, and perhaps this adds to lure enchantment. Individual fibres are thick and stiff, presumably because, for insulation purposes, each is hollow on the inside. Polar-bear-hair bucktails cost three times as much as other bucktails, and therefore are easy to recognize even when unlabelled. It makes good sense to keep them safe and dry to prolong their useful lives. Rinse them in clear fresh water. Never use soap: the residue leaves a smell on the bucktail and any gear it contacts. Dry bucktails thoroughly before storing them. I recommend devoting one clean, small, dry tackle box strictly to bucktails and the various bits and pieces of related gear.

Rust is particularly bad for bucktails. It corrodes the hooks, and as a bucktail is built around its hooks, once rusted a lure must be thrown away because new hooks cannot be mounted without destroying it. Furthermore, rust stains the hair of a bucktail and leaves a decidedly metallic smell. This cannot be removed and ruins the lure even if the hooks show no rust. Store bucktails in a dry place, your house being the best place unless the lures find constant use.

Bucktails should be stored straightened out and flat. Stored bent or coiled, they take on unusual kinks and resist being straightened for use. Whether curled or kinked, performance is marred. Solve the problem by making a piece of plywood with notches in one end and hook eyes at the other. Those bucktails permanently mounted to leaders can be saved straight and dry on this board. Put the hook in the notch and the swivel over the hook eye. Alternatively, one-inch segments of plastic straws will do in a pinch. They do not rust and the leader is prevented from tangling in the hooks. Do not use garbage bag twist ties; they rust.

Bucktailing reaches its peak in the fall months, when local waters teem with migratory coho. They can be deadly in winter months, too, when Island waters swell with bluebacks. Of course, bucktails will catch other species of salmon, and the occasional large chinook is brought in, particularly in areas of very shallow water over sandbars, or during early-morning hours. Pinks and sockeye will take bucktails occasionally. As with other salmon fishing techniques, though, catches of chum salmon are spottier than a hyena's backside.

FISHING WITH BUCKTAILS

Coho are the main quarry of bucktailing, and this influences technique: shortish leaders of 22 to 30 inches and 25- to 40-pound test attach to flashers. Flashers provide more snappy, coho-enticing action for these excitable fish. Usual depths range from the surface to 30 feet. For this reason, bucktails find most common use with 1 to 8-ounce slip weights or lead-ball weights. If you do employ a downrigger—and this is a less satisfactory way to use bucktails—let out 30 to 50 feet of line to get them away from engine noise. When weights are utilized, they should be 20 to 25 feet in front of the flasher. As always, watch the gear with a careful eye until it submerges unfouled.

Bucktail hair should flow evenly in a straight line behind the flasher. If the hair will not lie straight and insists on a chunky Coast Salish Indian-sweater look, bring the lure in and work on straightening it—or discard it. At home, try straightening the hair and mylar foil when wet. Let the lure dry stretched out in a warm place. Alternatively, iron the little devils, but do not melt the mylar to your iron. Your partner may not be happy. In any event, a lure that looks like a frazzled tongue covered with morning-after hair from the night-before bender fishes just about as well. Similarly, discoloured hair isn't going to do the trick either, unless the bucktail has proven to be a killer in the past. If it's a killer, place it in a velvet-lined tray and store it in a bank vault to keep it safe and sound.

Bucktails should run true. Good action does not include rapid spinning. A bucktail that revolves slowly or trails in an upright position will work much better. Some come with glued-on eyes, and hooks normally point straight up or down. Accordingly, well-balanced bucktails swim upright through the water. Trueness is less important when the bucktail runs behind a flasher; a fish doesn't get that close a look, its main consideration being to catch the darn thing. On the other hand, bucktailing sometimes produces more fish without a flasher. Spinners are used as an alternative. The traditional Cowichan Bay spinner is a number 4 or 5 abalone-shell teardrop shape. This small spinner, usually made of plastic these days, revolves in front of the bucktail. It serves to attract fish sonically and by flashing in the sun. Spinner fishing can be quite delightful because so little weight inpedes the line.

Spinners attach directly to a bucktail or to an extremely short leader. This short leader spans (brace yourself) a hefty 4 to 6 inches, so line and knot straightness increase in importance. Trim your knots close. Attach the spinner to a smaller-than-usual end swivel. In cases of clear water or spooked fish, dispense with the ball-bearing end swivel entirely, tying the spinner directly to the mainline. When dispensing with a swivel, you will note more line twist in your mainline. Make it standard practice to strip off 6 feet each day and retie the spinner to the line. In cases of extreme line twist, sacrifice simplicity and remount a small ball-bearing end swivel, or a small bead swivel some distance up the line. Once rigged, this setup also fishes 20 to 25 feet behind a weight, a useful place to tie in the bead swivel, thus avoiding the line-squashing nature of sliding weights.

For sheer, heart-palpitating, almost-unendurable fun, fish bucktails with a 6- to 7-foot trout rod. This makes for wild sport as the fish, caught on the surface, screams all over the place, yanking you along with it. Fish seem to bite surface-trolled bucktails with more vengeance than other gear. Try speeding up the boat to increase the jolt. Old-timers claim that coho bite while swimming away from the boat, rather than after the more usual chase from the rear. I doubt this is true . . . but who cares! Bucktails elicit a really hard bite followed by an aerial display that stops the heart, a condition best enjoyed once the fish rests safely in the boat.

LURE COLOURS
Choosing a producing lure colour is yet another area of fishing

artistry. Some individual colours work best in certain areas; local information will reveal these. Shade of colour can be important, too. For instance, some shades of green will not get a nibble in a bathtub full of fish. Other colours must be mixed in the body of the lure—the standby green-and-white hootchie should be in every tackle box. Every tackle box except mine. I can count the number of fish I have caught on this combination on one hand, yet all around me people pull them in by the thousands. Some general rules do exist, however, and throughout the text, I have alluded to many:

- *Lighter colours such as white in low light.*
- *Darker colours such as green in brighter light.*
- *Red and pink later in the fall.*
- *Pink lures whenever euphasiid shrimp abound.*
- *Darker colours as dusk approaches.*
- *Colour combinations that work on the surface will work hundreds of feet down where human eyes see nothing.*
- *Glow-in-the-dark lures for low light and deep fishing.*
- *Silver in metal lures.*

Take a look at the following chart of salmon species and colours. Please remember that it provides only an indication and is incomplete in that it lists preferences in individual colours, not combinations of colours. I am aware also that in many coastal British Columbia waters, strong local preferences may contradict this table. In addition, some combinations may work like a damn one or two months of the year and then stubbornly refuse to produce for another year. For example, day-glo solid green hootchies and pink Apexes work for bluebacks in Parksville, but only from April to June. Thirty-pound Saanich Inlet spawning chinook, to pick another example, prefer anchovy in September, a bait not heavily desired any other month of the year. Many lures mix three or four colours, and colours that don't work alone—yellow, for instance, can spell the difference in these lures, the 169 Tomic plug being a good example. In other words, plenty of anomalies exist. Refer to this chart when making or revising your plan or backup plan or when on the water, getting skunked and straining for clues.

	Coho	Chinook	Pink	Sockeye	Chum
Bait	xx	xx	x	x	x
Silver	x	x	x		x
Gold					
White	xx	xx	x	x	x
Yellow					
Pink	xx		xx	xx	
Red	xx		xx	xx	x
Orange			x	x	
Blue	x	x	x	x	
Purple					
Green	xx	xx	x	x	x
Brown	x	x			
Black	x	x			
Dark-glow	xx	xx			

x indicates a preference
xx indicates a strong preference

Do mix these basic colours. Silver and black stingsildas, for instance, can be killers some days. I have never found solid blue to be that effective; combine it with green and a few silver sprinkles, however, and you have one of the all-time greats in hootchies and squirts. Make sure all hootchie eyes glow in the dark. When using glow-in-the-dark baitheads, usually blue or green, shine a good light on them or expose them to the sun so that they get to the fish with a full load of radiant energy to expend. I feel like a nag, but check logs of past successes—even colours from ten years ago.

THE APPARENTLY INNOCUOUS JELLYFISH

The little white jellyfish found in the millions elegantly pirouette the seas like silent choruses of ballet dancers moving to their own ineluctable rhythms. Oblivious to one another, they squeeze their tutus and drift along. These benign creatures are completely harmless and pose no threat to anyone. You will see your rod bend and bend again as it passes through their bodies. When you retrieve your line, they will be pasted like clothes against a clothesline. Shake them off and inspect the terminal tackle. Clean off all residue, as salmon are not fond of jellyfish-smeared lures.

These harmless bits of mush are not to be confused with their much larger blood-red cousins, the Man'o War jellyfish. Man'o Wars are liquid fire to soft skin; treat them with exceptional care. I find myself cringing when we troll by one, its huge foot-wide maroon body like a gooshy heart, a mooshy corona of yellow and fifteen feet of bright purple stinging tentacles hanging below.

Avoid the tentacles like the plague. They are used to paralyze their prey—which could be people for all the poison in their nematocysts—where it hangs like a body in *The Big Chill* until lifted in slow motion into the yawning cavity of a mouth inside the body of the jellyfish. Since the tentacles can practically kill a human being, they must kill virtually any fish or other animal contacted. Needless to say, no lure covered with this purple slime will catch anything, and every last molecule must be removed by your own nimble fingers before the lure can be reused. Once you have finished, wash your hands meticulously until every last particle of tentacle is gone, and then dry them with a cloth.

The skin of your palms is usually calloused enough that these purple fire-breathers-from-hell will not cause great pain to your hands; however, any exposed flesh on your arms—and most particularly your face—will burn like fire for two or three hours if you are indeed unlucky enough to touch them. I suspect they could do serious damage to eyes or nasal passages. The first time my whole face went up in smoke, I thought I was going to die; I had no idea what had caused the pain, but it was excruciatingly sharp and deep. Anyone with a low pain threshold would find it unbearable. So take care while dealing with these most happily evolved of all God's creatures.

◆ 7 ◆
DRIFT-FISHING

THE BEAUTY OF DRIFT-FISHING

Picture a bright sunny afternoon. An eagle drifts like punctuation set free, and heat haze hangs over the blue mountains. Green and yellow spill down the black rocks. Boats are bits of crumpled paper that rise and slip over the ocean swell. Fishers are lifting and dropping their rod tips, lifting and dropping, eyes focussed lazily on the water, half wondering at the shafts of sun that drop like haloes behind their watery shadows to God knows where in the deep, deep green. You imagine a beautiful woman, the curling of forties smoke, Greta Garbo sighing, "I vant to be alone." And you are alone: with yourself; with the few people in your boat; with the kelp drifting like hair, like the bones of black people, their floats like small bulbous heads.

This is drift-fishing, one of the most beautiful and peaceful methods of fishing ever invented. No greasy oil. No gasoline fumes. No noisy boats jostling one another across the fishing grounds. It's just you and the imperceptible sound of nature, the sun slipping to the sea. Then your rod bends down and the line jerks. The ticks turn to a scream and the line knifes through the water until the fish erupts like fireworks 100 feet away on the other side of the boat. Holding the rod far, far out, you scramble out the side, cling to the stays and stick-walk around the outside structure of your boat. Standing on the bow, you watch the fish somersault across the surface.

And then the fish is twisting closer, flashing silver, purple and yellow, the greeny-black spots on its back. Life closes in on your net. Finally you dip for the played-out fish and it slips into the netting like a large, slippery arm. Sweat beads on your forehead. Both hands on the net, you heave the huge fish into the boat and stare, almost reluctantly, at the prize of your quest. Then the jolt of death shivers through its body. You stand puffing over the carcass. Fishing and death. The end of day.

THE THEORY OF DRIFT-FISHING

Drift-fishing may be described as an active variation of still fishing. Instead of a lead weight on the bottom, drift-fishing utilizes a lure that is a lead weight. The lead makes the lure drop through the water, imitating a wounded baitfish, one that has lost control over itself. As it falls, a wounded herring tries to right itself and its behaviour takes on a characteristic shimmy and flutter. Predators become highly stimulated by this behaviour because they key in on prey that is easier to catch: the dead, the dying and the weak. The action of a drift-fishing lure is intended to fool a salmon, or other carnivorous fish, into mistaking the lure for a weakened baitfish. Baitfish are wounded by many other animals. Salmon snap at herring balls or stun the smaller fish with a flick of their large tails; many varieties of gulls, terns and diving birds injure baitfish, as do dogfish. It is indeed a dog's life for a herring, and if your religious and metaphysical beliefs include reincarnation, you'd better pray not to come back as one.

A drift-fishing lure attracts fish in two ways. First, the behaviour of wounded baitfish sends sound waves through the water, a medium far more suited to passing the slightest vibrations than air. So, even though they cannot see the "wounded" lure, larger predators will be attracted from some distance away. Once they see the lure, its visual impact—the second attractant—takes over, and the strike reflex is stimulated if the fish are hungry or the lure has that indefinable something that triggers the tasty-morsel-I-simply-must-have-in-my-stomach instinct.

You can prove to yourself that drift-fishing lures send out vibrations by fishing one under a dock. Spot a bunch of perch, then walk down the dock and slowly lower your lure. Hold it still for a moment to extinguish all vibrations, then raise the lure and let it drop. Keeping your eye on the perch, you will notice that they suddenly become aware of something and begin turning toward your lure and swimming to the area, even though they cannot see the lure yet. In no time flat, all the other fish in the area will be attracted to the lure as well—even shiners that are smaller than the lure. Once you have attracted them, you can lift your lure and go back down the dock and attract them to a new site. These sound-emitting qualities can be further enhanced by sticking artificial eyes to the lure. The little eyes bang against the plastic bubbles in which they are encased, sending vibrations to the salmon. This is why some salmon lures are marketed with bulgy plastic eyes. If you are also a bass fisher, you will know already that the noise created by many bass lures—some of which look like helicopters invented by mad scientists, and absolutely nothing like natural bait—often makes them outfish "soundless" natural baits because their commotion says FOOD to Mr. Bass as he hangs in the weeds yawning at other offerings.

The well-known story indicating that drift-fishing lures send out fish-attracting vibrations comes from the development of the Buzz Bomb, which at the time was one of the truly revolutionary lures in salmon fishing. When Rex Field was testing it, he placed a plastic sheet in the water and discovered that fish on both sides of the sheet were attracted to the lure. The fish on the far side of the sheet could not see the Buzz Bomb, of course, but were attracted nonetheless and would wait there, patiently staring at the sheet even though they could not see what was on the other side. So it is important and quite exciting to remember that a drift-fishing lure is working even when the fish cannot see it.

Their attraction to noise may explain why in summer and fall fish with dings in their sides are caught. They may have been attracted to the turbulence of the prop and in their investigations gotten dinged before scooting off to lick their wounds and find your lure. I noted in Chapter 3 that sockeye and pinks are prone to such curiosity.

The second important factor in enticing a strike is that once you get the fish close enough, the drift-fishing lure must look convincingly like natural bait. If you have ever tried one of those whirring eggbeater-style bass lures on salmon, you will have gotten skunked. This is because they look more like streamered car lots than food and just don't stimulate that gotta-eat, Pavlovian response. So the lure must exhibit the proper behaviour, and it must also look like a real baitfish. Producing the proper "behaviour" will be discussed in upcoming sections on bending lures and fishing technique.

Salmon respond to other visual cues as well—for example, the tiny flashes of light coming from the lure. These flashes act as an attractant and, on a smaller scale, are similar in effect to the flashes sent off by the much larger flashers and dodgers used in trolling. As I've noted, anyone who has watched a school of herring will have noticed that some fish tend to twirl off in a tight spiral for a few feet as though suddenly palsied. During this instant of madness, these perfectly healthy fish reflect a dozen or so flashes as they spiral along. Accordingly, a successful drift-fishing lure should also send off flashes, as though the sun is glancing off scales. I have always thought that the spinning-off of schooled herring adds a touch of mystery to these small fish, a kind of mesmerizing magic that is one of the quiet joys of drift-fishing, particularly in the early morning when they innocently touch the surface like rain. Lovely. Those brought up on "Star Trek The Next Generation" may connect with a more contemporary metaphor. To the Trekkie, a school of herring probably looks like the positronic matrix of Data's brain when the skin's peeled back for a Level Three diagnostic. There're lights and action going on in there.

Lure shape also contributes to visual attraction; the lure must be shaped like a baitfish and also have a colour pattern that elicits strikes. Over the years, the Buzz Bomb has spawned a plethora of imitators, many of which look more like herring than the original lure. Current lures come in a range of colours, sizes and shapes, each of which may work on any particular day and then not catch a fish again for months. The standard colours are silver or white, although many lures have green or black backs and iridescent fish-scale patterns on their sides. White or light-grey lures are often productive, as are Buzz Bombs painted yellow or green. As mentioned earlier, though, local information will give you the best clues because fish taste is a transitory and local phenomenon.

RODS AND REELS FOR DRIFT-FISHING

The most important pieces of drift-fishing equipment are your rod and reel. Although any old cheap rod and reel will do, proper gear increases both fishing comfort and the number of fish hooked. I prefer a 7- to 8-foot rod with a semi-stiff tip.

A semi-stiff tip allows for proper hook setting, a necessity in drift-fishing, and is the feature of greatest significance. Soft tips lose many fish because the hook barbs cannot be secured in the flesh of the fish. I learned this one the hard way, losing a boatload of salmon before moving away from a soft tip. On the other hand, the rod does not have to be stout enough to raise Moby Dick. Stiff tips reduce fish-playing satisfaction and lead to lost fish; stiff rods have less give and hooks rip from mouths.

Next in importance is the length of rod butt below the reel mounts. Drift-fishing is the only method in which one arm bears the weight of the entire rod for the many hours of fishing. One foot of butt provides a place to rest your elbow, thus reducing arm strain. It also gives a good length of rod to stick into your gut while playing a fish. Anchoring the rod gives stability and leverage power. Salmon are heavy, and it's tiring to play one with a reel so close to the end of the rod that you cannot use your stomach to take the weight of the fish off your arms. More butt than one foot, however, simply gets in the way. Your arm will not be resting comfortably at a right angle during fishing. Instead, it will be stretched out and tired, even more so while playing a fish. Smaller people, or those with shorter arms, will find this problem magnified for them and will end up clumsily wedging the rod under an arm, a very insecure perch.

Once a rod has been selected, put a reel in the mounts and make sure that the combination is comfortable in your hands. As noted in Chapter 4, the balance point of a rod and reel can be determined by balancing the rod on your finger. This point should be where you would naturally hold the rod and, generally, will be located about a foot in front of the reel seats. If the balance point does not correspond to this spot, your arm—and this is particularly true for young fishers—will hurt in no time flat. You will not enjoy your fishing. A balance point more than a foot from the reel tires you out because your arm will be extended at an angle greater than 90 degrees. With shorter balance points, the rod jams into your stomach, and playing a fish is more difficult.

One might suspect that the preferred drift-fishing reel would be a casting variety, but this is not the case. Single-action graphite reels are best. These are light, durable and have considerably smoother action than other models. As discussed previously, they are far more fun and responsive when a fish is hooked. Twisting line causes problems in drift-fishing. This occurs because much of the time there is little or no tension on the line, and the twist acquired from trolling or from badly adjusted lures causes the line to wrap itself around the rod tip or reel. Single-action reels are the simplest around and the least likely to be fouled by twisting line. They are also best for accurately stripping off line, and it is crucial in drift-fishing to know exactly the depth at which you are fishing. Another useful feature is a reel with larger handles. Teeny handles are difficult to grasp with any strength or when wearing gloves.

There are times, however, when you will want to cast during drift-fishing. When a herring ball surfaces nearby or fish are rising all around, you will want to accurately place your lure, something that cannot be accomplished easily with a single action reel. Casting with single-action reels can be accomplished, of course, in the same fashion as with a fly reel—strip line into the bottom of the boat and cast this out—but it is most unsatisfactory. Purchase a casting reel that is made of graphite and has the largest drum you can find. Casting reels have one inherent weakness: they become badly fouled and are not really satisfactory for any purpose other than casting. Refer to the casting section of this chapter for further information.

LURES WITH FISH-CATCHING ACTION

Most drift-fishing lures come out of the package smooth and flat and require customization before they will catch fish. Either an "S" bend or a "C" bend must be introduced into the lure. The true artistes of the drift-fishing world are those lucky people who can regularly produce fish-catching action from any lure put into their

S BEND

hands. If your lures don't work well, ask a successful friend to bend them for you, because a hot drift-fishing lure is worth its weight in gold. A few lures, though, do come with action already built into them for (example, Buzz Bombs) and do not require bending. If one of these lures does not catch fish, try a bonk from a hammer or a jab or two from an ice pick to make it fishy.

The "S" bend modifies a drift-fishing lure for trolling or casting. Take the lure in both hands, placing your thumbs together on one side and your fingers on the other. Slowly introduce a slight bend into the first quarter of the lure. You want to produce a smooth bend along the lure, one that is not angled or kinked. Then turn the lure over and place your thumbs together on the other end of the lure (ie., on the opposite end and side from the one you have just bent). Once again, apply pressure until a slight, smooth curve appears in this end of the lure. The alternative method—and some people find this easier to do—is to bend the lure by pressing one end against a tabletop with your thumbs. Then the lure is rotated for the second bend. My attempts at doing this normally result in a kinked, over-bent lure, so I prefer to hold the lure in my hands while bending.

The resulting "S" bend gives the lure a slight spoon-like wiggle when retrieved or trolled through the water, imitating a healthy baitfish swimming merrily along its way. Lure rotation is not preferred because wounded baitfish action cannot be added successfully to "S"-bend drift-fishing lures very often. Rotation can be minimized by ensuring that all bends are at right angles to the length of the lure. And, of course, kinked or odd lure bends should be flattened and reintroduced. Do not worry if the factory finish cracks during bending; lure action is far more important to fishing than a cosmetically intact lure. I should add that I have never found drift-fishing lures to be that successful for trolling and do not use them for this purpose. However, there are circumstances, when casting from a dock or shore or from a boat at rising fish, in which you may want a straight cast-and-retrieve lure. This is the special domain of the "S"-bend lure. And remember that cast-and-retrieve lures grant a change in a day when you may tire of the endless up and down motion of drift-fishing.

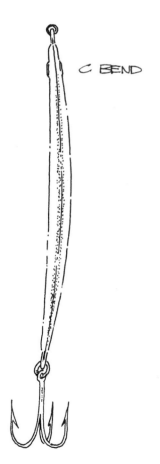

C BEND

The second type of modification, the "C" bend, is far more commonly used and will be introduced into every lure used solely for drift-fishing. Properly done, this bend looks more like the gentle curve of a camera lens or banana than a "C", and the general rule, in both "C" and "S" bends, is not to over-bend the lure: less is most definitely better. Once again, take the lure in your hands, placing both thumbs together on one side and your fingers on the other side. Slowly bend the first quarter in a slight, smooth arc. Without turning it over, take the other end of the lure and hold it in your hands as before. Press against the tail quarter of the lure, putting a slight curve in this end as well. The intention is to produce a gentle, smooth, unkinked curve along one whole side so the lure resembles a piece of bread curled by the sun.

Now the important moment comes: testing the lure in the water. Freely dropped, drift-fishing lures fall gently with a darting, shimmying, fluttering, haphazard action, emitting lots of sparkle in the sun. Drift-fishing lures should drop erratically in the way dying fish do, struggling vainly to stay upright and avoid predation. Hence, a lure with some variation in action is best.

A properly bent drift-fishing lure turns on one side, falling with the convex side facing down. Lures that drop flatly, evenly and ho-hum boringly are usually bent too much and should be flattened out a little. Under-bent lures often have an inconsistency in their fall, falling flat and smooth this time, sliding off here or there the next time. They seldom flutter evenly on one side and tend to slide into a downward spiral. A downward spiral in which one end leads the way to the deep, dark depths is the least productive action, and a lure should always be rebent to eliminate this. Either one end is bent too much or there is some drag on your tackle. Lay the lure on a flat surface and check that the lure is evenly curved along its length. Rebend to achieve a smooth curve. While it is still on the table, look down the lure from one end and make sure that it is not twisted. Rebend to eliminate twist. Having said this, it has to be pointed out that the indefinable factor in lure success can be the slight inconsistencies. The critical test is to put the lure in the water and assure oneself that it falls with that nice, tasty flutter, sort of slipping here and there in a zigzag way. Lures that do not catch fish after repeated use, or when everyone else is catching fish with grating regularity, should be flattened and bent once again. Also recall that the slower a lure drops through the water, the better; wounded fish do not plummet like rocks. In addition, the longer you can keep your lure in front of a fish, the longer it has to decide it must be tasty. Lures that go by like downrigger balls will go unnoticed unless they hit the fish in the head.

If all else fails, take your lures to successful friends and ask them to rebend them. Have friends show you examples of what they consider well-bent lures and also, if they will be so kind, to demonstrate a good fish-catching lure in the water for you. Have them test your lure until they think it will work. Ask them about their theories on what defines fish-catching action and try to memorize everything they do in the bending and adjusting process so that you can duplicate it later.

Some other circumstances can suggest that lures be rebent. If you catch a big fish or change a hook or add a swivel, recheck lure action and readjust. Similarly, if you catch the bottom and yank up the lure or do anything that may affect the lure's action, recheck it at the side of the boat. Remember, however, that any lure that is still catching fish should not be rebent. Another alternative is to have a bunch of lures ready to go and get to know if any work better under certain conditions—higher wind, increased tidal speed, upwelling or swirling water, for instance.

HOW TO DRIFT-FISH

Drift-fishing technique is so deceptively simple that it is, in fact, simple. Yet if done incorrectly, drift-fishing will yield nothing more than a tanned or wet neck at the end of the day. The gist of this method can be summed up in one phrase: get the lure to the fish and twitch them onto the line.

First comes descending to the fishy depth. Accomplish this by stripping line from your single action reel. Pull line directly from the reel in even-measured lengths. These are referred to in the complex lexicon of the fisher as "pulls." Put your free hand right at the reel and pull out a set amount, then measure this distance with a tape measure so that you know exactly how long a pull you pull. Be sure that every pull is exactly the same length. I use 2 feet per pull. Therefore, starting with the lure at water level, I know that after 15 pulls, my lure will be 30 feet beneath the boat. Be sure to use an accurate pull each time, because it is essential to know the depth of the lure. When a fish is caught, you want to be able to return the lure to exactly this depth, because fish tend to swim at a certain level as they cruise around scouting out your lure.

Accurate lure depth is vital because of the way salmon school. In clear water where salmon can be seen, you will be surprised how often they swim in an absolutely horizontal plane. This happens frequently with fall spawners. On hot days with the sun overhead, you will spot them swimming along in a flat plane while your drift-fishing lure—and this is an important image to form in your mind—dances in a vertical plane of 2 to 6 feet. If your lure is not at their level, they just will not encounter it. Err on the shallow side—say, 0 to 10 feet. As mentioned previously, salmon see ahead and up better than they see down, due to their facial features. Salmon also swim slightly below the bait, so they are long conditioned to look up for dinner; baitfish are easier to spot against a light background of sky than against a dark background of water.

Once the lure sits at the fishy depth, usually 30 to 80 feet and occasionally down to 120 feet, fishing time has arrived. Standard drift-fishing technique has two parts: a slow lift of the rod tip, followed by a quick drop of the rod tip to water level. This up and down motion of the rod is repeated endlessly, like a mantra. Once you have lifted the lure, let it freefall without tension until you feel a thunk. Then lift again. The slow lift wiggles the lure and, more important, keeps it in front of any fish that has been attracted to the area. The alternative—a fast lift—should be avoided. Imagine an intrigued fish closing in, and all of a sudden you yank the lure 6 feet and it vanishes from view. So be patient. Lift the rod slowly 2 to 6 feet, so that the fish has time to see and follow the lure.

After lifting the rod, the tip needs to be dropped. A quick drop allows the lure to fall unimpeded, thus establishing the tasty downward flutter of a dying baitfish. This couple of seconds is the only period during the cycle that the lure is working to catch a salmon. Therefore, the whole point of drift-fishing is to keep the lure falling as often and as long as possible. Very rarely will bites occur during the lift phase, and fish are almost never caught if the rod is put down and the lure hangs lifelessly in the water. In an area of high tidal flow, though, this can actually be good technique, provided the lure is light and the boat anchored. The lure trails along, fluttering slightly in the water.

After learning the straightforward technique, drift-fishing finesse arrives with experience. One tries to tease a fish into biting after it has been attracted sonically to the lure for a look-see. Baitfish do not march around like robots. When struggling, they behave erratically, first trying to right themselves, then getting tired and becoming still, only to try again once they are stronger. To imitate their behaviour, vary your lift-drop pattern. Throw in a couple of 2-foot lifts, then, for example, let the lure drop further by putting your rod tip down in the water. Follow this with a longer lift, say of 4 feet, followed by an even longer lift. Tantalize that fish with a slow 6-foot lift, making it appear that the lure is troubled but trying to get away. It is almost irresistible to a hungry predator when its prey seems to be getting away. So vary your lift and drop pattern and you will without a doubt catch more fish. West coast fishing guru Charlie White has pretty convincing underwater video proof that even 2-inch jiggles can excite salmon into biting.

When bringing in your lure, whether checking for weed or for resetting accurately to another depth, do not simply crank it in and strip it back down. Fish the lure to the boat. It is truly amazing how many fish will rise with a lure and bite somewhere on the uphill climb. They rise like mesmerized dirigibles until convinced the lure is trying to get away by swimming to the surface. Then the writing is on the wall. So fish a lure up. Lift and drop the rod tip; during the drop, reel in a couple of turns until the lure thunks to a stop. Then repeat the process. Add variation by stopping every 10 feet or so and fishing at that level for a minute before continuing up. This can also elicit a strike. The fish follows, the lure rises forlornly, trying to get away. It stops for a minute, seemingly too injured and waif-like to carry on, and bam, the salmon is on the line.

It makes sense to have a good idea of lure depth at all times during your retrieval process. Determine this by first measuring the amount of line your reel takes up on one revolution of the handles (ie., one revolution of the drum). To do this, hold the line in one hand, just below the last line guide on the rod. With the other hand, reel in one turn. The length of line between your hand and the last line guide gives the distance per drum revolution—about 1 foot on most reels. With this knowledge in hand, you will always know the depth of your lure, and hence, the fish. If, for example, you have been fishing at 50 feet and begin fishing your lure up, being lucky enough to receive a bite after 20 revolutions, you know then that the rest of the school likely will be found at 30 feet.

You should also try fishing at different depths. Start where you think fish are most likely to be found. Locals can tell you this information. Let's say that the likely depth is 50 feet. Over the first hour of fishing, start at 50 feet, then vary your fishing level anywhere between 20 and 100 feet. Now, if you know the length of line per pull and the length of line per drum revolution, you will always have a pretty good idea of lure depth. This straightforward method works in slower water and on calmer days. When the boat is pushed by wind or when surface water carries the boat at a different speed than the water at lure level, however, a different method of measuring lure depth must be used. I calculate depth using the angle the line descends into the water and length of line pulled out. For example, if the angle of your line from vertical is 22.5 degrees, then depth is one-quarter of the length of line pulled out. At 45 degrees, depth is one-half of the length of line pulled out, and at 67.5 degrees, depth is three-quarters of the line pulled out.

Using 100 feet of line as the length pulled out, the depths in these three examples are 25, 50 and 75 feet respectively. Unfortunately, this explanation works more accurately on the page than in practice. It doesn't work that smoothly with the variation you will find on the water—in high wind, for instance, where line streams out almost horizontally. In wind, it can prove better to anchor than drift, and therefore your lure will fish more directly under the boat as long as there is no current.

Generally speaking, it is best to fish a drift-fishing lure at a vertical angle (ie., directly under the boat). This gives the most accurate indication of depth and also the greatest amount of drop, or fishing time, per lift of the rod. Failing this, you should fish on the side from which the line naturally streams away, usually the side wind is coming from or current is going to. It is difficult, indeed, to fish and play a fish when the line disappears beneath the boat—invariably the line gets caught on the motor or another obstruction, leading to a cut line or a lost fish.

Once a fish has bitten, setting hooks is vital in drift-fishing. Setting hooks is easier when the line is taut at the reel at the moment of the bite. Tension must be set on the reel, and the rod hand's forefinger holds the line against the rod. If tension is not maintained, line simply strips off the reel and a startled fish swims away unhooked. Again, I would caution you to never wind line around a finger; a large salmon will snap it off. I mentioned in Chapter 5 that experienced fishers hold the line with their forefinger because fish and tackle action is transmitted much faster than in any other way, something that is particularly important in low light.

There is another reason for holding the line. During the time a lure drops in the water, residual line twist tends to wrap around the rod tip or the reel handles. A forefinger holding the line against the rod prevents problems at the reel. Tangles can also be minimized by purchasing a reel that does not have any space between its handles and their seats. This tiny space causes more tangles than you would believe, and ones that are next to impossible to free once a fish pulls on the line. As for line twist at the rod tip, this can be extremely frustrating when drift-fishing, as it binds the line when a fish bites, resulting in a lost fish. Fortunately, there are many ways of minimizing line twist.

 ♦ *Each time it is dropped, snap the rod tip to remove line twist.*
 ♦ *Use better-quality, nontwisting line.*
 ♦ *Dedicate one reel to drift-fishing.*

- *Use a swivel and 4 to 6 feet of leader at the lure end.*
- *Ensure lure action is not a downward spiral.*
- *Allow the lure to spin every time it is lifted from the water.*

GOOD LURE FEEL

We have discussed how to modify lures to obtain proper action. You should be aware, though, that lures can perform differently once out of sight below the boat. I can hear the existentialists asking how I can know this if I have not seen one way down there, and my answer is the Charles Dickens defence. Asked after writing *A Tale Of Two Cities* how he could know what happened at a guillotining, an event he had never witnessed, he answered, "I have been there many times in my mind." In equally fateful moments in the fishing arena, I have mentally apprehended the results of deviant lure behaviour, have felt it with my very own hands.

Many types of action indicate proper lure action at fishing depths. The most important is the length of time a lure takes to drop. If you drop your rod tip 4 feet, for instance, it is better for your lure to drop for 2 seconds rather than 1. In addition, a lure that has a soft thunk at the end of its drop, or has an indefinite drop period (ie., one that changes each drop), is probably working properly out of sight. A drift-fishing lure that appears to stop every now and then and then moves off again is often a killer. I consider it very lucky when one of my lures acquires this magic.

Good lure action at fishing depths depends largely on line drag. The longer the line, the greater the drag, and hence the greater the effect on your lure. Lures cease to work past a certain depth because lure weight cannot overcome line drag, and this is the reason I seldomly drift-fish deeper than 120 feet. Additions to the line such as weights, swivels or weed intensify drag, resulting in incorrectly performing lures. The greater the drag, the more likely it is that a lure will turn on its end and drop in a downward spiral, one end leading the way. Although there is one lure on the market specifically designed to drop vertically, generally speaking a downward-spiralling drift-fishing lure will catch fewer fish than a lure with any other type of action. Evidence of a downward spiral includes:

- *lure drop time decreasing with depth*
- *line twist accumulating on the water surface or rod tip*
- *lure stopping with a hard thunk*

Downward spirals can be avoided to some extent. The most common solution is to add a swivel and 4 to 6 feet of leader. Use a lighter leader, say 15-pound test, because subterfuge is important in drift-fishing; the fish should be paying attention to the lure, not to the long piece of plastic line rising from it. Unfortunately, swivels themselves add drag and, in some circumstances, cause more problems than they solve. So try one or more of the following ideas.

+ *Check lure action. Rebend until evidence of spiral action disappears.*
+ *Use a lower-pound-test mainline.*
+ *Use thinner-diameter, better-quality line.*
+ *Dedicate one reel for drift-fishing.*
+ *Use new line— one with few abrasions.*
+ *Use nontwisting line.*
+ *Either add or remove a swivel or bead swivel. Use a smaller one.*
+ *Use a larger lure.*
+ *Spin the lure each time it is lifted from the water.*

One other funny action can occur in drift-fishing. When the hook end of the lure drops a little slower than the line end, the hook can catch the line. This transmits itself as a small "strike" followed by a dragging feeling. The drag is caused by water pressure against the lure, rising horizontally, caught in a sling of line. I usually bring in the lure and unhook the hook from the line. But you don't have to. I have caught many fish with a lure that is fouled in its own line, and noticed on other occasions that the side-to-side shimmy of such a lure brings curious fish to the surface. In other words, the lure may have fish-catching action on the rise as well as the fall. Still, you are better advised to pull the lure and unfoul it. If the problem recurs, line twist is the likely curmudgeon, and you can check the list above for a solution. More often, though, an unbalanced lure causes this type of problem, and the solution is to rebend the lure. Alternatively, try putting the hook on the head end of the lure and attaching the line to the tail end. Lures such as Buzz Bombs can be turned around and the hook retied on the line.

Some fishers modify their drift-fishing lures in other ways. In the belief that salmon like to bite baitfish head first, some fishers always move the hook from the tail end to the head end. Some even put a hook on both ends of the lure, a modification that makes some sense with Buzz Bombs. Buzz Bombs, and a few other lures, slide freely on the line and sometimes can be found some distance up the line away from the hook. Without a second hook above the lure, a fish may be biting a lure as much as 1 to 2 feet away from a hook; of course, from the fisher's perspective, it is grabbing onto nothing.

In faster water, lure action can feel fine even though the lure is not performing properly. Smaller lures are much more sensitive to line drag than heavier lures, and unless conditions are calm, good action will not result. A lighter lure will not get down to the fish either. It will trail out to the side of the boat, and no amount of extra line will get it down in the water. The solution is to use larger, heavier lures than usual—2 ounces or heavier.

THE BITE

The drift-fishing bite can be so dramatic that it takes you completely by surprise, or so soft that you have no idea it has happened. As the lure exhibits action only as it flutters down through the water, most bites occur after you have dropped the rod tip. In other words, the bite occurs when there is slack line between you and the fish; exactly when you do not know a salmon has taken the lure, you need to set the hooks. In very short order, the salmon will discover that this chompy looks-like-an-injured-baitfish thing sure doesn't taste like one. Most drift lures are metal and have an electrical potential; if you leave a lure sitting in a fish's mouth instead of setting the hooks, it will be spat out within a couple of seconds. Consider for a moment your own reaction to electricity. Put your tongue on the end of a nine-volt battery and see how quickly that weird electrical sensation makes you spit it out. Fish feel the same way. More than other salmon species, chinook seem better able to detect electrical potential, thus necessitating quick action.

A salmon's sense of smell is just as exceptional. For this reason, many commercial trollers take special care to keep their gear absolutely clean. Many wear gloves to keep their scent off lures, especially those used for chinook. When you consider that smell isn't that important in trolling—salmon are more concerned with catching a fleeing lure than anything else—it is easily appreciated how smell becomes much more important in drift-fishing, where a fish can, at leisure, inspect a lure sitting in front of its nose. Researchers in Washington State have discovered that fishing scent applied to feed for penned salmon can increase the poundage yield by as much as 40 percent, an astonishing figure suggesting that far more bites will occur in drift-fishing

to the fisher who uses commercially available scent.
Because bites occur as lures drop, being alert is extremely important. Following are the most usual bites.

- *the line screams off like a freight train*
- *there is a small bump or tick or nudge to the line*
- *the lure stops before it ought to*
- *the lure doesn't hit bottom*
- *the line moves off slowly to the side*
- *there is a small tug, followed by a feeling of having caught the bottom*

Not surprisingly, the freight-train bite is the most satisfying of
the bunch, and also the one most likely to set the hooks for you. If
you have your forefinger on the line, the fish will set the hooks
itself nine out of ten times. Set the hooks anyway.

The bump-tick-nudge bite is also common and requires you to
set the hooks hard against a slack line. Seldom is there time to reel
in excess—which would be preferred—so remember that a rod tip
dropped to water level gives the most room for pulling. If you can
yank up 6 feet, yank away. Each time you fail to set a hook, don't
assume you've missed a huge salmon, though. Often this is evidence of undersized salmon snapping at the lure, or dogfish.
Dogfish are very clumsy and just can't catch that darn lure. They
will normally come up foul-hooked in the side or the tail from twisting unsuccessfully around the lure. You may want to consider moving
the boat forward into the current, because salmon are more powerful
swimmers than dogfish. To determine the presence of undersized fish,
slowly fish the lure to the boat, and they will follow. Thus you can
assure yourself that the taps are small salmon, and the lure need not
be checked for fouling on each tap. Try lowering your lure another
10 to 20 feet, where the larger salmon may be found.

Take a moment to observe small salmon snapping at drift-fishing lures. It's quite a shock to see how quickly salmon can swim.
Most of the time you will not see the salmon until it flashes past
your lure; then it may zap across your eyes and completely out of
sight in the same instant. This speed is the reason the lift portion
of the rod's lift/drop cycle ought to be slow. A quick lift when a
salmon is already on its speed-of-light rush makes the lure shift
and escape, like a halfback sidestepping a thundering lineman.

When a lure stops, your immediate reaction is to hesitate for a
moment, thinking your lure has hit bottom. This is something you

must not do. Get into the habit of setting the hooks regardless of the strange things happening to the line. If you are indeed on the bottom, there's no harm in lifting the lure before the hooks become completely ensnared. Also get into the habit of checking your charts or depth sounder, or even lowering your lure to the bottom once, so that you know when your lure ought not to be near the bottom. If the lure stops at 35 feet in 80 feet of water, you simply must be in contact with a fish.

The bite I like the most occurs when the lure does not hit the bottom of its drop. You stare at the line curling on the surface, and for a split second before setting the hooks, you are crazy as a werewolf, knowing a fish is on the other end and you are going into battle. Ah, the glee, the gush of adrenaline.

On rare occasions, your line will move off slowly from vertical. A moving fish has taken the lure and continued swimming in the direction it was going. Because the fish may be rising to the surface, I suggest you reel in as fast as possible until tension comes on the line. Then set the hooks. If the hooks can be set, fine and dandy, but when the rod comes up without a fish being encountered, drop the tip quickly and repeat the manoeuvre. Most often, however, a rising fish is spooked into dropping the lure, so be prepared to lose some of these fish.

The final drift-fishing bite results from a rock cod taking the lure and then a ling cod taking the rock cod. A weak, intermittent tug is followed by the feeling that you have bought a piece of underwater real estate. Refer back to Chapter 3 for ling cod netting technique.

SETTING HOOKS

As I've already mentioned, the hooks of a drift-fishing lure must always be set in the flesh of the fish. In trolling, fish inadvertently hook themselves while turning away from an essentially stationary lure; however, drift-fishing lures, like mooched baits, float freely and are picked up sideways or on end. They just sit there in the fish's mouth, hooks hanging free until the angler sets them.

Hooks should be set using the following procedure. With all slack out of the line, the reel's drag set on a medium level, a forefinger holding the line against the rod and the rod tip at water level, yank the rod as high as you can to drive the hooks home around the jaw of the fish. Simple enough. Unfortunately, hook setting does not work as easily in practice as it does in books. The bite usually happens when there is slack in the line, a horsefly on the end of your nose and an alligator coming over the transom. Adrenaline takes over and you try to yank the fish's head off. Actually, this is not such a bad situation, because anything that scares you into a bigger yank increases the likelihood of securing the fish. Setting drift-fishing lures takes skill, so do not be too disappointed if you lose a few fish along the way.

There are days when even the best fisher cannot set hooks any better than the beginner. On such days, give one of the following tactics a try.

+ *Sharpen all hooks.*
+ *Use a stiffer-tipped rod.*
+ *String the line through the second or third line guide to gain a stiffer rod.*
+ *Twitch the lure in 2- to 6-inch jumps.*
+ *Do not drop the rod quickly. Lower it a teeny bit slower than the lure.*
+ *Change from a lure that slides up and down the line to one that is tied to the line.*
+ *Mount a hook on both ends of the lure.*
+ *Change hook size. Try smaller ones, even though larger hooks set more securely.*
+ *Move from a treble hook to a single hook.*
+ *Use a larger lure to dissuade smaller fish.*

WHEN AND WHERE TO DRIFT-FISH

Salmon schooling behaviour determines the best times and locations to drift-fish. If, for instance, fish are swimming in loose schools in an area with a diameter of a mile or more, it makes more sense to troll around in search of them than to wait patiently for them to come your way. If a couple of fish are caught by 50 boats spread out everywhere, this does not indicate that drift-fishing is the best way to fish. With 100 lines in the water, it stands to reason that one or two lures will come in contact with fish. In addition, when the fish are more than 100 feet deep, the effectiveness of drift-fishing diminishes greatly, due to currents and line stretch.

Having said this, there are plenty of times when drift-fishing is more effective than trolling. Drift-fishing is more successful when salmon are bunched into a small area, relatively close to the surface. Any condition that pushes salmon into a small area should influence your decision to drift-fish. Consider the following favourable conditions:

- *tightly bunched feed*
- *high tidal flow encountering low tidal flow*
- *the entrance or exit to a narrow pass*
- *the presence of highly localized back eddies*
- *a spire of rock that rises from very deep water*
- *a mud bottom covered with needlefish*
- *a deep hole in the middle of an otherwise flat bottom*
- *the crack of dawn, when chinook salmon are often highly localized on shorelines after night*
- *jumping fish, most commonly the tight-schooling coho*
- *schools of summer spawners, on the move or holed up in front of spawning rivers, awaiting rain*
- *local information giving clues to lures, locations and depths*

Wind and current move feed into tidelines and push it against rocks and kelp. Salmon follow. A steady onshore or seasonal breeze, for instance, can markedly influence the fishing. In windy conditions, though, lures do not perform that well, and a move to heavier lures, or anchoring the boat, is advised. Tidelines are an area of preference for winter and spring bluebacks, as well as summer runs of coho, sockeye and pinks. You can successfully drift-fish miles off land provided you find a school of fish in a tideline. Screaming gulls, herring balls and patches of floating scales indicate a feeding spot.

Where needlefish abound, usually over a mud bottom, salmon fishing can be excellent. This is the case off Sidney at the Powder Wharf. Sand bottoms are virtual underwater deserts, but mud bottoms contain a higher concentration of plant and animal matter; eel grass provides cover and fishing productivity can be high. Salmon hang above the needlefish, and fishing within 15 feet of the bottom can prove deadly.

During the period of highest tides, fishing tapers off for a few days each month; however, the tide pushes salmon into slower flow behind islands and other land masses, where they may be found for the next few days. Passes between land masses similarly concentrate salmon. Sansum Narrows, Active Pass and Porlier Pass are all good drift-fishing and mooching spots. Rapid flow through a narrow space creates a venturi effect. Herring and salmon are pushed right up onto the rocks on the upstream side of a pass or carried through and deposited in the back eddy that forms on the downstream side of the land mass. You should also consider that it may be next to impossible to troll when everyone else is drift-fishing; you will be getting in everyone else's way and annoying them. When space is limited and fishers many, go with the flow and fish the same method.

Spires of rock rising from the seabed commonly attract salmon. Many banks exist off the west coast of Vancouver Island, and in Juan de Fuca Strait, Constance Bank juts up like an oasis in a surrounding desert, drawing rock and ling cod. The swirling waters move plankton around and herring congregate, attracting the salmon. Chinook salmon show great similarity to freshwater bass and most often are the salmon associated with rocks and reefs, even ones miles off shore. If herring are present in tight schools that stay in the area—and this happens often in areas of low tidal flow or when en route to spawn—salmon will stay with them and be quite localized.

Because chinook are prone to following shorelines, they are one of the more likely species for drift-fishing. Local information will reveal the kelp beds and points of land on which to concentrate. Chinook tend to hole up over dark and drift closer and closer to shore. They are often found in the same place day in and day out, year after year. So if the bait is close to the rocks, the chances of catching a chinook at the crack of dawn are quite high. Remembering that your lure must be close to the fish—even 100 feet away may be too far—pore over your charts and fish the nooks and crannies the fish move into overnight.

Generally speaking, drift-fishing is most successful in the summer and fall. The sea contains more fish, and they are often more tightly bunched, than in other seasons. Pressure on the finite bait resource is high, resulting in a greater percentage of hungry migratory salmon. In winter, only two of the five species of salmon feed on the resource: chinook and blueback coho. Consider also that winter drift-fishing is colder-than-the-last-ice-age-frigid and much less appealing than sitting around under cover drinking coffee while trolling. Let local information be your guide.

ALTERNATIVE DRIFT-FISHING METHODS

Thus far we have discussed drift-fishing in its most common form—stripping line from a trusty single action reel and fishing directly under the boat. Single action reels cannot cast, so it's not unlikely that most drift-fishing gets accomplished this way. Drift lures, however, can be cast or drifted behind a rowed boat.

Using a rod with an open-faced casting reel can be a real advantage when fish are swirling all around you on the surface. While

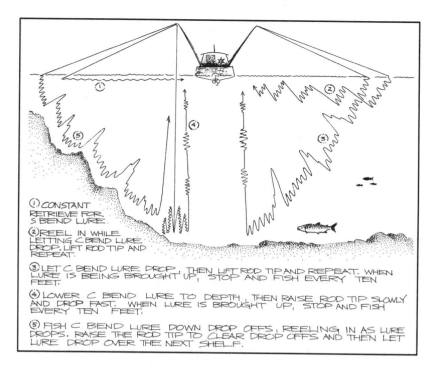

① CONSTANT
RETRIEVE FOR.
S BEND LURE.

② REEL IN WHILE
LETTING C BEND LURE
DROP. LIFT ROD TIP AND
REPEAT.

③ LET C. BEND LURE DROP , THEN LIFT ROD TIP AND REPEAT. WHEN
LURE IS BEING BROUGHT UP, STOP AND FISH EVERY TEN
FEET.

④ LOWER C BEND LURE TO DEPTH , THEN RAISE ROD TIP SLOWLY
AND DROP FAST. WHEN LURE IS BROUGHT UP, STOP AND FISH
EVERY TEN FEET.

⑤ FISH C BEND LURE DOWN DROP OFFS , REELING IN AS LURE
DROPS. RAISE THE ROD TIP TO CLEAR DROP OFFS AND THEN LET
LURE DROP OVER THE NEXT SHELF.

casting technique will be investigated more thoroughly later in the chapter, a few words should be said here. It is always better to have your lure near the fish in any kind of fishing, and it makes little sense to drift-fish under your boat when fish are on the surface. Fish rarely come close to large objects and your boat probably represents a sea lion or killer whale. In addition, fish have very good eyesight and easily see a hand and rod lifting and dropping over the water. For these reasons, casting can be preferred. Single action reels can be used in clumsy imitation of fly reels, but their range is limited and the lure tends to come plopping down on the water, scaring the fish. A casting reel allows much more accurate and quiet lure placement.

Retrieval of a cast lure can be accomplished two ways. To fish surface salmon with a "C"-bend lure, lift your rod, then during the drop reel in until the lure is contacted. Lift the rod once again and repeat the process. Remember to vary retrieval in order to tease fish into biting. You will also want to try your "S"-bend drift-fishing lures. This greatly increases fishable time per cast because the lure is being retrieved constantly and is thus fishing the entire time it is in the water. Try your brighter lures, the chromed or white ones.

When clasting at rising salmon, do not cast directly on top of where the fish boiled the surface. This simply scares the fish away. Cast a few feet to the side or a little past the fish so water noise is muffled and the lure is working properly as it moves past the centre of the rings on the surface. Fish begin moving off in search of fleeing bait, so placing your lure to the side of a rise makes good fishing sense. Bear this in mind when casting to herring balls, too. Roar over to where the gulls are squawking like crazy and park off to the side so as not to scare the fish. Cast right over to the far side of the herring ball and wait a few seconds. This allows your lure to drop beneath the herring ball where the salmon wait, much like sheep dogs rounding up sheep. One by one, they take turns slashing through the ball while the others wait for the injured fish to drift on down. And, of course, as you lift and retrieve, your lure moves right through the middle of them.

Another circumstance in which casting proves useful arises when there are a series of descending underwater shelves. Fish hang over the edges of shelves, and each time your lure goes over one, a strike is possible. A casted "C"-bend lure can provide the best way to fish ledges. You cast the lure and let it drop, then fish across the shelf, reeling each time the rod is dropped. When the lure comes to the edge of the next drop-off, let it drop more than it is retrieved and fish across the next ledge. See the illustration for a visual description of such fishing. As you fish the lure toward you, it slowly drops in the water so that it ends up right under the boat. Fish the lure to the surface and cast again.

Another more old-fashioned method of drift-fishing can be illustrated best with the original old standby lure, the Deadly Dick. This lure comes in a variety of shapes and has an action all its own, a sort of this-a-way-that-a-way wobble, like a combination spoon and drift-fishing lure. In my opinion, there is a market niche for another lure that is fished from a rowed boat and that has a tantalizing, crippled sort of indistinct wobble produced by a rubbery tail—a lure affected greatly by currents or change in boat speed.

As mentioned previously, I have had great success with very small herring in the summer in very calm water. I've rowed just enough to get the line to stream out behind the boat, then stopped and let the line drop to vertical. The drop may take as much as a minute, depending on tide and wind conditions. The bait drifts through the water in the most defenseless manner, its motion constantly changing. And this is the action of a Deadly Dick. Take your little rowboat and row yourself around. Take in the scenery, consider yourself a tourist for an afternoon. Above all else, it is the slowness of your rowing, the stopping and starting, the bringing your lure up and letting it drift down, that is the key. Take your time. Think of a pale-orangey nostalgic past when life was slow and easy and you've got the picture. Think of Norman Rockwell. And if you get a big northern coho on the line, it will scream away with a mind-jarring thrill better than winning the lottery. Well, almost better.

ANOTHER PORTRAIT OF THE FISHER
AS A SLIGHTLY CRAZED HUMAN BEING

One summery evening, I roared out with a Calgary friend to show him how fishing gets done on the coast. I wanted him to appreciate just how large a salmon can be compared to a prairie trout, and yet how delicately that bulk can be managed with only one small drift-fishing lure and an almost invisibly thin monofilament line. I stowed my wire line and planers, put away my downriggers and got out Buzz Bombs and Stingsildas. I went through the theory of drift-fishing and the practical how-you-do-it stuff. Half a mile off-shore, we settled in to fish beside a spire of granite that rose white and ghostly above our heads.

I explained that just the day before, two guys in an eight-foot dinghy had hooked a 40-pounder right where we were fishing. The two guys had rowed out all that way because they didn't have an engine, and once hooking the fish had no way of slowing it down. The salmon towed them across Saanich Inlet, a distance of four miles, before the sun went down. Then in the moist, dark mouth of summer night, plankton glowing like the Phantom of the Opera in their wake, the salmon towed them through the moonlight. They were yanked quietly through the dark, without navigation lights, without a horn. Large boats that would have cut them to pieces passed by completely unaware, leaving them bobbing in their wakes. The two guys were lucky enough to be towed back across the Inlet another four miles, almost to where they had started. In the middle of the night, they netted the monster fish by moonlight and lifted it over the gunwhale of the dinghy—its 4 inches of free-board. Salmon head hanging out one side of the narrow craft, tail stretched out the other, they rowed in, exhausted.

I pointed out that the boat they were in was very much like the extremely small and unseaworthy craft to our left, and went on to say that far too many people did crazily unsafe things by failing to respect the power of the sea. I told him it was hard to believe how few people get killed going out so underprepared. The boat to our side was a wooden punt, perhaps ten feet long, much like the ones students in straw hats pole down the shallow waters of Cambridge, girl trailing fingers, guy in black tie and twill pants, drunk with spring and willow bending down, forgetting the books languishing by their sides.

The boat off our port bow was made of plywood, the blue paint peeled from exposure. Flat-bottomed, it was made for calm water, not expeditions half a mile offshore. In the front end stood a woman, heaving out her lure. She was pretty and young, with blonde hair wound in a bun on the top of her head. Around her neck was a string of pearls. From her shoulders and her cleanly curved collarbones fell a lovely full-length black evening dress, sculpted down her long supple backbone and around the cleavage of her breasts. Here she was casting for salmon in the middle of the sea. The fellow with her was also dressed up. He wore good black trousers, a white shirt, black tie and a black sports jacket.

Why was this mirage here? My friend began chuckling and pointing his thumb. "Get a load of these guys." In our boat, we were the picture of typical guys doing the typical fisher thing, sitting in jeans with fish goosh smeared all over us, oozing day-old beards, smelling like half-dead armpits. My friend's T-shirt said "Sweat, Pain, Agony" in huge letters (presumably about the sports he endured, or perhaps about life in general). On his head he was wearing one of those baseball caps that has stuffed antlers hanging out the sides; he looked like Hagar the Horrible on a bad day. It crossed my mind that, in their tiny little punt, the partygoers were looking across at us as though at one of those unforgettable images epitomizing the oddness of others and thinking, "Boy, don't those guys look weird?" Such is the unending craziness of fishers. A craziness for which there is no explanation.

HOOKS FOR DRIFT-FISHING

Fish get a much better look at drift-fishing lures than trolled lures, so the need for natural presentation increases in importance. Thus hook size should be more closely considered. I use 5/0 and 6/0 hooks for trolling and seldom vary from them. In drift-fishing lures I am more inclined to use a smaller, less-visible hook—for example, a 3/0 single, a 1/0 Siwash or as small as a 4 in trebles. Smaller hooks do not hook as well as larger ones, but induce more strikes.

One can also ponder the use of treble barbed hooks in drift-fishing. Drift-fishing lures come with treble hooks and are intended to be fished this way. As mentioned, though, most undersized fish are killed by the time one gets the barbs out of them. In addition, much time is consumed getting trebles out of bigger fish, as well as out of your net and your fingers. To avoid these problems, I use single hooks about half the time. When small fish are thicker than mosquitoes in Winnipeg, I use singles. When large fish are prevalent, I use whatever hook comes with the lure.

Treble hooks do, indeed, have their place in drift-fishing. Any lure that slides up the line rather than being attached to it, such as the Buzz Bomb, fishes better with a treble hook. The lure flops away from the hook, and it increases your chances of snagging a fish by having three barbs. And remember that sliding lures create problems for all types of hooks. They put a great deal of stress on the knot at the hook end. Over time, the relentless thunk-thunk of the lure will break the knot. Solve this by retying the knot each time out. Cut the last 10 feet of line to remove nicks and abrasions. If you get in the habit of retying hooks, it will occur to you in no time flat that a swivel may not be very useful because you are constantly shortening the leader. I would not recommend using a leader shorter than 3 feet. It's just too close to the lure. A leader longer than 6 feet, on the other hand, makes netting difficult.

LURE WEIGHT, FISHING DEPTH AND SEASONAL VARIATION

Line drag affects lure performance, so as you go deeper, you will want to increase lure weight to counteract drag. The smallest drift-fishing lure is about 28 grams, or one ounce, and may be successfully fished to about 35 feet. The next and most commonly used size is 40 grams (1.5 ounces); it performs properly down to about 80 feet. I move to 60-gram (2 ounces) sizes or larger to fish 80 to 120 feet, and do not drift-fish deeper than this.

Feed size dictates lure size. Gut a fish on the spot and check the size of bait in its stomach. Try to match bait size with your lure. Growing to twelve inches, the largest herring appear in the winter months from January to April when they move in close to weed beds for spawning. Hence you will use your largest lures this time of year. By the end of June, the ocean begins filling with tiny 1½-inch newly hatched herring, and the smaller lures will be more successful until the end of July. By August, the mid-size 40-gram (1.5 ounce) lure comes into its own. Use it for the fall and into winter.

If you open a fish and find it crammed with shrimp rather than herring—most often a coho—it may be a good idea to switch to a red or pink drift-fishing lure. Alternatively, paint dots with red fingernail polish on a lure. This lure will also be successful on sockeye and pink salmon.

LURE FOULING

Drift-fishing lures catch nothing when fouled. Check them at least every twenty minutes for contaminants. This includes fouling with weed, jellyfish, algal bloom or even small herring. When you are fishing near herring balls, herring quite often become impaled on treble hooks. Surprisingly enough, they must be removed; salmon will not bite lures with their natural food hanging from them. One of the common tricks when freshwater trout fishing for splake is trailing a piece of bacon on a Len Thompson spoon, so it seems doubly surprising that salmon will not take a lure with a herring or needlefish on it, but they will not.

If you are fouling continually with baitfish, consider changing fishing method to mooching. Salmon bite most readily on the natural bait in the water, and these bright herring are killers. I have caught salmon with herring still wriggling and dripping from their mouths and had a whole day's mooching from the throat contents of one fish. Even those taken fresh from the stomach of a fish can be effective. Do not, however, use herring that are at all dull. Stomach acids have begun working on them and their smell will repel other salmon.

TYPES OF DRIFT-FISHING LURES

More types of drift-fishing lures exist than you can shake a sack of apricots at. Go in and familiarize yourself with them all. Just some of the lures in this expansive market include Buzz Bombs, Reef Raiders, Rip Tide Strikers, Pirks and Pirkens, banana jigs, hootchie and weight rigs for halibut, Stingsildas, Zingers, Deadly Dicks, Magic Lures, Cod Kings, Spinnows, Phishes, King of Diamonds, Lucky Jigs, etc. Virtually all of these are designed to flutter down on their sides.

The most commonly used are the Buzz Bombs and Stingsildas. If you're low on clams, you can't go wrong buying a few of these two lures for the tackle box. In the Buzz Bomb, get the white, the white with a grey stripe, white with green, and white with pink. In the Stingsilda, get the green one as well as the black one. The 40-gram (1.5 ounce) size will work effectively most of the year.

Drift-fishing lures are easily customized, and this ease may account for the many different models vying for tackle-store shelf space. One common alteration is scraping and chroming the lures. This makes them highly reflective, and a fluttering, reflective lure can only spell e-a-t-s to a fish. Another common modification is spray-painting. Consider using blue, green, red or pink. If you want to try a Buzz Bomb in fresh water, try black with yellow dots. The colour combinations are endless, and you should try any combination that works for you in another lure. For example, if a blue-and-green hootchie with a pink stripe works well in your area, then spray the base colour on the drift lure and put the other colours on by hand with a paintbrush and hobby paints. Finish your masterpieces with reflective tape. There are also eyes that rattle and eyes that glow in the dark. There are hooks of different colours. Spray-paint a hook red when sockeye are around. Do anything that works. The possibilities are limited only by your imagination. Imagine that.

Once one gets into modifying lures, the next step is almost irresistible—putting out one's own line of lures. Let me add one more suggestion at this point. Pick up a freshwater bass jig, the one comprised of a long-shank hook with a weight built around the eye end. Slip a hootchie over the lead weight or mount one of those ever-so-slippery wiggly tails and use it like a typical drift-fishing lure. This range of lures will be limited only by the colour combinations that can be molded into the wiggly plastic tails. Some brands of plugs, for instance, have over 700 colour combinations. Think about the numbers for a moment. Do a few profit calculations and you'll soon realize why anglers are continually inventing new lures. Say you heard it here first and, er, send me some royalties.

REVENGE OF THE SEA CUCUMBERS REVISITED

Those of you who like to eat sea cucumber (though I've never met one of you), take heart. Sea cucumbers have a real affection for drift-fishing lures. Strangely enough, these spiny-bags-of-nearly-nothing that don't seem to have fins or muscles or any other way of moving themselves through the water seem to be able to spot a drift-fishing lure simply miles away and glom onto it.

If you are fishing over a fairly flat, shallow, calm, weed-covered mud bottom, sooner or later you are going to catch a sea cucumber. Either they are lying there cheek by jowl like Canadian tourists on a Hawaiian beach, waiting to be snagged, or these creatures are the most deceptive low-flying blimpy denizens of the sea. I have caught dozens of them over the years, and though they lie in your hands like a pod from *Invasion of the Body Snatchers*, they have deadly accuracy when it comes to locking sensors onto a drift-fishing lure. On a particularly boring day—and it would have to be pretty boring—you can amuse yourself by catching them one after the other when it seems that the salmon have also departed for Hawaii.

MOOCHING

THE EXCITEMENT OF MOOCHING

You are leaning back contemplating the wonders of the universe, as can only be appreciated through the bottom of a bottle of beer. The sun is making a beeline under the rim of your baseball cap into your brain, and the sandman is sprinkling sand in your eyes. As your eyelids grow heavy, you see your rod tip rise imperceptibly, as though even from it the weight of the everyday world has been lifted. Now you leap to action, reeling in like crazy, and lo and behold feel the heft of a huge salmon on the other end of your rod. With nothing between you and the fish but a small banana-shaped weight, the battle is on.

This is the appeal of mooching, the laziest, most relaxing form of salmon fishing, which, in the right spot, can be by far the most productive. The rods are long and limber, the tackle light and agile. There is the constant bobbing of your tip and the understanding that you are using the best possible lure—the salmon's natural food. Mooching is the use of some form of bait, most often live or dead herring, that just floats in the water, somewhere below the boat, while the rod sits in the rod holder waiting for action. This is peaceful, Huckleberry Finn stuff; you can take a magazine or spend the day talking to someone as you wait for that telltale lift or "pop-up" of the rod. This fishing is much like still fishing in fresh water—or halibut fishing—where bait wafts in the current on short leaders attached to a mainline, at the end of which is a weight that sits on the bottom. You are simply waiting for the fish to come along and pick up the bait. Most often the motor is off, the quiet beauty of the B.C. coast takes over and the magic of nature trickles in: the arbutus leaning like liquid gold, the cormorants sitting on rocks like undertakers waiting for a bus.

JIGGED HERRING

The most productive bait is live baitfish that have been obtained fresh on the fishing grounds. These small fish are the food on which the salmon are actually feeding and will usually outfish purchased bait that you have brought along. They are shiny, fresh, lithe and have that drip-through-your-hand softness that previously frozen bait cannot match. Live herring are steak to a fish.

There are three ways of obtaining fresh herring: buy it at a marina before setting out; use a herring rake; or use a herring jig.

Live herring is available at some marinas, but not nearly as often as you might like; it was more common in years past. Many new boats come delivered with a tank for keeping herring alive, complete with a pump that circulates salt water in and out of the tank. Whether you can save time by buying live herring or must catch it yourself, it is a great advantage to keep bait alive as long as possible.

A herring rake is a long, thin, paddlelike instrument about 12 feet long which has pins sticking out one side for about half its length. The design allows the rake to be swept through a school of herring quickly enough so that herring get stuck on the pins. In the same motion, the rake is brought up over the gunwhale and turned over, thus dumping the herring into the boat. The person running the boat makes a tight turn and quietly takes the rake-handler back through the herring ball for another pass. A homemade herring rake can be made from a paddle grafted to a wooden extender, using piano wire for pins. Ready-made herring rakes can be purchased as well. Usually made out of metal, they sink like rocks, and you are strongly advised to tie them to the boat. If that is too restrictive, tie a float to the rake so that if you drop it—something that is very easy to do—it can be retrieved.

Herring rakes can only be used when the herring or other baitfish are on the surface. When the herring are deeper, a herring jig must be used. A herring jig is a six- to eight-foot piece of fishing line which has about six short leaders bearing small flies with hooks along its length. The rod end of the jig ends in a swivel, and a weight is attached to the far end. This setup is lowered to the depth of the herring. If they are too deep to be seen, your depth sounder will be able to spot them for you. Lift your rod tip up and down among the herring—hence the name "jig"—and soon you will feel the tiny tugs that indicate herring on the line. Bring them in and keep them alive in your herring well or even in a bucket of salt water.

Jigged herring stay alive longer than raked herring because they do not have holes stuck through their middles, so if you have the option, jigging for herring is preferable to raking. Whichever method is used, please remember to take only the herring you need. This helps conserve the resource for other fishers and, more important, for the salmon and other fish stocks that depend on herring for food.

MOOCHING ROD AND REEL

The preferred mooching rod is the longest employed in any method of salmon fishing. Ten and a half feet long, fiberglass or graphite, this rod has a very soft tip. The reel is the standby single action graphite reel. A long rod is required because the rods are all fairly close together, and thus the baits are close together under the boat. The extra length allows for more spreading of lines and less tangling. Reread the section on rods in the drift-fishing section of this chapter. Many of the same considerations apply. Also refer to the section on rods in Chapter 4.

A fisher who wants to take a more active role in mooching will hold the rod in his or her hands while slowly working the bait up and down. This technique demands a well-balanced rod that fits easily under the arm but does not have a butt end more than a foot behind the reel seat. On the other hand, mooching can be the easiest of all fishing methods. Simply let the line out, put the rod in the rod holder and voilà, it be fishing. It's that simple.

BAIT SETUPS

The real skill in mooching is in rigging the bait for fishing. I suggest taking more care in setting up mooching baits than in setting up any other type of fishing tackle. In mooching, there is no room for error, no subterfuge too arcane to be considered. Your only ticket to a salmon is a four-inch piece of meat that the fish can study all day long if it wants to before deigning to pick it up. And after the first nibble, fish do not just grab the bait and scram. They mouth it softly and sit there for a moment. When you consider that boat electrical potential affects fishing in ranges well below 1/10 of a volt, the electrical potential of hooks must be sensed by fish, even if they somehow overlook this hard crunchy presence in something they know ought to be a soft, luscious, oozy, tasty treat. (Consider, for a second, how long you hold a bite of pizza in your mouth if you crunch down on something.)

There is more variation in mooching setups than in any other type of fishing lure. This is because the hooks can be inserted almost anywhere in the bait, imparting any characteristic roll that a particular fisher desires. In fact, you don't have to get the bait to roll at all for it to be successful. A flop every now and then can suffice, as can a semi-conscious drift through the water. I will describe the usual setups, but I suggest you go fishing with someone who catches a lot of fish and memorize his or her mooching rigs which may not agree with mine at all.

There are four types of bait setup used in mooching: cutplug herring; live herring; whole dead herring; and strip and slab-cut herring.

I will describe how to rig these setups, but you will learn far more by examining the illustrations closely. (In addition, refer back to Chapter 4 for the sliding hook instructions.) I should also add that it is far easier to work with frozen herring because it is harder than unfrozen herring. Unfrozen bait tends to lose scales in handling, even if your knife is sharp enough to slide right on through, giving a crisp, even slice. And, above all else, an ultra-sharp knife is an absolute necessity. Anything less, and every piece of bait will be ruined. One final comment: where I use the word herring, you may substitute anchovy or, if care is taken, needlefish.

Cutplug Herring

Take a whole, lightly frozen herring and lay it on its side on a cutting surface. Using your ultra-sharp knife, slice off the head and gills. Be very precise in this cut: the knife should be held so as to pass through the fish at a 45-degree angle from one lateral side to the other lateral side, and pass through the fish at a 45-degree angle from the dorsal side to the ventral side. Got that? If not, reread the sentence until it sinks in. Once this single clean cut has been made, put the herring in salt water for a few minutes to thaw out, then remove all the entrails. Work carefully so as to avoid cutting the belly of the herring, thus ruining its action.

Now attach the bait (in some areas referred to as "plugcut" bait) and tackle together. Taking the sliding hook arrangement you have previously tied in a shiny new leader of 15 to 20 pound test, and insert the leading hook into the dorsal meat at the point of the cut, barb pointing up. Take the trailing hook and insert the barb just before the tail, slightly above the lateral line. The slow roll of a cutplug herring is achieved by modifying a number of factors:

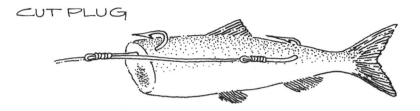

CUT PLUG

- *the angle of the cut in the cutplug herring*
- *the position of the leading hook in the meat*
- *the distance between the leading and trailing hooks*
- *the position of the trailing hook*
- *the use of treble versus single hooks*
- *hook size, usually 1/0 to 3/0*
- *boat speed and variations in boat speed*
- *actively fishing the bait by moving the rod*

Over the years, you will gain an understanding of each factor. Take your time and make changes in a methodical way. Remember to write the modifications that work for you in your logbook. The two factors that make the biggest difference in cutplug fishing are the angle of the bevel cut and position of the leading hook. Increasing the angle of the bevel increases the speed and snap of the roll. A slow roll is best for chinook, the usual quarry in mooching, and a snappier roll will attract more coho. As for hook position, the leading hook should be be placed in the top third of the cutplug and in the leading-edge side of the bevel (the meat side). The closer the hook is placed to the lateral line, the slower the roll, but never place the leading hook below the lateral line of the bait. It may not roll, or may roll backwards. If you prefer to let the bevel do most of the work, place the leading hook into the meat right in the middle of the bait under the backbone, barb pointing up.

Improve the appearance of your cutplug, and all mooched baits, by ensuring that hooks lay parallel to the sides of the bait. Present a smooth, fishy-looking morsel, not a crunchy-looking sputnik with things sticking out at weird angles. Smooth out excess line as well. And, of course, always check the bait's action at the side of the boat.

LIVE HERRING

Live herring aficionados have good reason to believe theirs is the most productive type of fishing on the coast. What could be better

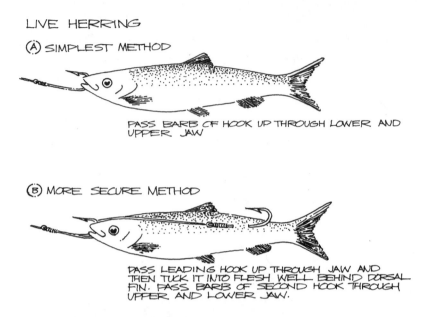

LIVE HERRING

(A) SIMPLEST METHOD

PASS BARB OF HOOK UP THROUGH LOWER AND UPPER JAW

(B) MORE SECURE METHOD

PASS LEADING HOOK UP THROUGH JAW AND THEN TUCK IT INTO FLESH WELL BEHIND DORSAL FIN. PASS BARB OF SECOND HOOK THROUGH UPPER AND LOWER JAW.

than fishing with a salmon's actual food—a live herring that is swimming around? Some days the results can be spectacular, and so very satisfying if you have caught the herring yourself. The most important factor in fishing live herring is to hook up the baitfish so that it stays alive as long as possible. The natural swimming action of the live bait attracts the salmon as no artificial lure can. Be gentle with the bait, inserting hooks as lightly as you can. Do not impale vital organs or impede breathing or swimming. Smaller single hooks will aid in achieving this: a 1/0 or 2/0 hook is not too small—indeed, sometimes I use much smaller.

Most fishers use a variation of the standard live herring setup, and I am no exception; however, regardless of your style, may I suggest using the simplest arrangement that suits you. See the illustration for a typical rigging. Usually, the trailing hook is passed upwards through the jaws and pulled through. This hook tucks lightly under the skin, well behind the dorsal fin. The leading hook then passes upwards through the jaws. Attached this way, the herring is able to open and close its mouth, thus forcing water over its gills. A slightly more secure arrangement can be fashioned by pulling the leading hook completely through the jaws, just as the trailing hook was, and then passing the barb through the nostrils of the herring. Another variation is simply slipping the leading hook on the line without tying a knot to it. It will be kept on the line during a bite by the trailing hook. In this case, the usual technique includes using a treble hook and hooking one barb through a jaw or the nostrils.

Having said all this, I have had my most successful live bait mooching using a single, size 10, freshwater snelled hook, hooked only through the front lower jaw of a teeny-weeny 1½-inch newly hatched August herring. The only thing holding the whole fragile affair together is the tiny hook at the extreme front edge. And, of course, the hook rips out easily. If you are watching like an eagle, though, and have the patience to leave the bait in the mouth of the salmon a little longer than usual before striking the hooks, you will hook nearly every salmon that takes your bait. Waiting is critical because small snelled hooks will not hold that often in a salmon's hard mouth parts and need to find their way into the softer tissues deeper in the throat. The trick is to hold off until the line starts to bear away from the boat briskly, meaning the salmon has finished eating and is back on the move. Strike the hooks hard, and in playing the fish, remember that the small hook is holding on for dear life to just a nip of flesh.

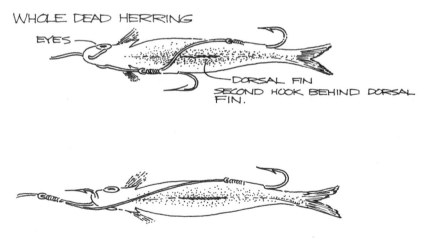

WHOLE DEAD HERRING
EYES
DORSAL FIN
SECOND HOOK BEHIND DORSAL FIN.

Whole Dead Herring

In due course, every live herring becomes a dead one. A whole dead herring can also be used for mooching and is much easier to handle than a live one because you are not concerned with being gentle enough to keep it alive. One good squeeze of a live herring can kill it, whereas a dead herring can't be killed anymore.

Although dead herring do not have the action of live or cutplug herring, more can be done to bury hooks within their flesh. The trailing hook, once pulled through the jawbone, can be inserted behind the dorsal fin and completely buried except for the tip, so that the salmon contacts meat rather than a mouthful of metal. Bury the hook—and this can be done in any type of bait—by first inserting the barb pointed in the direction of the tail. Carefully slide the curve of the hook around and through the bait, including the shank. Once the eye of the hook is buried within the body, take hold of the barb and push the shank back up into the body past the point where the hook first punctured the side of the fish. If you have followed this explanation, all that should remain outside of the bait is the barb of the hook. The leading hook is then hooked through the jaws in an upward direction. Make sure the line is smoothed out and the leading hook pulls the herring directly forward. This causes the bait to flutter forward as you move your boat, rather than towing to one side.

In whole dead herring fishing, the action is provided by the boat or the rod; you have placed the leading hook in a location where it will not make the fish roll as it is moved. If desired, roll can be added to the bait by:

- *Attaching the leading hook to one side of the head.*
- *Positioning the trailing hook so it makes a slight curve in the bait.*
- *Using a trolling baithead.*
- *Shortening leader length between the leading and trailing hooks.*

STRIP MOOCHING

If you are a strip fan and prefer a bait that rolls, the fourth method of mooching is for you. Either you can cut the strip yourself or use the ready-made variety. The next illustration shows the strip and slab-cut patterns for the do-it-yourselfers. Frozen or brined bait is far easier to cut, and fewer scales are lost. If, however, you are using just-caught bait and cut off a strip or a slab (which comes with a nice wiggly tail), take great care in handling the bait and great care in cutting it. Your knife must be razor-sharp or you will go crazy before producing a single usable piece of strip. One final thing to tuck away in your mind is that bait shrinks after cutting, so don't cut bait too small.

To be honest, I don't have the patience for cutting bait this way. If you are as imprecise and impatient as I am, take along a package of strip. It has already been cut in perfect slices ready to use, and much grief and effort can be saved. In the trolling section, I explained how to

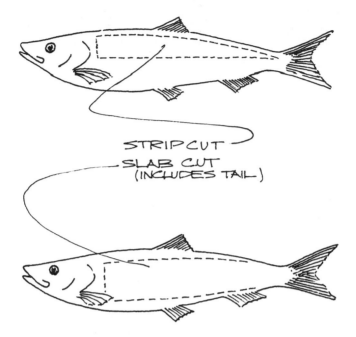

STRIPCUT
SLAB CUT
(INCLUDES TAIL)

take a herring strip and rig it up in a strip teaser head. Simply prepare this setup and attach it on a 6-foot leader to your sinker. You
will notice right away that it does not roll in the water the way it
does when you are trolling. This is because you are moving more
slowly. I should add that in my experience, using a strip head is
the least effective method of mooching. I surmise that the plastic
head makes the bait seem unnatural to the fish when it has the
good, long look afforded in the slow-motion world of mooching.

If desired, you can achieve a roll from a strip teaser head at
lower speed by:

- *Using only one hook so as to reduce gear and reduce drag.*

- *Inserting the hook through the meat side of the bait about two
  thirds of the way back, at or above the lateral line, and taking up
  slack so as to introduce a curve into the bait.*

- *Bending the plastic tab on the head at an angle away from the strip.*

- *Using one hook, pulling it right up to the teaser head and cocking it
  at a right angle away from the strip.*

- *Working the rod tip up and down, forward and back.*

If all else fails, go back to cutplug fishing, the tried-and-true traditional method of mooching for salmon. Alternatively, dispense with the

strip head and attach a single hook directly to the strip's leading edge. Many readers will disagree with the methods I have suggested here and be just as, or more, successful. If you have a successful moocher in your area, listen to him. Buy him a beer, and he'll tell you what you want to know.

OTHER MOOCHING TACKLE

Because the fish get a very good look at a mooched bait, it is important to make everything look as natural as possible. This includes:

+ *Using smaller hooks than usual, such as 1/0 to 3/0 single hooks and 4 to 6 trebles.*
+ *Smoothing all slack and line kinks out of the leader.*
+ *Using a lighter leader of 10 to 15 pounds.*
+ *Using 6 feet of leader.*
+ *Using one of the "invisible" leaders.*
+ *Burying, where possible, hook barbs in bait.*

Once you have rigged up a mooching bait, it needs to be attached to your mainline. This is accomplished by attaching the leader to a mooching weight that has a swivel conveniently placed at each end. Mooching weights are very functional items and are virtually tangle-free due to their swivels and shape. Tangles will happen from time to time, though, when you are letting out line. Here are two solutions:

+ *Add a rubber-core weight two feet up from the main weight. This will make your leader go down two feet away from the mainline, making it less likely to tangle.*
+ *Let line out more slowly. The faster that line is let out, the more likely it is that bait will double back into the mainline.*

Bait will also sometimes tangle in the line during fishing, usually because of too much rod action. Remember that soft, slow movement, or no movement at all, is enough. Even moving from side to side in the boat can lift the bait a foot or two, and this is plenty tantalizing.

On any given day the weight will vary from 1 to 8 ounces, depending on current speed, boat speed, wind speed and depth.

Weights now come with bright orange plastic coverings, which make them rather indestructible. Chromed weights might also be a good idea as fish attractants, but I have not yet seen them on the market.

Another factor in mooching is boat noise. As the boat is not moving, a footfall or the sound of pliers being dropped is transmitted instantly through the water, and fish swim away from the boat. Ghetto blasters are definitely out when you are mooching.

MOOCHING TECHNIQUE

Once a mooching setup has been prepared, it is time to get fishing. Strip out line in 2-foot pulls, taking care to avoid tangling the bait around the mainline. Fish your way at 10-foot intervals down to and below where fish are expected. If you can determine bait depth on your depth sounder, some of the guesswork has been eliminated. Salmon have a tendency to cruise around below the baitfish, so your lure is best placed 0 to 15 feet below them. Usually this implies fishing at depths of 30 to 100 feet. Now you put your rod in the rod holder and wait. It's that simple.

Mooching technique is both easy and subtle. The easy method involves leaving the rod in the rod holder. The subtle method involves giving a bait its own irresistible action. The aim is to produce a lazy, rolling, drifting bait that may have a soft twirl, or a very slow rise and fall, or a slide-off to the side, or an imperceptible twitch—any kind of very slow action that indicates a dead or almost dead herring swirling along naturally with the water. Rapid movements are out; you do not want the bait to jump and leap about like a Punch and Judy show. Slow and easy wins the day. Tease the fish onto the line. I have seen expert old codgers outfish everyone just by keeping the rod in their hands for hours and slowly, ever-so-gently changing the action they give to the tip so the bait is constantly changing its dance.

Actions you may want to try include:

+ *Pulling a couple of feet of line and letting it go.*
+ *Dropping the rod tip to the water and raising it.*
+ *Conducting a lullaby, rod tip used as a conductor's baton.*
+ *Moving your rod to the opposite side of the boat.*
+ *Slowly walking around the boat with your rod in your hand .*
+ *Twitching the rod tip up and down.*
+ *Leaving your rod where it is, getting up and walking to the other side of the boat.*
+ *Slowly lifting your rod six feet and then letting it drop.*
+ *Row, row, rowing your boat and then stopping.*
+ *Putting your engine in and out of gear.*
+ *Anchoring in a current, letting the flow work the bait.*

The possibilities are endless. The key is that the bait should not hang like a rock beneath the boat: you are after variation. Keep the boat moving in calm water or anchored in moving water. As long as boat and current speed differ, you will find that line does not drop straight down, but wafts down at an angle. In calmer water, one of the perfect boats for mooching, surprisingly enough, is a rowboat. You can row and then stop, row and then stop, without the disturbance of engine sound, while your line streams out behind the boat, lifting the bait toward the surface. When you stop rowing, the line descends slowly, taking the bait fluttering down with it. The image of the bait in my mind is so irresistible that if I were a fish, I would jump out of the boat and bite the line. The other small craft that makes a lot of sense for mooching is a kayak. Palpable is the only word to describe the excitement when a large salmon tows you all over the place.

In a larger boat, control over bait motion is exerted largely through boat speed. Mooching is a much slower form of fishing than trolling, and when using your engine to motor-mooch, use it sparingly, putting the boat in and out of gear to keep the bait swimming along in a rhythmic crest-and-trough pattern. If you end up having the engine in gear all the time, you are actually trolling, and should consider using the bait setups described in the trolling section.

WHERE TO FISH

Mooching will be successful virtually anywhere that drift-fishing is hot, so you may wish to reread the pages on drift-fishing locations. In a nutshell, anywhere that fish are highly localized should be a good place to mooch. Normally this will involve an association with land structures—either above or below water. Most of these locations will concentrate the passively transported plankton, the baitfish that eat them, and the salmon.

Anywhere that consistently holds herring schools is a good bet for mooching. Finding these locations sometimes takes years; however, it is worth taking the time to understand the nuances of any particular fishing ground—catch results increase dramatically. Herring tend to hang around the same places year in and year out. If you can get a handle on their annual cycle, you have a guide to the moochable water on a year-round basis. Keep your eye open at the crack of dawn for that delicate dimpling as the nose of herring after herring touches the sky. Later in the day, the school will descend, and you can obliviously pass right over them. Remember the spots that you have seen herring—and the season—for they will return. Look for herring:

- *in front of lighted areas at night, such as deep sea docks*
- *in tidelines*
- *in back eddies*
- *right on shore where a tide or wind pushes onto the rocks*
- *between arms of reefs, over top of a reef or offshore in a direct line with a reef*
- *behind islands, pushed by fast-moving water*
- *in front of kelp beds*
- *where seagulls, cormorants, mures, grebes, auklets and pigeon guillemots are diving*
- *where the beautiful bonaparte terns are dipping*
- *on the edge of drop-offs close to shore*
- *underneath docks*
- *in winter, in schooling areas near herring spawning beds*
- *over spires of rock that rise from the ocean bed*

This is a short list, similar to that for drift-fishing. Remember, in mooching, the presence of herring or other baitfish is essential, as is a well-defined area where salmon are likely to congregate.

THE BITE

As already mentioned, the bite in mooching can be the most unusual encountered in all salmon fishing. In other methods, the salmon bites, then heads off in another direction as soon as it feels the hooks. In mooching, however, the bite is like a teenager leaning in front of the fridge, munching on something while deciding what else can be raided from the larder.

The usual quarry in mooching is the chinook salmon. Chinook will move up to the bait slowly, take a look at it and then take the morsel in their mouths for a few seconds before swallowing or drifting off. They are, after all, in a location where there may be much more food just hanging around, and it makes no sense to take off out of the area. It should be noted that the larger the chinook, the more slowly it will move toward the bait, take it and swallow. There is something downright professorial and dignified about a larger chinook, something related, I suspect, to its girth. In any event, a larger chinook is more deliberate in its actions and, once on the hook, moves off like a locomotive rather than a firework.

One comment about mooched chinook: they tend to sound—head for the bottom—once hooked, and the pressure of your rod, in this case a soft-tipped one, must be kept constant so that over time they can be dislodged from the depths. Unlike many freshwater fish and the coarser saltwater fish, salmon do not display the behaviour of purposefully seeking the bottom. Thus, tangling lines on rocks and weed is not common. A sounded salmon generally just needs pressure or line tweaking to be raised.

Having said that chinook sound after biting, it must be pointed out that most mooching bites begin with the opposite behaviour. Normally, the salmon will take the bait and rise slowly, presumably looking for more to eat. This shows at the rod tip as a slight upward movement of an inch or so. This is the reason for a very soft tip: it informs you that a bite has occurred. If a harder tip were used, most bites would be missed because the rod would not be telegraphing the bite to the fisher.

The lift of the rod tip during a bite is referred to as a "pop-up," and what you do in the next few seconds will likely determine whether you land the fish or not. First, of course, you must be watching your rod to actually see it pop up. The slight downward bow in the rod tip prior to this is attributable to the heft of the mooching weight. When the fish takes the bait and begins rising from the depths like the Good Year blimp, it lifts the mooching weight, and the line pops up. Quickly take your rod and, without making any jarring movement that may send a vibration down the line, wind in all the slack. At the same time, lower the rod tip to the water. When the line goes taut, set the hooks hard. You have a very long, very soft-tipped rod in your hands and will have to yank up hard and high to drive the hooks into the fish on the other end. As soon as the fish feels the hooks bite home, it will be off. If it is a chinook, it will tend to turn and go back down. If it is a coho, more than likely it will come straight to the surface for an aerial display.

The other commonly encountered mooching bite occurs when the line moves off horizontally and keeps moving as though with a mind of its own. In this circumstance, strike home hard as soon as the slack is out of the line; it is only a matter of seconds before the fish figures out something is wrong with the bait and spits it out. I noted earlier that I have had great success with fall-run northern coho mooched on tiny summer herring. In the warm, calm afternoon, the line veers quietly, the hooks are set and before I can say "fish," a 15-pound coho takes a 100-yard run, 1 foot below the surface. Time and again, I have had fish take the equivalent of a football field of line before I can move, and then take another 100 yards before I can start the engine and race off in pursuit.

In netting a mooched fish, a partner can make all the difference. Because mooching rods are long, it is difficult for one person to keep a fish at the side of the boat and net it as well. You may have as much as 10 feet of line to contend with, and it is hard indeed to keep the rod high in the air with one hand, while netting with the other. Two arms are really needed for both procedures. The best advice when mooching alone is to play the fish until it has rolled on its back and can fight no more. It must be still during the time you are fumbling with the cumbersome net.

MOOCHING ETIQUETTE

Most fishers aren't likely material for tea with the queen. They are grimy, slime- and blood-splattered, unshaven. In their eyes is the hardened gleam of the gambler down to his last chip. When mooching, the boats of such individuals are often in close proximity. As it takes no time at all for a fish to head directly for the lines of such desperados, alert everyone that you have a fish on. They then have the option of pulling in lines or edging away. In your own boat, you should immediately decide whether you are dangerously close to other lines (and crazed, knife-wielding, non-tea drinkers) and begin looking for a passage to freedom. Providing the fish will come with you, the best course of action is to begin moving with the tide. This will take you away from other boats as quickly as possible, where you can fight the fish unobstructed. There is nothing that leads to frayed tempers more readily than a fish that tangles another line, particularly when the fish is ultimately lost.

If you do tangle with another boat, ask the fishers—politely—to let you do the work of bringing in the fish, and to keep their boat clear, playing out and retrieving line as necessary. Most good fishers will do this without being asked; they understand the importance of keeping tension on the fish and that the person with the fish needs to be in contact with it at all times.

After tangling, and getting your line (and hopefully the fish) in the boat, cut your own line in an attempt to hand the other person's line back unbroken. When this is not possible, simply cut both lines above the mooching weights. Ninety percent of the time, line above the weights can be easily zipped apart by running a hand down one of the lines. Then you are left only with the problem of untangling the last six feet. Cut your own leader or offer the other fisher another already-rigged-up double sliding hook setup. Hand it to him along with his or her weight and an apology. Then beat him back to the fishing ground and catch the next fish, too!

SUBMARINE FISHING

One day in the hunt for the not-so-elusive and not-so-wily pink salmon—the same day I cut my foot to the bone with my gutting knife and my blood still swilled in the bilge—I and a fishing buddy were heading back to port feeling rather sheepish. In the excitement of it all, a ninth pink had somehow insinuated itself among the other eight legitimate fish in our fishbox, and we were feeling rather badly about it. We couldn't fathom how it got there and, knowing the laws, wanted (a shade desperately) to share our good fortune with someone.

Imagine our surprise when, rounding the last corner, we almost ran smack into a huge black submarine blocking our way. We knew the Fisheries Department was tough, but this seemed a bit Draconian. Getting closer, and less paranoid, we discovered that this was the Australian Navy, and not the Fisheries guys at all. I have no idea how a submarine got so many thousands of miles off course, but there it was, black-uniformed guys sitting all over the deck, casting into the water. I guess they had heard the pink run was on and had come straight across to get in on the gold rush. And, of course, they were right: a pink salmon run is big excitement, every second year, as the fish pile through the Strait shoulder to shoulder, begging to be caught.

The Navy boys were catching nothing. They needed to be trolling from their submarine, three lines over the stern like everyone else, rather than lamely jigging away with blue-and-green barracuda-like lures. Being goodwill ambassadors (like all Canadians since Lester B. Pearson know in our heart of hearts that we are), we offered up our renegade fish. It was gladly accepted with a "Good on yer, mate." The fellow who took the fish, pleased to have fresh salmon for dinner, reemerged from the conning tower with a gunnysack full of beer. We roared off with our vast selection of genuine Australian beer, brought directly to our doorstep by an obliging Navy. We concluded that the offending extra fish was actually a sign from God that we were exceedingly fine fellows. That evening, this explanation grew more and more plausible, the more Australian beer we drank.

♦ 9 ♦
CASTING FOR SALMON

THE ATTRACTION

Casting for salmon will appeal to the thrifty at heart and to those who cannot afford a boat. While one can cast from a boat, most casting is done from breakwaters and wharves, at river mouths and from rocks. On the southernmost tip of Vancouver Island, at least one person a year catches a 50-pound chinook Buzz Bombing at Beechy Head, while thousands of boats catching nothing mill about right in front of him.

Casting from shore exudes nostalgia and is the fishing method of true romance. It's just you, your rod and the fish—real "Father Know's Best" stuff. A short drive from home, you can be at any number of shore-casting spots in the area. And though you may be on shore, the fish, as noted above, can be every bit as big as those caught from a boat. Considering that chinook hug the shore, it is hardly surprising that some very large fish are caught from the rocks with little more expense than the cost of a Buzz Bomb. In places where current or wind pushes herring and, hence, salmon onto the shore, fishing from the rocks can be almost as productive as from a boat, and a lot less hassle.

Every boat-owner knows that a boat is the proverbial hole in the water that you fill with money. A moored boat runs up thousands of dollars in expenses every year. In fact, in the fifteen years that we have had our boat, I do not recall a single day when it has been completely trouble-free, nor a day when something did not need to be repaired or cleaned or sanded or polished or etceteraed. As you are forking over all those clams, it dawns on you like a nice, new summer day how lovely it might be to sit on a rock fishing, your pockets full of money.

ROD AND REEL AND LINE

Good casting rods have a few key characteristics, most of which can be found in modestly priced gear. Select a rod at least 8½ feet long and with a "snappy" tip. The tip is the most important portion of the rod. A soft tip absorbs too much of the energy you are trying to transfer to the lure; a hard tip will not transfer energy to the lure because there is no force-multiplying whip. When looking at rods, try a few casts in the store. If the tip has little action, it is too hard. If it bends quite noticeably, it will be too soft. Select the one that snaps. Take each tip in your hand, bend it and release it. You will see quite readily how different tips behave.

The next consideration in a casting rod is being able to cast as far as the moon if possible. The more distance you get, the closer you get to the fish. Line guides are an important component that can help you in this quest. Generally, I am not a fan of ceramic line guides, because the ceramic rings are easily knocked out—particularly in trolling, where bead swivels pass through, knocking out one after the other; however, ceramic inserts are a real advantage in casting because they drastically reduce the friction of the line whizzing through. Huge line guides—and fewer guides—are also important in reducing friction. Anything that reduces friction will take you that one step closer to the moon. And remember to couple antifriction features with a good, stiff butt extending at least a foot below the reel seat.

When matching a reel to a casting rod, there is only one main criterion: buy the biggest reel on the market. The larger the reel, the further it will cast. Large reels have less friction because the line is flying off a larger drum. They do not foul as often, either, something of great importance in casting; you don't want to be untangling line frantically in the few seconds it takes your favourite drift-fishing lure to drift to the bottom, where it will remain snagged forevermore.

Also check the reel for line capacity. The greater the capacity, the better. Sometimes you are casting from a dock twenty feet above the water and need the extra distance. Try to resist solving this problem by putting extra line on the reel. A drum filled to the rim is a problem waiting to happen; casting reels foul too often, and overfilling one is asking for trouble.

Graphite reels, which are light and rustproof, are also worth considering. Make sure the bale is large, too. Again, try out a few in the store. Check for ball bearings and a smooth, trouble-free action. Select the smoothest one, as this will aid in casting. Do not buy the most costly. My reel has all the important features, but was not expensive. (It is also too big to fit in my tackle box, which suits me fine because it works like a charm.)

Once rod and reel are found, line must be purchased. I am not a fan of expensive fishing line; however, I recommend it for casting. Better line is thinner than poorer-quality line of the same pound test. Consequently, it is less likely to bind on rod guides during casting. You also may want to consider line of lower pound test, say 15 to 20 pounds. The downside of such line is that it breaks more easily when caught on the bottom. This is particularly important to the caster who fishes from shore, because most locations require casting and retrieving over kelp. In these situations, it's really helpful to have 25-pound test to rip your lure through the stuff without losing it. I leave this decision to you. If you fish in a weed-free area, choose lighter line. It will cast further.

CASTING TECHNIQUE

The purpose of casting is to place your lure far out in the water where fish lurk in toothy anticipation. Good technique makes all the difference between a lure that is launched in strange and possibly dangerous directions and one that sails way out there to land with a satisfying kerplop. You may wish to perfect one or more of the following three methods: Dennis's cast, the one-handed cast or the two-handed cast.

Not surprisingly, Dennis' cast was invented by me. After opening the bale on the reel, hold the rod in one hand and the line in the other. When casting, let go of the line an instant after the rod's energy has been fully transferred to the lure and it is snapping forward—not up—from the tip. I use this method because it is simple and by far the most accurate cast around. Employ it when a lure must be placed within 1 to 2 feet of an intended target. The downside to this cast is its inefficiency. One can cast comfortably only 50 to 75 feet, not anywhere near as far as with the other two types of cast.

In the one-handed cast, after the bale is opened, the rod and line are held in one hand. When the rod is snapped forward from the ten o'clock position and the energy tranfers completely to the lure at about two o'clock, the line is released from the hand, and away sails the lure. This cast is by far the most commonly used, and one can cast considerably further than with my cast. Accuracy is lower, but you should be able to cast a 1.5 ounce drift-fishing lure more than 100 feet with little trouble.

In the two-handed cast, after the bale is opened, the rod and line are held in one hand. The second hand is placed below the reel seat on the rod butt. Turn sideways, drop the rod parallel to the ground behind your body (ie., nine o'clock) and begin a terrific swing up and over your head, using both arms and torso. Push the top hand toward the sea while pushing the bottom hand in the opposite direction and, of course, release the lure at about two o'clock. Adept casters reach 200 feet with this cast. This cast has much to offer when fishing over a great distance of shallow water—for example, traversing a sandy bottom before deeper fishable water is reached.

Each of these casts differs in the amount of force transferred to the lure. Of the three, my version is the gentlest, the one-handed less so and the two-handed cast downright violent. Remember this difference when casting any type of bait; the more violent the cast, the more likely it is that the bait will snap off. In addition, stronger casts more frequently break off lures when line becomes fouled in the rod or reel; casting reels are prone to tangling because line twist creeps into the fishing line, making it twist into loops and catch on handles or anything exposed. I have launched more Buzz Bombs to Mars by snapping them off this way than I care to remember.

Before moving on, one variant of these casts should be mentioned. When casting to rising fish, try to avoid slapping the lure on the water, and thus scaring the fish. Utilize a side cast in this instance: instead of arcing the lure directly overhead, flip it from the side of your body. Hold the rod to the side of your body with any of the three methods and snap it out. The lure will travel out much closer to the surface of the water and, as it has less vertical distance to drop, will hit the surface much more quietly. Distance is drastically reduced with a side cast, but accuracy increases.

CASTING FROM A TROLLING BOAT

Although the same three casts are employed, casting from a trolling boat requires slightly different technique. Since the boat is moving through the water and there are trolled rods over the stern, the problem for the caster is to avoid tangling in the other lines. The best position for casting is standing on the bow, where the lure can be aimed safely ahead of the boat. Any lure cast to the side will be swept into the trolled lines. This problem also surfaces any time the boat is anchored in fast-moving water and lines descend off the back end—for example, in halibut fishing or mooching.

One difficulty in casting from the bow becomes immediately apparent. The boat moves directly toward the lure, leaving the fisher little time to fish on any cast. One spends most of one's effort reeling in line so as to maintain contact with the lure should a fish bite. In addition, as the line is fairly slack most of the time, big glumpfs of it are far more prone to tangle on the rod tip or reel. Refer back to the drift-fishing section for solutions to this problem. Making sure that your casting line is brand new should result in fewer tangles. As mentioned in Chapter 4, keeping a rod and reel on board dedicated solely to casting can ensure line in good condition for many years.

Casting from a trolling boat is most successful from late July to early October, when the migratory runs muscle their way home, quite often milling about the surface. Since your lure cannot penetrate deeply when cast from a trolling boat, success will be far higher when you are certain fish are about. Obvious signs include:

+ *A school of finning salmon.*
+ *Jumping salmon. Do not, however, chase the non-biting chum, distinguished by alternating yellow and purple bars and a pattern of four to six successive jumps that describe a lazy curve.*
+ *Herring balls.*
+ *Herring that come flying out of the water as though shot from a cannon.*
+ *Fish mouthing the surface.*
+ *Herring scales in the water.*
+ *Diving birds oozing bait from their bills and sitting among impatient seagulls; the herring below are just out of reach of the seagulls.*

CASTING FROM SHORE OR A WHARF

Those fishers not lucky enough to afford boats usually fish from shore or wharves. Because the tide constantly sluices one way or another, one can count on casting into moving water, and this requires one to fish as though fishing a stream. The usual stream technique is to cast the line directly out across the stream at a 90-degree angle to the current or slightly ahead. One never casts far upstream because by the time control of the lure is regained, it will have snagged on the bottom. Similarly, when fishing in the ocean off rocks or from a shallow shore, snagging is a constant worry. And this is also true at the tail end of your cast. The lure slowly carries with the current past you and swings into the shoreline on the retrieve. As the lure nears shore, you may want to speed your return to avoid catching bottom.

Another complication arises when boats fish close to shore. The main consideration in shore casting is achieving a good, long cast; however, if you tangle with a boat trolling by in moving water, you can kiss your lure goodbye. A boater finds it next to impossible to untangle a line in these circumstances, and usually your line will be cut. Even if he wants to, the boater has little chance of getting close enough to toss back your lure.

Having mentioned the caveats first, I should now state quite clearly that the most important aspect of shore fishing is determining where to stand. This location should be determined largely by analyzing past success—of both yourself and others: stand in the spot from which most fish are caught.

When I was a kid in Alberta, I used to fish the Bow River just below Bearspaw Dam. I and a couple of old guys fished there almost every day, and we caught 95 percent of the fish. Our success was related partly to technique, but mostly to our fishing the exact right spot. We knew the bottom contours intimately from long experience, even though we could not see them. We knew the gear-catching rocks. We knew the right size of hook and bait and so on. We knew precisely the path the fish would swim up to the penstock, then turn and be carried by the outflowing water; they would turn at a certain point and get carried back towards us by the back eddy. There was a foot-wide, six-foot-long stretch of bottom angling from ten to twelve feet offshore. Nearly every single fish was caught in this tiny space. We knew this.

We also knew how each of us fished. Much like racecar drivers in a pack at 200 miles per hour, we learned to rely on knowing exactly what the other two people were going to do so that all three could place our still-fishing gear on the bottom in a row. We also knew we could count on the other two when we got a bite. We seldom tangled lines and we always caught fish. No one else ever caught a thing. One could mark with a felt pen the exact rock on which to sit along a 100-foot section of shoreline where nearly every single fish would be caught. We knew also the second and third most successful rocks and our sitting position was determined by who got there first. If others arrived before us, we simply positioned ourselves close by and cast onto a dime where we wanted our gear to end up. Not easy in a fast current.

Fishing from shore into the ocean is just as specific. You may be fishing from a breakwater a mile long but there may be only half a dozen ten-foot stretches where fish are caught regularly. To locate such spots:

+ *Ask someone who catches fish.*
+ *Remember where every single fish is caught, and the tidal flow at those times.*
+ *Draw a chart in your logbook. Dot in each fish until a pattern emerges.*
+ *Note a spot where the kelp clears.*
+ *Pore over charts and memorize the bottom.*
+ *Bump a hookless lure along the bottom until you can form a 3-D image of the area where you fish.*
+ *Note where reefs approach the shore or where there are drop-offs.*
+ *Note where eddies occur or where fast water slows.*
+ *Note underwater weed growth and where it provides cover close to shore.*
+ *Know current patterns in both a flood and ebb tide. Study the water.*
+ *Know how the current moves your various lures and how different weights of lures are moved.*
+ *Note whether more fish are caught at a bend in or at the end of a breakwater.*
+ *Fish into open water if possible.*

Although not exhaustive, this list should give you some ideas. Your mind must remain open and actively thinking in order for you to become successful. Match the tackle of successful people. Hook size is critical in well-fished areas where fish are often extremely tackle-shy. Do whatever it takes to catch a fish.

Of all the fishing techniques, shore casting has the strictest sort of etiquette. To stay on the good side of your fellow fishers, please observe it—who knows, you may need them to help you land your 50-pounder. When casting from heavily used rocks or wharves, you will find that space is limited, and the potential for tangles huge. Bear in mind the following entirely-unwritten-but-ignored-at-one's-peril set of rules and you can't go too far wrong.

+ *Be pleasant to your fellow anglers.*
+ *Do not move into a spot that has less than six feet of space on either side of it. More is required where casts must be long.*
+ *When tangles occur, tanglees should reel in cheerfully— oh sure— and separate lines. Offer to cut your own. Whether or not it is your fault, suggest that you may possibly be sorry.*
+ *Do not take over a fishing spot without asking if the person is leaving. Taking someone's spot is the cardinal sin of shore fishing.*

- *Cast in the same place as other anglers.*
- *Do not cast across other lines.*
- *If a number of people are casting, wait your turn. Order is determined by the order lures are retrieved, much in the way cars move from a four-way stop.*
- *Call "Fish on" when you have a fish.*
- *Haul in your line when someone else calls "Fish on."*
- *If someone offers to shoot you, decline politely and compliment him on his nifty gun.*
- *Glare at someone who breaks the rules, particularly someone who is a wild caster. He is a problem waiting to happen to you and everyone else.*

And one final comment. Wet rocks and shoreline can be dangerously slippery, and if waves are high, falling in can end your life. Please get a good pair of boots that have good wet-weather grips if you are going to fish from rocks.

CASTING LURES AND RETRIEVAL TECHNIQUES

Virtually any lure can be used for casting, provided it has enough weight and your technique is gentle; bait, for instance, tears easily. Having said this, strip casting, one of the most traditional methods of fishing, can in moving water provide a very fishy roll from a stationary spot. The most common lures, of course, are drift-fishing lures because these are made of lead and have the weight to be casted. Casters should have some that have been modified with an "S" bend. They can be fished with a constant retrieve rather than the lift-and-drop method of the traditional "C" bend lure. In addition, many factory-bent lures come into their own while casting.

Spoons are light and seldomly used in shore casting; however, casting distance can be increased by mounting a small rubbercore weight ahead of the spoon. In circumstances where a breakwater or wharf is built into the water at right angles to the current, a spoon may be fished simply by playing out line and letting it sparkle away inches under the surface, awaiting a hungry fish. This is a rather nice method of fishing if it can be found, because you just let the lure sit there, rod propped against the railing, and that's all there is to it. Mooching setups would also be effective where the current moves the bait away from the shore and over a drop-off.

The traditional banana jig for cod is useful for a sand or mud bottom. An updated version of this lure that will not snag the bottom can now be purchased. After being lifted, the lure flutters back down to the bottom. The hook comes to rest on top of the lure and therefore cannot catch on rocks or whatever.

Do not overlook freshwater casting lures when fishing the salt chuck. Slender Len Thompson spoons will take salmon. Once, as a kid, I looked down into the raging tidal flow below the dock of The Dolphin's Lodge in Campbell River. I could see a five-pound chinook under the dock, and all I had was a red-and-white Len Thompson. I marched up and down, up and down, dangling the lure in front of him until he couldn't take it anymore. He shot out faster than I could see, and the fight was on. The larger flatfish lures will also work. Remember, though, that freshwater lures need to be wiped off after each use, otherwise their hooks will rot off with electrolysis in no time.

Whichever lure you try, vary retrieval technique. Tease those salmon onto the line. Variation often triggers that strike response.

+ *Try a fast retrieve followed by a slow retrieve, or mix up the speed within the same cast.*
+ *Twitch the tip of your rod or shake it a good one.*
+ *Move the rod tip to one side and then to the other.*
+ *Drop the tip.*
+ *Vary the length of lift and drop of your rod, as you would when drift-fishing from a boat.*
+ *Consider using freshwater still fishing technique (ie., the weight sits on the bottom and the bait sways in the current on leaders attached 1 to 2 feet apart on the mainline). Add action by raising and lowering the rod tip.*
+ *Tap a stationary rod with your fingernail.*
+ *Take up slack line, then let it go.*

One other trick may come in handy. Anytime you use bait from a shore position, it's worth the effort to bury hook-barbs inside the meat. This allows the lure to ride over weed without becoming stuck. Kelp is rather slippery anyway, and many lures will slide past if hooks are buried. Alternatively, quicken your retrieve as the lure approaches weed or other obstructions. This causes it to rise in the water. Just before the lure comes to the weed, give a really good yank and it will come flying out of the water like a projectile, right over top of the weed. Of course, it will be going like a bullet for your face, so duck and reel like mad. Another market opportunity awaits an enterprising type: a weedless stainless steel hook, either with a fin before the barb or a shape that allows the hook to slide across weed but does not prevent a fish from impaling itself.

Freshwater bass fishing is about the most snag-filled experience in an angler's life, and many products and techniques have been developed to alleviate the frustration of hang-ups. You may wish to adapt some of these to saltwater use. For example, one artificial worm setup uses a specifically designed hook—the Messler—with an extra curve and bend so that it will slide around the shank of a lily pad. Once the barb is embedded inside the plastic worm, only plastic or smooth hook shank will make contact. Properly set up, the hook rolls the bait over so that the slipperiest part will be presented to the weed and thus will slide over every time. I've seen this work time and again. Give it a try.

PLAYING AND NETTING A FISH

Landing a salmon from shore normally involves a journey past weeds into your net. The solution to this difficulty is to play the fish completely before attempting to lead it through the weeds. You will get only one chance, for if it rolls and takes another run, line will wrap around kelp or other weed and the hooks will rip out. A long gaff would help, provided you are proficient with gaffs.

The options are few: lead the fish to water free of obstructions, or play the fish until it croaks.

The first option may only be employed when open water presents itself nearby and the fish is cooperative. You also need the cooperation of other fishers to let you pass by to the intended netting spot. In any event, you should play the fish until it is half dead. The second option may be your only choice when the fishing area is surrounded by weed. Play the fish well out from shore until it is so tired it simply can't roll off its belly.

Once you have a dead-tired fish, netting time nears. Keep the rod tip high so that the fish's head will be slightly out of the water. This keeps it under control, prevents it from nosing down into the weeds and allows you to lead it in a straight line, headfirst into the net. Once retrieval has been initiated, draw the fish in one continuous movement, allowing momentum to help you. Prior to this, your helper—or you—should have placed the net in the water under the surface. Do not lift the net until two thirds of the fish has passed over the rim. At this point, the fish's centre of gravity is already in the net, and as long as you lift the far edge of the net first, it has no choice but to slide in even further; a last bit of thrashing can only propel the fish deeper in.

A WHARF NET

When you are twenty feet above the huge fish on your line, lunacy is the word to describe lifting hand over hand, hoping it will stay on until safely deposited beside you on the wharf. Either the line will break or the fish will snap its tail and rip out the hooks. A sad feeling it is, indeed, to stand with limp line in your hands watching that huge dream drift off, knowing that your poor decision was the reason. Even if you are successful—a rather unlikely outcome with any fish 10 pounds or heavier—the line strain will result in the loss of other fish.

Since the usual net comes with a six-foot handle, you are in a real pickle as to how to get the fish up to you. Some fishing wharfs have nets on long handles, but when they don't you may have to lead the fish on a long and dangerous journey to the shore, where you attempt to nab it. Many times this is not practical. Solve the problem by making a wharf net. While many designs will suffice, obvious ones include a large, square crab trap with a lid or a bicycle tire rim with netting attached.

The trick to the net is to make one that is well balanced at the midpoint. Using a bicycle tire as an example, at least three pieces of rope will need to rise from the rim and join some distance above the water. At this joint, tie the pieces to the mainline that will rise to the wharf. Make sure to tie the mainline to the railing. Suspended in the air, the rim must rest absolutely horizontally. The three ropes will have to be adjusted where they join to achieve this. An improperly adjusted net will simply dump the fish back into the water. The alternative is to use a deep net. With the fish at the bottom, it can thrash all it likes but can't jump out. More importantly, it will always return to the centre of the net, keeping the net rim horizontal. Wharf netting is tricky, and leading a fish safely by the various ropes without catching a hook or getting tangled up is immeasurably easier when it's well played-out.

♦ INDEX ♦

L. Brock

Dennis Reid has spent a large portion of his life fishing for salmon on the West Coast and has had phenomenal success hooking the prized fish. With degrees in biology, philosophy and public administration, and a burgeoning literary career in poetry and fiction, Dennis seems to be particularly suited to the mental and physical battle that is salmon fishing.

Dennis makes his home in Victoria, British Columbia, and is very active in the local fishing and literary communities.